THE REFERENCE SHELF (*Continued*)

Volume XVI. $6

Volume XV. $4.80

Volume XIV. $3.60

Volume XIII. $3.00

THE REFERENCE SHELF

Vol. 20   No. 6

FEDERAL INFORMATION
CONTROLS IN PEACETIME

Compiled by
ROBERT E. SUMMERS

THE H. W. WILSON COMPANY
NEW YORK   1949

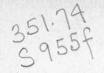
PREFACE

Federal information controls have gradually assumed the character of a Frankenstein monster in recent months. Those favoring such controls have been kept busy explaining why such controls exist, while their opponents have stirred up a storm of protest throughout the nation against the asserted violation of individual rights.

Actually, the present problem is linked with the drastic changes in thinking generally which the American people are undergoing in these first years of the "atomic age." Opinions are confused and contradictory, with the large majority of the public completely at sea to know what to believe. Until new definitions of rights in this changed postwar world can be evolved, federal control of information will probably continue to be a real problem.

This volume is not intended to offer any solution. Its purpose is merely to present, as clearly as present circumstances permit, the basic issues and the various implications involved. The underlying forces which have brought the issue to the fore could possibly be traced to the early days of the New Deal, or to trends in changing thought in the world as a whole. Such a task, however, is beyond the scope of this volume, which deals specifically with the situation as it exists today, and the status of opinion regarding it.

For their kindness in permitting the reproduction of copyrighted materials which appear in these pages, the compiler is deeply indebted to the editors of the following periodicals:

American Political Science Review, American Bar Association Journal, Bulletin of the Atomic Scientists, Christian Science Monitor, Editor & Publisher, Fortune, Forum, Harper's, Harvard Law Review, Liberty, Newsweek, The New York Times, Nieman Reports, Plain Talk, St. Paul Pioneer Press & Dispatch, Saturday

Evening Post, United States News & World Report, University of Chicago Law Review, and the *Yale Law Journal.*

And to the following individuals and organizations:

Ellen D. Ellis, Anthony Leviero, Allan Nevins, John Lord O'Brian, and James A. Wechsler; the Public Affairs Committee, Inc., and the University of Chicago Press.

ROBERT E. SUMMERS

December 10, 1948

CONTENTS

THE THREEFOLD PROBLEM

DISCUSSION

Rarely in the history of this nation have the American people been confronted with a problem which is as complex, as multi-faceted, as the present problem of security of information.

Every nation has secrets of one sort or another (usually military) which must be preserved. Every nation in the last twenty years has had to worry about the possible threat of communism, even to the extent of becoming worried over the loyalty of government employees. No other nation, however, has had these two problems plus that of the control of atomic energy to contend with.

The United States, feeling the heavy responsibility for the ultimate safety of mankind, as well as this nation, is presently faced with these problems all at the same time, each complicating a situation which is none too simple at best. The three together loom up like a Frankenstein monster, to some threatening the very foundations of our nation, to others equally menacing to our civil liberties and democratic processes.

This then is the situation in which we find ourselves.

THE POSTWAR SITUATION [1]

We have learned in two world conflicts that war, by its very nature, is a menace to civil liberty. War usually makes it necessary to forbid people to say or do many things which, in time of peace, would be harmless. . . . Military authority must take control of many things which were before beyond its reach. In

[1] From "New Threats to American Freedoms," by Robert E. Cushman, professor of government, Cornell university, and authority on constitutional law. *Public Affairs Pamphlet.* no. 143:2-7 September 1948. Reprinted by permission of the Public Affairs Committee, Inc., 22 E. 38th St. New York 16.

wartime most people agree that national security—i.e., military success—must come before everything else. But this idea is only a step removed from the brutal slogan that the end not only justifies the means, but justifies *any* means. There is constant danger that we shall sacrifice more civil liberty to the cause of national security than is really necessary. . . .

As after World War I, the present postwar period has been a troubled one. Although the Axis has been destroyed, and the fighting is over, we have not recovered our sense of national security. Our enjoyment of peace is troubled by great fears and uncertainties. As a result of those fears the American people today face more serious threats to civil liberty than at almost any time during their entire history. There are a number of reasons why this is true.

In the first place, we are badly scared, and with reason. We are engaged in a "cold" war with our former ally, Soviet Russia, and we are fearful lest this might lead us into another "fighting" war. The thought of such a war is peculiarly frightening because it threatens civilization with destruction by the atomic bomb and other devastating new weapons of war. Not only are we worried about our relations with Soviet Russia in world affairs, but we are also worried about the possible growth of communism in this country. Many of us fear that an undisclosed number of people in our midst are seeking to undermine our institutions by placing men and women whose first loyalty is to Soviet Russia in key positions in our political and economic life. Troubled over what seems to be a serious threat to our national security, we are groping for ways to deal with that menace.

In the second place, we possess the secret of the atomic bomb, and we assume that other countries do not as yet possess it. It is clearly necessary to surround our work in the field of atomic energy, as well as work on other new military weapons, with absolute secrecy. This secrecy, however, provides an opaque screen behind which a vast range of governmental operations are carried on, and it makes it impossible for the public to judge how necessary the restrictive methods and procedures that have been adopted actually are. In other words, the need for atomic secrecy may be used to withdraw from public scrutiny and public criticism official activities about which there is no real need for secrecy. There are signs that we are building up in the minds of responsible officials and in the minds of the people generally the conviction that the more restrictions we have, and the more strictly they are enforced, the safer we are, and the more patriotic we are. . . .

In the third place, we are in serious danger of losing sight of the vitally important social stake that the community as a whole, and every individual member of it, has in the preservation of our freedoms. . . .

A fourth danger to civil liberty in our postwar situation arises from the difficulty of discovering which persons and groups are an actual menace to the national security and ought to be restrained or punished. Public opinion believes that Communists are a public menace. But how do we define the term "Communist"? What is the difference between a Communist and a non-Communist radical or liberal? What do we mean exactly by the term "subversive" or "un-American"? There is no official definition of any of these terms. They are so general that each of us defines them in terms of his own fears and dislikes. We have invented the labels "front organization" and "fellow traveler" to describe groups and individuals who are in any way associated with Communists or share any of their views, and it is a strong and constant temptation to pin the label of "fellow traveler" on anyone who holds political or economic opinions more radical or liberal than our own. . . .

THE PROBLEM OF LOYALTY [2]

Two persuasive premises guide the thinking of the men who are now shaping government policy in this elusive realm. The first is that we are engaged in a worldwide diplomatic and ideological struggle with Russia, with little prospect that the conflict will be swiftly or easily resolved; the second is that one of Russia's most valuable weapons—present and potential—is an

[2] From "How to Rid the Government of Communists," by James A. Wechsler, former staff member of *Nation* and *PM*, now in the Washington Bureau of the *New York Post*. *Harper's Magazine*. 195:438-43. November 1947. Reprinted by permission.

international army of agents organized as "native" Communist parties. Reasonable men must be legitimately frightened by the dimensions this two-world conflict has reached and the danger that it will end in the ultimate catastrophe of war; but unless one argues, as Henry Wallace appears to, that the burden of guilt in this duel rests on America and unless one dismisses as fantasy the modern record of the Communist parties, the need for minimum safeguards seems inescapable.

Obviously the American Communists are incapable of staging a revolutionary coup in the foreseeable future; and only true disbelievers in the democratic process assert that American society lacks the strength to combat the large-scale promotion of Communist ideas. J. Edgar Hoover himself has publicly opposed the outlawry of the Communist party and only the lunatic fringe in Congress has clamored for the suppression of Communist propaganda. In some measure, at least, hysteria over the Communist issue has been deliberately exaggerated by the Communists themselves to obscure the real problem. That problem is the exclusion of Communists from government—not because they are nonconformists, not because they have read the works of V. I. Lenin, not because they agitate against the poll tax, but because the Communist parties are organized instruments of Russian espionage, disruption, and—in the event of war—full-fledged sabotage.

What the Communists will do in wartime at signals flashed from the Kremlin was tragically demonstrated in France—and on a less calamitous scale in the United States—during the Nazi-Soviet pact. Political strikes in American defense plants were a miniature of the more grandiose betrayal staged by the powerful French Communist machine after Molotov proclaimed that fascism was "a matter of taste." There is little historical quarrel on this point outside of the orthodox journals of the shifting Communist theology. Even more relevant now is the story of Soviet espionage in Canada unfolded in the report of the Canadian Royal Commission. The suspensions of civil rights that accompanied the Canadian spy inquiry have been justifiably decried by lawyers and libertarians alike. But the ultimate findings are grimly meaningful to a country seeking to deal with the same problem in a democratic context.

For the Canadian report is a fascinating and revelatory study in the psychology as well as the pattern of Communist behavior. It demonstrates beyond dispute the link between the Soviet intelligence network and home-grown Communist parties. It also depicts in detail the strange process by which men who are drawn to the Communist movement by devoutly idealistic symbols become full-fledged spies in the service of a foreign power— not for monetary reward and usually with the loftiest rationalizations of their conduct. They are stirred by the concept of internationalism. They are taught to identify the welfare of humanity everywhere with Soviet national interests. They learn to regard concealment of their own political identities and transmission of official secrets as noble tricks against the pillars of society. Finally, when the political hypnosis is completed, they have resolved all inner doubt. They are agents. Describing the systematic "education" which transforms well-intentioned "fellow travelers" into useful cogs in the espionage machine, the Canadian report said:

Indeed a sense of internationalism seems in many cases to play a definite role in one stage of the courses. In these cases, the Canadian sympathizer is first encouraged to develop a sense of loyalty, not directly to a foreign state but to what he conceives to be an international idea. This subjective internationalism is then usually linked almost inextricably through the indoctrination courses and the intensive exposure to the propaganda of a particular foreign state, with the current conception of the national interests of that foreign state and with the current doctrines and policies of Communist parties throughout the world.

And further:

The evidence we have heard shows that at each stage of "development" the adherent is kept in ignorance of the wider ramifications and real objectives of the organization, to one of the fringes of which he has allowed himself to be attached.

In these Koestlerian fragments we glimpse the real nature of the dilemma facing the democracy that is the direct target of this enterprise. For the Communist movement—like the Nazi international—is essentially an underground society. Its moral codes and its habits of thought are often remote and implausible to people steeped in a democratic tradition.

When Mr. Wallace professes doubt that Communists are actually agents of the Soviet government, he really articulates his own disbelief that anybody schooled in Western democracy could act like a character in the Canadian spy drama. When liberals exhibit reluctance to accept the proposition that Communists must be barred from government, it is because they regard the earnest Communists they have known as simply another, if peculiarly fanatic, species of left-wing thought. What they underestimate are the subjective rationalizations which skilled and cynical Communist operatives offer their new subjects; the extent to which the novice may be used—unwittingly—in the early stages of his "development"; and the ultimate intellectual corruption that marks the final triumph of the commissar.

Any "purge," however circumspect and limited, involves risks to democratic institutions. The hazards must be balanced against the consequences of wide-eyed innocence and simple-minded incredulity. To European social democrats the nature of the Communist thrust is infinitely plainer than it is to us; they have faced the full fury of what Harold Laski called the disciplined secret battalions. In the light of the European story of the past two decades and the Canadian disclosures of 1945, the rule of reason would seem clear: Communists (no less than Fascists who operate in any remnants of the Nazi International and in such units of potential Fascist resurgence as the Christian Front) must be excluded from government—while their rights to raise hell through the public channels of democratic debate are vigorously reaffirmed. Ideas are not the enemy; an awareness of the distinction between communism as an idea and the Communist parties as battalions of Soviet espionage and sabotage is essential to any national wisdom. It is that distinction which both Congressman Rankin and William Z. Foster try to blur. Rankin, and the frightened men around him, would destroy all dissent as an expression of "communism." Foster publicly depicts the Communist party as a native American voice of dissent.

To say that these ambiguities are overwhelming and that any "loyalty" procedure in government is intrinsically doomed to become a replica of the Palmer raids in 1920 is in effect to let reaction run the program as it pleases. For the Communist apparatus does exist in the real world. If liberals cannot face the reality of Communist intrigue as they once recognized the scope of the Fascist fifth column, the Congressional cops will run the show; if liberals cannot offer an affirmative, clearly defined plan of democratic self-defense the witch hunt may truly be upon us.

THE ATOMIC ENERGY PROBLEM [3]

During late 1945 and extending over to something more than the first half of 1946 our government, and indeed most of those who were our allies in the last war, operated in an atmosphere which from today's viewpoint seems to have been almost rosily optimistic. The United Nations were organized with high hopes for immediate solution of some of the world's most troublesome problems. The bills which were introduced into our Congress for domestic control of atomic energy, and the act which was eventually passed, provided for a subordination of many of our domestic interests to the international agreement which it was expected would soon be reached. The Board of Consultants of the State Department issued the so-called Acheson-Lilienthal Report outlining principles of international control which it seemed might well be acceptable to all nations. Mr. Baruch, our representative on the United Nations Atomic Energy Commission, made for the United States a concrete proposal which offered a great sacrifice on the part of the nation in order to achieve a workable program for international control. If that plan, or any modification of it, had been agreed to by the United Nations and accepted by the Congress under procedures detailed in the Act, we would now be operating under Section 8 (b) of the Atomic Energy Act of 1946, usually called the McMahon Act, which reads as follows:

Any provision of this Act or any action of the Commission to the extent that it conflicts with the provisions of any international arrange-

[3] From "The Work of the U.S. Atomic Energy Commission," speech by Commissioner Sumner T. Pike before Cooper Union Forum, New York City, January 13, 1948.

ment made after the date of enactment of this Act shall be deemed to be of no further force or effect.

One intent of the Congress was clear—the United Nations would handle international problems, while the United States Atomic Energy Commission would operate in only the domestic field. It was clearly the hope and belief of the Congress that long before tonight the threat of the atomic weapon would be obsolete. The declaration of policy in the preamble of the McMahon Act states in part:

It is hereby declared to be the policy of the people of the United States that, subject at all times to the paramount objective of assuring the common defense and security, the development and utilization of atomic energy shall, so far as practicable, be directed toward improving the public welfare, increasing the standard of living, strengthening free competition in private enterprise, and promoting world peace.

Since the expected international agreement has not been reached, what the lawyers call the "saving clause"

Subject at all times to the paramount objective of assuring the common defense and security

has attained an importance far beyond what the Congress expected when it passed the Act.

Now, what does this Act do? It uses the familiar device of an independent commission to administer the terms of an act passed by Congress. In a way this Commission is an arm of the Executive Branch but is a creature of the Congress. The Commission is charged as agent of the people of the United States with the ownership and operation of a vast property representing the expenditure of many hundreds of millions of dollars a year. It is charged with a heavy responsibility in determining the fitness on the basis of loyalty, character and associations of the nearly fifty thousand people who work in this nation's atomic energy program, either on the Commission staff or as employees of its contractors. It is charged with manufacture of fissionable material and the many by-products of the nuclear reactor and it is finally charged with the manufacture of bombs. It is directed to conduct, direct and encourage research in the many wide fields which open up from these great discoveries. It is also charged with letting people know what it is doing, all the way from furnishing the most complex basic scientific data as raw material for nuclear scientists to supplying either on its own motion or application of the citizens of the United States, the things which they should legitimately know in order to make the decisions which they will inevitably have to make as time goes on. Paradoxically, of course, it is entrusted with weighty secrets which must be carefully guarded until the world can be sure that no evil use will be made of them.

Due not only to the unique nature of the subject, but to the fact that in the words of the Act, "The effect of the use of atomic energy for civilian purposes upon the social, economic, and political structures of today cannot now be determined," Congress provided a special set of auxiliary machinery to insure the closest possible coordination of those agencies of the government having direct responsibility in this field.

There is a Military Liaison Committee consisting of six high-ranking military officials. This Committee lives with us a good deal of the time, has a staff of its own and effects a continual give and take between our job and the National Military Establishment. A Joint Congressional Committee of nine Senators and nine Representatives also has its own staff which keeps in constant touch with us, and the Committee holds frequent meetings either by itself or with our Commission and its staff so that a continuous understanding between the legislative body and our Commission can be maintained.

There is also a General Advisory Committee, consisting mostly of eminent scientists in this field. . . . This Committee is appointed by the President, meets with us at stated intervals and through subcommittees is constantly at work in its role, which is something akin to that of elder statesmen.

Last, and possibly least, is the Commission itself, consisting of a chairman and four other members, a general manager in complete charge of operations, and four statutory department heads, covering research, production, engineering and military application. To go farther into the organizational machinery would, I am afraid, lead to more confusion than enlightenment at this point.

As you probably know, on the first day of 1947, this Commission took over, lock, stock and barrel, the enterprise conducted during the war, and in the interim after it, by what was known as the Manhattan Engineer District. The Manhattan District, headed by Major General, now Lieutenant General Leslie R. Groves, was a war enterprise and completed the job for which it was organized on the target date and in an impressive fashion. It also carried on for well over a year while policies were being made, minds were being made up and laws were being passed. It fulfilled the discouraging task of keeping the various elements functioning when everybody was sick of war and wanted to go home, as a good many did.

Now what did the Atomic Energy Commission take over? Well, we inherited at once one of the largest manufacturing organizations in the world, representing almost all of the elements of a complex countrywide business organization, except one item, which is fairly essential to anything called a business; that is, income from sales, of which we have practically none. . . .

Until it does come to pass that this nation has no need, in the common defense and security, to manufacture weapons or to accumulate and hold materials from which weapons can be made, the Commission's responsibility on behalf of the people is crystal clear. It is to push weapon development as fast and as far as may be possible. That responsibility is being discharged. . . .

One [problem causing] great and immediate concern refers to the people who either work directly or through contractors on our projects, and especially those who live in these artificial creations, our company towns. Each one of these people is subject to thorough investigation by the FBI as to his character, associations and loyalty. Naturally in as large a group as fifty thousand people, some of the reports which come to us raise doubts as to the suitability of the employee to work on such a vital national enterprise. On the other hand, in dealing with human beings, one must remember the inevitability of certain fallibilities and also that testimony which is given without possibility of cross examination or confronting the accused wth his witness, can be biased and sometimes downright cruelly malicious.

The power which may amount to that of making or breaking a person's career is one not to be used frivolously. We are not satisfied with the stop-gap methods which we have been tentatively using and are taking steps to make the necessary improvement. . . . The maintenance of proper security or secrecy in certain of our operations is one of the most difficult and puzzling problems which the Commission has to face. Under wartime conditions with quite complete control of personnel and material and a highly keyed up sense of urgency in our population, the problem was much simpler, but even then difficult decisions had to be made.

If we were dealing with a static situation where a formula known to but a few people could be locked up and securely guarded, the measures for secrecy could be simple and complete. The fact is that in a constant and necessary attempt to improve both methods of operation and product, the cooperative efforts of large groups of people are necessary and these people must, in order to further the common cause, be able to talk with each other, compare notes, lay out and fulfill programs.

As the armed services have found through bitter experience, when large numbers of people share information over a considerable period of time, it is inevitable that leaks occur. They occur in spite of the best intentions. There need be nothing subversive or inimical in the motives of the people who spill information. The usual sources are indiscretions and inadvertent errors which having once occurred cannot be recalled. You may remember how our OSS in the recent war was able to trace the operation of German synthetic oil plants and refineries through the publication in an obscure official journal of the freight rates for oil products from these locations. It is my feeling that this situation must be accepted as one of the facts of life inevitably involved with the make-up of human beings. This does not mean, however, that real security need be lost or even impaired. With groups of competent people working intelligently on new processes and improvements on present ones, it is not only possible but probable that despite the inevitable seepage of so-called "secret information," the group or nation which pursues the positive plan will continue to be further ahead of the field than the one which sits with a bunch of keys in its hand, each key representing a locked up, unproductive, secret fact or formula.

This problem has an analogy to the one which the ship owner and captain face in the operation of a vessel. It is almost inevitable that any ship in operation on the high seas will leak. In fact, any ship captain will tell you that he doesn't feel comfortable until it takes a few strokes of the pump each day to clear the bilges of seepage. There is an old seafaring expression, "She doesn't leak enough to keep her sweet." Theoretically it would be possible to put the ship in dry dock at each port and completely stop every leak, but this would defeat the main object of operating a ship which is to carry cargo and people from place to place expeditiously and efficiently. A ship that has no leaks, but cannot make voyages, is effectively no ship at all. So a compromise has to be made accepting the fact of the slow seepages and pursuing the main purpose for which the ship was built.

This is I believe something of our situation in atomic energy. We have to go somewhere. We have to learn things. We need large groups of people working on various phases of the project. This is our main objective. In attaining that objective we have to accept, however reluctantly, the fact that bits and pieces of information which we would rather keep secret will inevitably leak out, but we do hope and expect to move fast enough along our course so that we will be much farther ahead of our competitors than if we stayed in dry dock, devoting our main energy to the hopeless task of keeping a large organization completely leakproof.

Another problem . . . is that of a general, broad, countrywide understanding of the elements of this business which people are going to need to have in order to make up their minds as to how they want to have this thing handled. During the last century we have had to make up our minds how to regulate railroads, although few of us could lay a piece of track, or biuld a locomotive. We have had to learn how to control our electric utilities although few of us know or care much about the technical problems of power production. We have tried not too successfully to handle the public problems involved by the coming of the automobile, although today few of us know what to do when we open the hood, or when we get down under the transmission. We have set up a system of public regulation for the radio, although few of us are experts in electronics.

The developments in the nuclear field—some of them are here, more of them are coming—they must be handled in the public interest and by the voters through the Congress which passes the laws and us who administer this particular law. To deny the existence of the problem and hide our heads in sand, or to let chilly panic take hold of us when the name of atomic energy is mentioned, is just the worst possible procedure. These things as they come up are susceptible, as most questions are, to calm, sane, common sense and to debate on lines to which we are perfectly accustomed, and to decision by democratic methods to which this country is used. This is one of these problems where the Commission cannot come forward with the solution. We hope to be of considerable help. It is a problem which deserves the best thought of the people who have concern about the future of this country and the world. If we fail, all our beautiful dreams of the future will be but as ashes in our mouths.

INCREASED GOVERNMENT CONTROL [4]

There are . . . deep-seated causes for grave anxiety about the future of the freedom of the press. Modern democratic society is in the greatest crisis of its history, because new conditions have been rapidly created by a technical civilization . . . which have an indirect but strong tendency to increase governmental control over the distribution of news and opinions. . . . [Among these is] *the growth of functions, range of activities, and interventions of government generally.*—Technical instruments make for a more complete control of many social activities by the government. . . . The same instruments make for a state control of public opinion. . . .

[4] By Zechariah Chafee, Jr., professor of law, Harvard University, and author of *Freedom of the Press in the United States. Government and Mass Communications: A Report from the Commission on Freedom of the Press*, Vol. I. University of Chicago Press. Chicago. 1947. p. 4-29. Reprinted by permission.

In many subjects the complexity of the pertinent facts increases. Equal access to the facts becomes more and more difficult. The power of governments over the sources of information tends to grow. Hence the misuse of this power by governments becomes a more and more serious danger. Governments withhold one part of the facts and use the other for sales talk. This tendency is fostered by general worship of efficient salesmanship. Hence we observe an increasing amount of government activity in the field of what is called "propaganda," viz., the creation by government of various kinds of information and publicity, thus emphasizing and stimulating public interest and response in certain directions at the expense of other interests and ideas. Even when completely devoid of such intentions to falsify and propagandize, governments must make increasing use of communications. . . .

On the other hand, a modern government makes great demands for secrecy. Of course, state secrets are nothing new. Military information was always guarded from the enemy, and bureaucrats have often invoked public safety as a protection from criticism. What is significant is the enormous recent expansion of the subjects which officials are seeking to hide from publication until they give the signal. If persuasion fails to prevent leaks, they are tempted to use threats. The result may be a hush-hush attitude, likely to extend beyond the real public need for silence. . . . A direct consequence of secrecy in the ordinary press may be great activity of the subsidiary press in disseminating the concealed material, and this is more dangerous than frank discussion in the general press. One may add that Drew Pearson's rumors are a poor substitute for frank official disclosures. Too often we get as gossip what ought to reach us as regular news.

No doubt there are many matters which ought not to be disclosed for a time, but the officials should not have a free hand to determine what those matters are or to lock them up forever. It may be human nature for them to want their mere say-so to be decisive on the need for secrecy, but the possession of such a power would allow them to hoist public safety as an umbrella to cover their own mistakes. Secrecy has other dangers. The controversy over atomic bomb control shows how the claim of military security may possibly be used to hamper civilians in proper scientific activity, the progress of which depends on public communication in lectures and learned periodicals. In short, official encroachments on freedom of the press will be probable unless the boundary line between secrecy and publicity is very carefully demarcated. And officials must not do the demarcating. That is a job for the representatives of the people in Congress. . . .

The belief is growing that freedom of the press is so important to the state that it cannot be irresponsibly exercised. . . . But . . . the meaning which our ancestors gave to liberty of the press, namely, freedom from the will of legislators and officials, is just as vital today as it was in 1791. . . . This does not mean that all state activity in the field of communications is necessarily bad. . . . The point is that unwise state activity must be steadily resisted.

AMERICA'S CONTRADICTORY POLICY [5]

The developments of the last two years have been contradictory—in the field of atomic energy as in the wider realm of human affairs. . . . Militarism rises in traditionally civilian America, and nationalism in the Soviet Union, originally dedicated to intransigent internationalism. Generals and admirals admit that national security is an obsolete notion, but military budgets swell as never before. The atomic bomb has much to do with these contradictory trends. Opinion polls show that a substantial majority of Americans is ready for extreme sacrifices of national sovereignty, if these could buy freedom from fear of an atomic war. . . .

At the same time, the feeling of overwhelming power which the bomb gives the United States contributes largely to the callous nonchalance with which a new war is often discussed. Apprehension of the time when America will not be the sole posses-

[5] From "Two Years After Hiroshima," editorial. *Bulletin of the Atomic Scientists.* 3:233-4. September 1947. Reprinted by permission.

sor of the Absolute Weapon, breeds thoughts of a preventive war. The fear of losing atomic secrets endangers the fabric of American civil liberties. . . .

We want a world free of the threat of atomic weapons; but we also want to keep our bombs as long as possible. If international control is established, we might still want a few bombs to be left at the disposal of the United Nations—in the hope that if the worst comes to the worst, these bombs will be "on our side."

In the general field of world politics, the American policy also has a double set of objectives. We work both for the strengthening of the United Nations, and for the acquistion of outlying bases; for universal disarmament and for secret development of new methods of mass destruction; for rehabilitation of war-devastated Europe and Asia, and for such distribution of our assistance as would strengthen our allies and weaken our potential enemies. In brief, we try to abolish war and to be in a position to win it.

THE POLICY OF SECRECY AS TO ATOMIC ENERGY

DISCUSSION

The whole issue of security of information would have little or no importance if this nation had no particularly vital information to keep "secure." Quite understandably, the far-reaching implications of possible misuse of the atom bomb have placed the United States government in a difficult position.

During the war, development of the atom bomb was a closely guarded military secret, kept even from the American public and Congress. It is doubtful if any person in the United States could seriously argue against the policy of secrecy enshrouding the initial military development of the atom bomb.

But with war's end, control of the atomic energy program passed from military to civilian hands. The vast potentials for the enhancement of civilization were eagerly discussed and the public sat back expecting great new things to come. But in three years' time little had been added to public knowledge. The great strides in technological advancement, predicted with the first announcement of the bombing of Hiroshima, the promised "atomic era" still haven't materialized. So far, there has been little protest from the public, but criticism is becoming stronger from more informed groups such as science and the press.

The question is not that of giving away the secret of the atom bomb. No one questions that the secret of the bomb must be preserved as long as it proves militarily expedient. The real question is how far secrecy should extend. The scientists as a group seem to believe that much of the hush-hush over atomic energy is needless and that it hampers scientific research and investigation, that through over-exercise of secrecy precautions, we are delaying the advancement of technological progress in the use and control of atomic energy for peacetime productive purposes.

A partial answer to the question may be found in the development of the governmental policy with regard to information about the atomic energy program. Let us go back to the first public release of information—Hiroshima—and bring the story up to date.

THE FIRST STATEMENT: PRESIDENT TRUMAN [1]

Sixteen hours ago an American airplane dropped one bomb on Hiroshima, an important Japanese army base. That bomb had more power than 20,000 tons of TNT. . . . It is an atomic bomb. It is a harnessing of the basic power of the universe. . . . The fact that we can release atomic energy ushers in a new era in man's understanding of nature's forces. . . .

It has never been the habit of the scientists of this country or the policy of this government to withhold from the world scientific knowledge. Normally, therefore, everything about the work with atomic energy would be made public. But under present circumstances it is not intended to divulge the technical processes of production or all the military applications, pending further examination of possible methods of protecting us and the rest of the world from the danger of sudden destruction.

STORY BEHIND THE BOMB [2]

The requirements of security do not permit any revelation at this time of the exact methods by which bombs are produced or of the nature of their action. However, in accord with its policy of keeping the people of the nation as completely informed as is consistent with national security, the War Department wishes to make known at this time . . . the story behind this tremendous weapon. . . .

[1] Excerpts from the statement by the President of the United States, August 6, 1945, in first announcing the use of the atomic bomb at Hiroshima.
[2] Excerpts from a statement by the Secretary of War, Henry L. Stimson, August 6, 1945, Washington, D.C.

The chain of scientific discoveries which has led to the atomic bomb began at the turn of the century when radioactivity was discovered. Until 1939 work in this field was worldwide, being carried on particularly in the United States, the United Kingdom, Germany, France, Italy and Denmark.

. Before the lights went out over Europe and the advent of war imposed security restrictions, the fundamental scientific knowledge concerning atomic energy from which has been developed the atomic bomb now in use by the United States was widely known in many countries, both Allied and Axis. The war, however, ended the exchange of scientific information on this subject and, with the exception of the United Kingdom and Canada, the status of work in this field in other countries is not fully known. . . . Thus it was evident when the war began that the development of atomic energy for war purposes would occur in the near future and it was a question of which nations would control the discovery. . . .

Late in 1939 the possibility of using atomic energy for military purposes was brought to the attention of President Roosevelt. He appointed a committee to survey the problem. Research . . . was put on a full-scale basis as a result of the recommendations of various scientific committees. At the end of 1941 the decision was made to go all-out on research work. . . .

From the outset extraordinary secrecy and security measures have surrounded the project. This was personally ordered by President Roosevelt and his orders have been strictly complied with. The work has been completely compartmentalized so that while many thousands of people have been associated with the program in one way or another no one has been given more information concerning it than was absolutely essential to his particular job. As a result only a few highly placed persons in government and science know the entire story. It was inevitable, of course, that public curiosity would be aroused concerning so large a project and that citizens would make inquiries of members of Congress. In such instances the members of Congress have been most cooperative and have accepted in good faith the statment of the War Department that military security precluded any disclosure of detailed information.

In the appropriation of funds, the Congress has accepted the assurances of the Secretary of War and the Chief of Staff that the appropriations made were absolutely essential to national security. The War Department is confident that the Congress will agree that its faith was not a mistake. Because it has not been possible for Congress to keep a close check on the expenditure of the funds appropriated for the project which to June 30, 1945, amounted to $1,950,000,000, key scientific phases of the work have been reviewed from time to time by eminently qualified scientists and industrial leaders in order to be certain that the expenditures were warranted by the potentialities of the program.

The press and radio of the nation, as in so many other instances, have complied wholeheartedly with the requests of the Office of Censorship that publicity on any phase of this subject be suppressed. . . .

It was early recognized that in order to make certain that this tremendous weapon would not fall into the hands of the enemy prompt action should be taken to control patents in the field and to secure control over the ore which is indispensable to the process. Substantial patent control has been accomplished in the United States, the United Kingdom, and Canada. In each country all personnel engaged in the work, both scientific and industrial, are required to assign their entire rights to any invention in this field to their respective governments. . . . All patent actions taken are surrounded by all safeguards necessary for the security of the project. . . .

Because of the widespread knowledge and interest in this subject even before the war, there is no possibility of avoiding the risks inherent in this knowledge by any long-term policy of secrecy. . . . Every effort is being bent toward assuring that this weapon and the new field of science that stands behind it will be employed wisely in the interests of the security of peace-loving nations and the well being of the world.

THE NEW POLICY CONCEPT [3]

The discovery of the means of releasing atomic energy began a new era in the history of civilization. . . . Never in history has society been confronted with a power so full of potential danger and at the same time so full of promise for the future of man and for the peace of the world. . . . The first and most urgent step is the determination of our domestic policy for the control, use, and development of atomic energy within the United States.

We cannot postpone decisions in this field. . . . Atomic force in ignorant or evil hands could inflict untold disaster upon the nation and the world. Society cannot hope even to protect itself—much less to realize the benefits of the discovery—unless prompt action is taken to guard against the hazards of misuse. . . .

Measures . . . may seem drastic and far reaching but the discovery with which we are dealing involves forces of nature too dangerous to fit into any of our usual concepts.

In international relations, as in domestic affairs, the release of atomic energy constitutes a new force too revolutionary to consider in the framework of old ideas. We can no longer rely on the slow process of time to develop a program of control among nations. Civilization demands that we shall reach at the earliest possible date a satisfactory arrangement for the control of this discovery in order that it may become a powerful and forceful influence toward the maintenance of world peace instead of an instrument of destruction.

THE TRIPARTITE AGREEMENT [4]

We recognize that the application of recent scientific discoveries to the methods and practice of war has placed at the

[3] Excerpts from a message from the President of the United States to Congress transmitting a request for the enactment of legislation to fix a policy covering the use and development of the atomic bomb, October 3, 1945.

[4] Excerpts from the three-nation agreed declaration on atomic energy, Washington, D.C., November 15, 1945, issued by President Harry S. Truman, Prime Minister C. R. Attlee of the United Kingdom, and Prime Minister W. L. Mackenzie King of Canada.

disposal of mankind means of destruction hitherto unknown, against which there can be no adequate military defense, and in the employment of which no single nation can in fact have a monopoly.

We desire to emphasize that the responsibility for devising means to ensure that the new discoveries shall be used for the benefit of mankind, instead of as a means of destruction, rests not on our nations alone, but upon the whole civilized world. Nevertheless, the progress that we have made in the development and use of atomic energy demands that we take an initiative in the matter, and we have accordingly met together to consider the possibility of international action:—

a. To prevent the use of atomic energy for destructive purposes;

b. To promote the use of recent and future advances in scientific knowledge, particularly in the utilization of atomic energy, for peaceful and humanitarian ends.

We are aware that the only complete protection for the civilized world from the destructive use of scientific knowledge lies in the prevention of war. No system of safeguards that can be devised will of itself provide an effective guarantee against production of atomic weapons by a nation bent on aggression. . . .

We believe that the fruits of scientific research should be made available to all nations, and that freedom of investigation and free interchange of ideas are essential to the progress of knowledge.

We have considered the question of the disclosure of detailed information concerning the practical industrial application of atomic energy. The military exploitation of atomic energy depends, in large part, upon the same methods and processes as would be required for industrial uses.

We are not convinced that the spreading of the specialized information regarding the practical application of atomic energy, before it is possible to devise effective, reciprocal, and enforceable safeguards acceptable to all nations, would contribute to a constructive solution of the problem of the atomic bomb. On the contrary we think it might have the opposite effect. We are, however, prepared to share, on a reciprocal basis with others of the United Nations, detailed information concerning the practical industrial application of atomic energy just as soon as effective enforceable safeguards against its use for destructive purposes can be devised. . . .

POLICY ON INFORMATION CONTROL [5]

A very serious question arises . . . when we reach the stage of exchanging detailed information about the industrial application of atomic energy. The thought to be borne in mind is that up to a certain rather advanced point, the so-called "know-how" of production is the same whether atomic energy is to be stored in bombs or harnessed as power for a peaceful industrial purpose. And so it was necessary . . . to determine in the light of this fact, how soon information concerning the practical application of atomic energy could be disseminated.

Only one answer was possible. Until effective safeguards can be developed, in the form of international inspection or otherwise, the secrets of production know-how must be held, in the words of the President, as a sacred trust—a trust in the exercise of which we are already under definite international obligation. . . .

While we consider it proper and necessary, therefore, to continue for a time to hold these production secrets in trust, this period need not be unnecessarily prolonged. As experience demonstrates that the sharing of information is full and unreserved, it is to be hoped that the exchange, for peaceful purposes, can be extended to some and eventually to all the practical applications of atomic energy and of other scientific discoveries. This is the objective we seek.

If we can move gradually but surely toward free and unlimited exchange of scientific and industrial information, to control and perhaps eventually to eliminate the manufacture

[5] Excerpts from an address by James F. Byrnes (then Secretary of State) at Charleston, South Carolina, November 16, 1945.

of atomic weapons and other weapons capable of mass destruction, we will have progressed toward achieving freedom from fear.

PUBLIC REALIZATION OF THE ISSUE [6]

In the months following President Truman's declaration of a protective trusteeship over the methods of large-scale atomic fission, the nation was preoccupied with the change and readjustment entailed in the transition from a wartime economy. In the general desire for swift demobilization and in the perplexities of the first efforts to resume prewar patterns of living, the atomic energy developments received only a portion of the public attention they were to absorb in later months. . . .

It was some time before the general public came to understand that the atomic bomb could not be demobilized along with the other weapons of war, that deactivating it safely would require effective international safeguards of a novel character, and that the desirable peaceful developments of atomic energy would raise unusual economic and social questions.

Secretary of War Patterson's order of October 20, 1945, was a decisive aid to a wider understanding:

Public discussion of great issues such as the dissemination and regulation of knowledge of atomic science is one of the basic principles on which democratic government is founded. In it all citizens have a right to participate. American scientists in particular, because of their knowledge of the technical matters involved in the achievement, can contribute powerfully to it. Security, of course, still requires that nothing beyond the specific subject matter contained in the Smyth Report be brought into discussion, and the use of due care that matters outside the content of this report and still under security regulations be not inadvertently encroached upon. With this sole restriction, however, which applies to all citizens, our scientists should feel that it is proper for them as citizens to join actively in public consideration of this question.

Privately sponsored proposals for national action in this period ranged from the suggestion that the United States keep

[6] From "International Control of Atomic Energy: Growth of a Policy." Department of State Publication. 2702:11-21. 1946. Government Printing Office. Washington, D.C.

permanently the "secret" of atomic fission and the atomic bomb, to the suggestion that all information held by the United States be turned over immediately to the Security Council as a gesture of confidence in the United Nations organization.

Nationwide and statewide polls conducted by various organizations in the summer months and published in September and October summed up these reactions. . . .

Question: Do you think the secret of making bombs should be put under the control of the new United Nations Security Council, or should the United States keep this secret to itself?

Answer:	September per cent	October per cent
Put under United Nations control	14	17
U. S. should keep control.	73	71
No opinion	13	12

Polls summarized in November indicated some shift in opinion. Although 85 per cent of the individuals questioned thought the United States should keep the "secret" as long as possible . . . 51 per cent would share the "secret" *if* the United Nations could control atomic weapons so that no country could use them to start a future war. Confidence in the ability of the United States to retain for any considerable length of time the secrets of atomic bomb manufacture dropped sharply between October 1945, and February 1946. . . .

As public awareness of the alternative to effective international control deepened, there was a remarkable effort made to understand the scientific realities of atomic energy. The effort was stimulated by the early release of . . . the first technical study of the Manhattan Project . . . by Henry DeWolf Smyth. On the new atomic explosive Mr. Smyth wrote:

Here is a new tool for mankind, a tool of unimaginable destructive power. Its development raises many questions that must be answered in the near future. Because of the restrictions of military security there has been no chance for the Congress or the people to debate such questions. . . . In a free country like ours, such questions should be debated by the people and the decisions must be made by the people through their representatives. This is one reason for the release of this report.

The extended Senate and House hearings on atomic energy proposals brought the conclusions of the country's foremost scientists, statesmen, industrialists and military leaders to bear upon problems of control. In the Senate this information was brought together before a single body . . . [the] Senate Special Committee on Atomic Energy. . . .

Hearings were begun late in November [1945] and the Committee published its report on April 19, 1946. . . . On the basis of this testimony the Committee decided that it seemed evident that certain facts relating to atomic energy, including all technical data on the design and construction of the bomb, ought to be kept secret, "at least until effective and reciprocal international safeguards could be devised." Legislation, however, should "facilitate as far as possible (1) international agreements on atomic energy which would themselves be a step toward international understanding and good will, and (2) the rapid scientific development of atomic energy which would promote both the industrial prosperity of the world and the improvement of our own instruments of national defense." . . . The result was a bill that sought to create a system of domestic control "designed to protect the common defense and security, without constituting an obstacle to the attainment of satisfactory international controls," . . . [which] was signed by the President on August 1, 1946.

THE SCIENTIST AND THE SECRECY POLICY [7]

Freedom of investigation and discussion has been the cornerstone of scientific progress. Continued scientific progress is today not only important to the scientists, but in many fields it is necessary to the long-range success of the atomic energy development. Since the withholding of information in certain fields, pending certain international arrangements, is a declared national policy written into law, the scientist is confronted with

[7] From "The Physicist and the Future Development of Atomic Energy," by Robert F. Bacher, member of the United States Atomic Energy Commission, in an address before the American Physical Society, New York City, January 30, 1948. Press release.

major problems in following his profession. These problems are an immediate concern of the Atomic Energy Commission since progress in the related fundamental science is vital to the long-range success of the atomic energy project. . . .

At the end of the war, large numbers of the scientists who had been engaged in the war work returned to their normal prewar pursuits. We were eager to get back to the free and unrestricted scientific atmosphere in which we had lived before the war. We were all tired of working at classified projects Moreover, most of us felt that the war was over and that many of the subjects considered classified during the war would no longer need to be kept as such. Indeed, many articles on subjects which had not been mentioned aloud for years soon started to appear. Electronic developments in radar and the proximity fuse, nuclear physics and particularly neutron physics, and a host of other subjects began to appear in scientific journals.

In the atomic energy project, a committee of scientists was set up to recommend policies of declassification. This committee, which was headed by Dr. Richard Tolman of the California Institute of Technology, first met in the fall of 1945. At that time the committee set apart a considerable number of scientific and technical subjects which it felt could be immediately declassified without prejudice to any vital secrets of the Atomic Energy Project. The subjects recommended for declassification included certain sections of basic physics, chemistry, metallurgy, biology, and certain technological developments, many of which have today appeared in various scientific and technical journals.

In addition, the committee considered that there were other questions more closely connected with the production and use of fissionable material which must be reserved for later consideration. In particular, there was a further group of subjects clearly connected with the development of atomic weapons which it was felt could not be considered for possible declassification until a satisfactory international arrangement for the control of atomic energy had been developed. At that time, most scientists felt that there would soon be progress toward international understanding, and we all shared some hope that the policy of declassification was an interim policy which would be largely unnecessary upon the establishment of suitable international arrangements.

In the summer of 1946, the United States advanced a proposal for the international control of atomic energy in the first meeting of the United Nations Atomic Energy Commission. These proposals have been debated pro and con for something over a year and a half. With some minor exceptions, they have met with approval by the majority of the countries which have been, or are, members of that Commission. Unfortunately, a small minority has held a quite different view on the fundamental nature of a proposal for the control of atomic energy. This difference is not just a minor one but goes so deep that it would be naive to think that an agreement is just around the corner.

While every effort should be made to attempt to resolve these difficulties, it would certainly be unrealistic at this time for us to continue to regard the subjects of declassification and the prosecution of unclassified and classified research as ones which will soon be resolved in the light of a far reaching international agreement. Whatever policy is adopted now for unrestricted research and the continuation of research and development in the classified areas must be more than just an interim policy. . . .

For the development and production of fissionable materials and weapons, it is now necessary, and it will probably continue to be necessary, to maintain strict security and secrecy. Such security safeguards will, necessarily, have to carry over into certain of the peacetime uses of atomic energy. For example, the development of nuclear reactors is closely tied to the production of fissionable material and will need to be classified. On the other hand, many of the uses of these reactors are unclassified. Radioactive isotopes produced in the Oak Ridge reactor are now distributed in this country and to foreign countries, and efforts are being made to promote their use in a wide range of scientific and technical researches. Many fundamental physical and chemical experiments have been made possible by the strong neutron sources which these reactors provide. Results of numerous such experiments have appeared in scientific journals. . . .

During the past year several requests have been made to the Commission for an exact demarcation between classified and unclassified information. Some people have construed the Atomic Energy Act to mean that all information touching on nuclear physics is classified until declassified. The Commission does not believe that all nuclear physics is or should be classified. It is not possible, however, to offer a flat guarantee to anyone that, in pursuing a certain course of investigation, he will not come upon information which should be restricted under the terms of the Act. For work in most areas which do not touch upon fissionable materials or other special products of the Atomic Energy Project, the probability is great that classified information will be avoided. It is just this conviction which prompts us to place emphasis upon the creation of unclassified areas in the national laboratories and upon the pursuit of unclassified research in the universities.

Under the Atomic Energy Act, access to restricted data ordinarily will not be granted to any individual "until the Federal Bureau of Investigation shall have made an investigation and report to the Commission on the character, associations, and loyalty of such individual and the Commission shall have determined that permitting such person to have access to restricted data will not endanger the common defense or security." It is upon this statement of the McMahon Act, and upon other statements of that Act which are somewhat more detailed, that the clearance policies of the Atomic Energy Commission are based.

During the past year there has been considerable hardship occasioned by the clearance procedure required by the new law. The tremendous amount of work to be done by the Federal Bureau of Investigation in the investigation of all project personnel required by law has led to many unavoidable but quite serious and costly delays. The Commission believes that the orderly process of clearance will in the future be much faster.

For scientists in particular, the question of clearance raises definite problems. In any project involving restricted data, the scientists are usually the ones who must have those data. Moreover, a significant fraction of scientists in certain fields are at present associated to some degree with restricted information. Under those circumstances, failure of clearance for an individual may exclude many possibilities for employment and may, unfortunately, influence an employer not to employ that person on a completely unclassified project. Yet, it is very likely that there will be some who do not meet the requirements for clearance stated in the Atomic Energy Act.

Under these circumstances, the greatest care must be taken to avoid injustice and to provide an opportunity for any person to be heard and to learn the reasons for the action in case of denial of clearance.

MEASURES TO PRESERVE THE SECRET

DISCUSSION

Once having determined that the secret of atomic energy should be held by the United States for as long as possible, or until international controls over its use could be established, the next step logically was to institute specific measures to control the flow of information relating to the program.

During the war, under the military, the atomic energy program was 100 per cent secret. Its very existence was known only to a few high-ranking officials. Congress had appropriated money for atomic development with scarcely more than the word of military leaders that it would be used to develop a powerful new weapon. Ordinary secrecy was simpler to maintain during the war.

Under the newly created civilian Atomic Energy Commission, the problem was not so simple. Purely for expediency, the entire security program of the military operation was continued under civilian management. But during the war the military authorities could justifiably classify almost any type of information as potentially dangerous if published. But the civilian AEC was in no such position. The war was over, in the minds of most people at least, and the public was reluctant to accept the word of the civilian authorities that secrecy must be maintained. Of particular concern, in view of the magnitude of this greatest of government monopolies, were the measures actually put into effect to preserve the secret.

Basically, they were of two types: rigid controls over release of news and information about atomic energy, and equally rigid controls over the personnel handling any phase of atomic energy.

The first, controls over information, was in the nature of censorship at the source, i.e., actual suppression of all information felt to be harmful if released. To offset the handicaps to scientific progress this program entailed, the AEC was to "declassify" as much material on atomic energy as fast as possible. Upon "declassification" that particular item of information would be channeled to the press and other interested parties.

The second, controls over personnel, required some further improvising. The military had carried out extensive investigations of all personnel employed on the atomic projects before they were ever hired. But Russia was then an ally. Our enemies were clearly Germany and Japan and Italy. Security clearances were employed primarily to trace spies and saboteurs, rather than evidence of pro-Communist leanings. Now, the enemy was merely a potential one. Loyalty investigation required extensive probing into political convictions and past associations, with a different enemy in mind. None of the clearances developed during the war could apply any longer, and the whole procedure had to be revamped accordingly.

The basic fundamentals of the control measures and their operation are explained in the pages immediately following.

THE ATOMIC ENERGY ACT OF 1946 [1]

SECTION 1.

a. FINDINGS AND DECLARATION.—Research and experimentation in the field of nuclear chain reaction have attained the stage at which the release of atomic energy on a large scale is practical. The significance of the atomic bomb for military purposes is evident. The effect of the use of atomic energy for civilian purposes upon the social, economic, and political structures of today cannot now be determined. It is a field in which unknown factors are involved. Therefore, any legislation will necessarily be subject to revision from time to time. It is reasonable to anticipate, however, that tapping this new source of energy will cause profound changes in our present way of life. Accordingly, it is hereby declared to be the policy of the people of the United States that, subject at all times to the paramount objective of assuring the common defense and security, the de-

[1] From "The Atomic Energy Act of 1946," Public Law 585—79th Congress.

velopment and utilization of atomic energy shall, so far as practicable, be directed toward improving the public welfare, increasing the standard of living, strengthening free competition in private enterprise, and promoting world peace.

b. PURPOSE OF ACT.—It is the purpose of this Act to effectuate the policies set out in section 1 (a) by providing, among others, for. . . .

2. A program for the control of scientific and technical information which will permit the dissemination of such information to encourage scientific progress, and for the sharing on a reciprocal basis of information concerning the practical industrial application of atomic energy as soon as effective and enforceable safeguards against its use for destructive purposes can be devised. . . .

SECTION 10.

a. POLICY.—It shall be the policy of the Commission to control the dissemination of restricted data in such a manner as to assure the common defense and security. Consistent with such policy, the Commission shall be guided by the following principles:

1. That until Congress declares by joint resolution that effective and enforceable international safeguards against the use of atomic energy for destructive purposes have been established, there shall be no exchange of information with other nations with respect to the use of atomic energy for industrial purposes; and

2. That the dissemination of scientific and technical information relating to atomic energy should be permitted and encouraged so as to provide that free interchange of ideas and criticisms which is essential to scientific progress.

b. RESTRICTIONS.

1. The term "restricted data" as used in this section means all data concerning the manufacture or utilization of atomic weapons, the production of fissionable material, or the use of fissionable material in the production of power, but shall not include any data which the Commission from

time to time determines may be published without adversely affecting the common defense and security.

2. Whoever, lawfully or unlawfully, having possession of, access to, control over, or being entrusted with, any document, writing, sketch, photograph, plan, model, instrument, appliance, note or information involving or incorporating restricted data—

A. Communicates, transmits, or discloses the same to any individual or person, or attempts or conspires to do any of the foregoing, with intent to injure the United States or with intent to secure an advantage to any foreign nation, upon conviction thereof, shall be punished by death or imprisonment for life (but the penalty of death or imprisonment for life may be imposed only upon recommendation of the jury and only in cases where the offense was committed with intent to injure the United States); or by a fine of not more than $20,000 or imprisonment for not more than twenty years, or both;

B. Communicates, transmits, or discloses the same to any individual or person, or attempts or conspires to do any of the foregoing, with reason to believe such data will be utilized to injure the United States or to secure an advantage to any foreign nation, shall, upon conviction, be punished by a fine of not more than $10,000 or imprisonment for not more than ten years, or both.

3. Whoever, with intent to injure the United States or with intent to secure an advantage to any foreign nation, acquires or attempts or conspires to acquire any document, writing, sketch, photograph, plan, model, instrument, appliance, note or information involving or incorporating restricted data shall, upon conviction thereof, be punished by death or imprisonment for life (but the penalty of death or imprisonment for life may be imposed only upon recommendation of the jury and only in cases where the offense was committed with intent to injure the United States); or by a fine of not more than $20,000 or imprisonment for not more than twenty years, or both.

4. Whoever, with intent to injure the United States or with intent to secure an advantage to any foreign nation, removes, conceals, tampers with, alters, mutilates, or destroys any document, writing, sketch, photograph, plan, model instrument, appliance, or note involving or incorporating restricted data and used by any individual or person in connection with the production of fissionable material, or research or development relating to atomic energy, conducted by the United States, or financed in whole or in part by Federal funds, or conducted with the aid of fissionable material, shall be punished by death or imprisonment for life (but the penalty of death or imprisonment for life may be imposed only upon recommendation of the jury and only in cases where the offense was committed with intent to injure the United States); or by a fine of not more than $20,000 or imprisonment for not more than twenty years or both.

5. A. No person shall be prosecuted for any violation under this section unless and until the Attorney General of the United States has advised the Commission with respect to such prosecution and no such prosecution shall be commenced except upon the express direction of the Attorney General of the United States.

B. i. No arrangement shall be made . . . , no contract shall be made or continued in effect . . . , and no license shall be issued . . . , unless the person with whom such arrangement is made, the contractor or prospective contractor, or the prospective licensee agrees in writing not to permit any individual to have access to restricted data until the Federal Bureau of Investigation shall have made an investigation and report to the Commission on the character, association, and loyalty of such individual and the Commission shall have determined that permitting such person to have access to restricted data will not endanger the common defense or security.

ii. Except as authorized by the Commission in case of emergency, no individual shall be employed by the Commission until the Federal Bureau of Investigation shall have made an investigation and report to the Commission on the character, association, and loyalty of such individual.

iii. Notwithstanding the provisions of subparagraphs (i) and (ii), during such period of time after the enactment of this Act as may be necessary to make the investigation, report, and determination required by such paragraphs (a) any individual who was permitted access to restricted data by the Manhattan Engineer District may be permitted access to restricted data and (b) the Commission may employ any individual who was employed by the Manhattan Engineer District.

iv. To protect against the unlawful dissemination of restricted data and to safeguard facilities, equipment, materials, and other property of the Commission, the President shall have authority to utilize the services of any Government agency to the extent he may deem necessary or desirable.

C. All violations of this Act shall be investigated by the Federal Bureau of Investigation of the Department of Justice.

6. This section shall not exclude the applicable provisions of any other laws, except that no Government agency shall take any action under such other laws inconsistent with the provisions of this section.

c. INSPECTIONS, RECORDS, AND REPORTS.—The Commission is—

1. Authorized by regulation or order to require such reports and the keeping of such records with respect to, and to provide for such inspections of, activities and studies of types specified in section 3 and of activities under licenses issued pursuant to section 7 as may be necessary to effectuate the purposes of this Act;

2. Authorized and directed by regulation or order to require regular reports and records with respect to, and to provide for frequent inspections of, the production of fissionable material in the conduct of research and development activities.

THE PATTERN OF SECURITY [2]

The successful prosecution of the vast atomic energy program depends upon the contribution of many and varied segments of American life. Government agencies, industrial concerns, universities, and other educational and research organizations are now participating in the Commission's research and production program under contracts and agreements with the Commission. Through such participation the recognized managerial skills and scientific and technical talents of many organizations are available to the enterprise. The Commission has more than a hundred contractors, and these in turn have several hundred subcontractors. . . .

To provide security for properties and restricted data involved in the program, the security regulations in force when the Commission assumed operating responsibility on January 1, 1947, have been maintained, and a survey of their effectiveness has been instituted. As this very extensive survey and inventory of practices proceeds, changes to provide for greater security and workability have been made. Other changes will be made as required. This is a matter receiving continual review and consideration by the Commission. . . .

The maintenance and improvement of the United States position in the field of atomic energy requires a careful balancing of control and dissemination of information. In our desire to prevent unauthorized transmission of scientific information of military importance we must not go to the extreme of permanently locking up all our information. We must inspire talented

[2] Excerpts from the letter of transmittal of the second semiannual Report of the United States Atomic Energy Commission to Congress, July 22, 1947. Senate Document No. 96. 80th Congress, First Session. p. 3-19. U.S. Government Printing Office. Washington, D.C. 1947.

men to enter the new field and we must give them the information they need in order to proceed. To overconfine today's knowledge is to stifle the development which would provide security tomorrow.

The Commission's program for the protection of restricted data is being ably supported by the Federal Bureau of Investigation and other agencies. Advice has been obtained also from the Congressional Joint Committee on Atomic Energy. The security measures in effect when the Commission assumed operating control have been maintained; in addition these measures have been in process of careful review and they have been strengthened in a number of instances.

At the same time effort is being made to facilitate the appropriate declassification and distribution of information not essential to national security. The Commission's Technical Information Branch is currently studying and clearing for public release approximately a hundred technical articles each month; a group of more than a hundred leading scientists cooperate in this work. Articles are declassified only if determined to conform to carefully established criteria which were codified by the Manhattan Engineer District on the general basis of the report by the Committee on Declassification under the chairmanship of Dr. R. C. Tolman. The Commission has reaffirmed the declassification policy established by the Manhattan Engineer District. . . .

The Commission is responsible for guarding the restricted data involved in the program and for protecting production plants, laboratories, and other facilities costing in aggregate more than $2 billion. In addition, there are special materials and products which must be protected. As previously stated, the Commission, when it assumed responsibility for the atomic energy program on January 1, 1947, immediately issued instructions to its entire organization to continue in full force the security system which had been in effect under the Manhattan Engineer District. It also initiated a comprehensive survey of security practices, and as a result many security practices have been strengthened. Protective measures are being constantly studied and reinforced.

Acting pursuant to the Atomic Energy Act of 1946, a program has been instituted, in collaboration with the Federal Bureau of Investigation, under which some 6,500 applicants for employment by the Commission, or by the Commission's contractors and licensees (where access to restricted data would be involved) have been investigated and screened. In addition, all individuals still employed who received clearance under the Manhattan Engineer District are being reinvestigated by the Federal Bureau of Investigation as rapidly as possible. Some 1,500 investigations of this latter type have been completed. The Commission believes that the investigations performed in this program by the Federal Bureau of Investigation represent the most thorough and comprehensive effort of this type ever made.

In connection with physical security, the Commission has established a continuing inspection program under which more than 400 facility inspections have now been completed. A thorough inventory of classified technical documents and the establishment of sound uniform document accounting procedures have been ordered. In addition, certain studies have been undertaken in collaboration with the Army relating to the physical protection of Commission facilities. Details of the entire security program have been, and will continue to be, discussed with the Congressional Joint Committee on Atomic Energy.

ACCOMPLISHMENTS: THE FIRST YEAR [3]

Directly supporting not only the research and training activities of the Commission's facilities, but also the work of educational and industrial institutions throughout the country, is the provision of technical information on work done in the atomic energy program.

The Commission established late in 1947 a unified Public and Technical Information Service to insure, in accordance with the Atomic Energy Act, adequate control and dissemination of

[3] Excerpts from the letter of transmittal of the third semiannual Report of the United States Atomic Energy Commission to Congress, February 2, 1948. Senate Document No. 118, 80th Congress, Second Session. p. 24-31. United States Government Printing Office. Washington, D.C. 1948.

the information that is the lifeblood of scientific and engineering progress—and of public understanding of that progress and its implications. The Public and Technical Information Service combines five interdependent functions relating to the control and dissemination of information:

1. Preparation, reproduction, and controlled distribution within the project of classified reports to personnel requiring such information.

2. Declassification through analysis by qualified scientific reviewers of material which then becomes available for public use.

3. Editing, preparation, and reproduction of technical information materials, including indices, abstracts, project reports, and declassified papers.

4. Security guidance service—aid to publishers, editors, reporters, broadcasters, leaders of citizen groups, or others issuing material relating to atomic energy—in order to prevent compromise of restricted data; and assistance to contractors of the Commission and other agencies of government to safeguard restricted data.

5. Public information service—assisting representatives of the press, radio, picture services, citizen and trade organization, and educational agencies, in obtaining the full range of declassified and unclassified data currently available from the national atomic energy program.

Declassification of information: The declassification system developed under the Manhattan District and continued under the Atomic Energy Commission during 1947 received some 1,200 documents for declassification. Of those, the 120 scientists and engineers serving as reviewers recommended declassification and general release of over 1,000, after the making of necessary changes and deletions. A number of these declassified documents have been published in scientific and technical journals and have also been made available to the public through the Office of Technical Services of the United States Department of Commerce.

In order to insure uniform application of declassification policies with respect to information shared by the United Kingdom, Canada, and the United States, as a result of their combined wartime efforts, and in the interests of maintaining maximum security of information, the Commission arranged a three-day conference between representatives of the atomic energy agencies of the three nations in November 1947. The conference was concerned with the application of uniform declassification policies for atomic energy information. Discussions were limited to technical data jointly held by the participating nations as a result of their cooperation during the war. Canada and the United Kingdom now use the Declassification Guide developed in the United States and made available to them in April of 1946.

Technical information: Congress in the Atomic Energy Act recognized that the dissemination of scientific and technical information relating to atomic energy should be permitted and encouraged so as to provide that free exchange of ideas and criticisms which is essential to scientific progress. The system for providing information to the scientific and technical community, both inside and outside the Commission and its contractors' organizations, developed extensively during the year.

Of prime importance in this program is the distribution of restricted data originating within the atomic energy project to those within the project who have need of such information and are authorized to receive it. In 1947, an average of 50 copies each of 3,000 such classified reports were distributed in accordance with distribution lists carefully compiled. Each laboratory received those categories of information it needed for the successful accomplishment of its program. In addition to this routine distribution, 34,000 individual copies of such reports were distributed to laboratories requiring them, after careful screening to insure that no unnecessary distribution of restricted information resulted.

To insure that project laboratories have access to all information in the field of atomic energy which originates outside the atomic energy project, a continuing Guide to Published

Research on Atomic Energy and allied fields was prepared in
the Technical Information Service by assembling abstracts in
this field from all of the published abstract journals. During
the year, 2,223 such abstracts were assembled and circulated
throughout the Commission's contractor groups.

In order to make certain that all project scientists have
access to the information contained in the Research and Development Reports prepared at each laboratory, the Technical
Information Service prepares abstracts of each of these reports
that can be circulated to all project laboratories; 507 such
abstracts were prepared and incorporated in the Abstracts of
Research and Development Reports which was issued monthly
during the year. This publication is classified Secret.

To furnish adequate reference service for the mass of information contained in the 18,000 individual classified research
and development reports deposited in the Commission's libraries,
an extensive card index system was developed by the Technical
Information Branch; 906,000 index cards were prepared and
distributed in the past year.

Over the past year also, nearly 1,700 individual declassified
documents were distributed, including those declassified prior
to January 1947. So that the information contained in these
documents would be of maximum usefulness to the scientific
community, the documents were reproduced and distributed to
project laboratories, government agencies, and 150 depositories
of the Library of Congress, and were made available to the
public through the Office of Technical Services of the Department of Commerce. Nearly 162,000 copies of these documents
were distributed.

A program was instituted to make the information in these
declassified documents more readily accessible through abstracts,
700 of which have now been prepared for the same distribution
as the documents themselves.

Much progress was made toward completion of the National
Nuclear Energy Series, a 110-volume compilation of scientific
treatises based primarily on research in the field of atomic energy
conducted under government auspices. By the year's end, material for six volumes had been declassified and prepared for

reproduction and public sale. An additional twenty classified volumes are ready for reproduction and distribution within the project. The Commission entered into a contract with Columbia University to handle the publication of the series, and it is expected that a publisher will be announced shortly. The first issuance of the National Nuclear Energy Series will be known as the Manhattan Project Technical Section, covering work done under the Manhattan project. Approximately half of the total number of volumes are expected to be declassifiable and available for public use and will aggregate approximately 25,000 pages.

Public information: In response to the very great public interest in and concern with the progress of the nation's atomic energy development program, the media of public communication and information during 1947 continually devoted large amounts of space and time to reporting all that could be reported on the program, explaining the basic nature of atomic energy, and counseling readers and listeners on public policy toward control and use of this new force. At the Commission's offices in Washington and the five Offices of Directed Operations, there was a mounting volume of demand by reporters, editors, broadcasters, picture men, and leaders of citizen groups, for information from the Commission and for guidance on the security aspects of information on atomic energy obtained elsewhere.

To meet this demand the Commission authorized a small public information staff—four professional employees in Washington and one at each of the five Offices of Directed Operations. Through the declassification system this staff obtained for all who asked such service—writers, publishers, periodicals, newspapers, broadcasters, citizen groups—judgment on whether copy proposed for publication contained restricted data. The volume of requests for such service grew steadily. It was—and is— evident that the public communications media of the nation desire overwhelmingly to avoid harm to the national defense and security through publication of restricted data. There is a heavy continuing demand for security guidance service in Washington and at the Offices of Directed Operations.

Security guidance service constituted only a part of the public information requests handled by the Commission's offices. An even larger volume of requests called for positive information, declassified or unclassified, to be used as news, in radio broadcasts, in books, pamphlets, periodicals, or talks by a great range of people. Additionally, the Commission issued at its Washington office 75 statements for press and radio giving the facts about new developments in the national atomic energy development program. Through such public releases the Commission is able to discharge to some small extent the public accountability which rests upon all government agencies and which is especially important in the case of an agency under heavy security restrictions.

The public demand for information direct from Commissioners and staff members through talks upon numerous occasions was far greater than could be satisfied, and only a small fraction of the requests could be filled.

It is the Commission's hope that the contractor organizations and the associated universities and colleges will redouble their efforts to provide speakers, visual materials, etc., to help satisfy this intense and extensive public demand for basic information on atomic energy and the progress of the national program for its development. The Commission's own activities in this field were small in 1947 and will be on a limited scale in the future. This educational need can and should be met by the press, the radio, the schools and colleges, and the organized groups of the country.

The extent and the urgency of the demand for both security guidance and positive information service from the publishing group in the United States was indicated by three developments of the last quarter of the year: (1) the appointment by the American Society of Newspaper Editors of a special committee on atomic energy to develop recommendations for editors and for the Commission on how to give fullest service to readers on atomic energy development and at the same time to avoid breaches of security; (2) the appointment of a special committee on atomic energy by the American Textbook Publishers' Institute to speed the development of textbooks dealing with this field; (3) the appointment of a special committee by the Association of Secondary School Principals to develop a broad program for school and community education in the fundamentals of atomic energy development and control through a project called "Operation atomic vision." . . .

Soon after taking office, the Commission enlisted the services of Rear Admiral Sidney W. Souers, USNR, former Deputy Chief of Naval Intelligence and first head of the United States Central Intelligence Group, and of Frank J. Wilson, former Chief of the United States Secret Service, as special consultants to assist in a survey of the long-term security problem. Meanwhile, the security system of the Manhattan project remained in effect.

As a result of the study, the Commission established in its staff headquarters an Office of Security and Intelligence to direct all of the security activities of its program. The Office maintains close liaison with the Central Intelligence Agency, the Federal Bureau of Investigation, and other security and intelligence agencies of the government, as well as with the staff of the Congressional Joint Committee on Atomic Energy.

Following its establishment, the new Office took many significant measures to insure the security control of plant, personnel, documents, and information in addition to the establishment of standards, policies, and procedures.

The policy and procedures with respect to administrative review of personnel clearance decisions were developed to a point where by the year's end a five-member Personnel Security Review Board, composed of prominent citizens, was being established, to make recommendations to the Commission for further definition and codification of standards and criteria used in determining ineligibility for employment by the Commission and its contractors and to provide for administrative review. . . . All Commission employees are given full background investigation.

In order to protect restricted data and at the same time allow maximum progress in construction at the Commission's installations, access to restricted work is allowed to as few cleared construction workers as possible, the security and construction plans being so integrated as to provide for classified work being started only after the nonclassified construction has been completed.

Considerable progress was made in 1947 in reducing the number of construction workers who have access to restricted work.

In connection with the information control and security education program, a Classification and Document Control Board was set up to establish criteria for the classification of restricted data, to supervise procedures involved in the accounting for classified documents, and to define such areas of Commission information and activity as should be free from security restrictions. Field units were set up by the managers to work closely with the Board.

There was no complete inventory of classified documents available when the atomic energy program was transferred to Commission management. The task of inventorying such documents was begun in July 1947. The magnitude of the inventory may be illustrated by an operational and statistical outline. In the highest category of classified data over 25,000 documents were identified and are in the process of inventory. Technical and scientific reports totaling over 450,000 are also in the process of a detailed inventory and were about 75 per cent complete by the end of the year. Part of the problem involved in inventorying documents is the several million less highly classified papers, which must be scanned in various repositories, to separate the two named groups of material from other less highly classified documents being studied, and to set up an improved system for handling and accounting for documents. One location has more than 25,000 linear feet of files in which 20 per cent of the material is estimated to be classified.

In the security education activities, vigorous efforts were made to indoctrinate all personnel having access to restricted data with a full knowledge of their duties and responsibilities. At regular meetings, local security officers achieved, through personal contact, the cooperation of plant and laboratory personnel in understanding and executing the requirements of security. Security kits containing training material and copies of Security Education Outline, a guide to the procedures involved in security, were distributed to all managers of Directed Operations.

Ten thousand copies of a general manager's instruction, "Responsibility for Security," were also distributed. This document describes precisely the personal obligations of all Commission and contractor personnel for security obligations. It defines the responsibilities of administrative officers—the Director of the Office of Security and Intelligence, the managers of Directed Operations, and the heads of Washington divisions and offices.

REPORTING TO CONGRESS [4]

The Congress recognized that under the provisions of the Atomic Energy Act of 1946, which placed this vast enterprise in the hands of a commission to operate, there was being created the greatest administrative monopoly with the most far reaching power ever set up in this country; but there was no other course. The authority of this commission is greater than any other commission or bureau either heretofore or presently established in government. It ramifies throughout industry, management, labor, and natural resources. Its authority extends into the international field of atomic energy. Because of the secrecy necessary to preserve the knowledge essential to the production of atomic weapons the operation of this vast setup is clothed with restrictions and mandates for security, and the opportunity for public examination and evaluation of its progress and of the impact of its activities upon our normal peacetime or even potential wartime economy is nonexistent. This situation is unique in administrative policy of our nation. . . .

The Atomic Energy Commission is presently operating on an annual basis of over $600 million in cash and $300 million in contract authorizations. It has unlimited discretion in the types and kinds of goods and raw materials it buys; it has complete control over the extent to which private enterprise may venture in this field; it preempts patents; it has full authority over all phases of production and activity in atomic energy; it has, subject to certain responsibilities of periodic direction by the President, complete discretion and control over the production of atomic weapons; it can make foreign contracts and arrange-

[4] Excerpts from the report of the Joint Committee on Atomic Energy presented to the U.S. Senate by Senator Bourke B. Hickenlooper of Iowa, May 17, 1948. *Congressional Record.* 94:6045-6. May 17, 1948.

ments; it can contract with state and local governments; it operates municipalities, is the landlord, and subsidizes many local services traditionally within the province of private enterprise; it has the duty of extensive participation in the fields of public health; it is authorized to participate and is participating in agricultural and industrial research and development and may give or withhold its aid in its discretion. Its broad powers enable it to establish and maintain countless programs which are not clearly defined. It employs, either directly or through its operating contractors, over 55,000 people who with their families probably total 200,000; it has discretionary authority over the release or the withholding of information affecting the program.

The Atomic Energy Commission, because of the nature of its duties and the extent of its power, can exercise decisive control over the destiny of our nation and the lives of our people.

The Congress, under the Atomic Energy Act, and in consideration of the inherent dangers and problems involved, deemed these broad powers essential for the protection of the public and in order to prevent, if possible, the devastating use of atomic weapons in war. In addition, these powers have been deemed initially essential in order that we may make the greatest progress and maintain our preeminence in the advancement of the science of atomic energy. . . . These powers . . . illustrate the magnitude of the social and economic area within which atomic energy operates. . . .

Because of the unprecedented monopolistic control of atomic energy set up in the government through the Commission, the Congress, in section 15 of the act, created the Joint Committee on Atomic Energy composed of nine members of each house. This committee has a responsibility to "make continuing studies of the activities of the Atomic Energy Commission and of problems relating to the development, use, and control of atomic energy."

This section further provides that "The Commission shall keep the joint committee fully and currently informed with respect to the Commission's activities."

It was intended that by setting up such a joint committee, necessary secrecy of the project could be preserved, but at the same time a responsible body of Congress would be constantly kept informed so that it would be able, from time to time, to make such recommendations for legislation affecting the policy and operation of the atomic energy program, and to make such report as might be indicated in the public interest. . . .

In a number of areas the joint committee has requested, from the Commission and other vital coordinating agencies, information, conclusions, and recommendations which will aid in evaluating the national program and its operation. Information has not as yet been furnished to the joint committee enabling it to fully comprehend or determine long-range goals of production and operation policies of the Commission. This reference is not made by way of criticism but merely to indicate that the composite circumstances involved in our public affairs and within our economy create a certain indefiniteness that needs time and the unfolding of events before long-range policies can be fully justified. . . .

Due to the nature of the Commission's operation, its budgetary and accounting problems are ramified and very extensive. The accounting situation has been more complicated because of the fact that under previous wartime operation of this project necessitating complete secrecy, utmost speed, etc., standardized accounting procedures were not in effect; therefore, historic detailed costs are not fully available. A satisfactory system has not yet been set up. This fact is recognized by the Appropriations Committees of the Congress as well as by the Commission itself in its most recent report of February 2, 1948.

The importance of establishing satisfactory and adequate personnel programs in the operation of this project is evident. The necessity for security cannot be disputed. Policies for assuring the personnel security of the project under conditions of fairness to individuals but at the same time protecting inviolate the rights of the public and the integrity of this national venture, have been and still are in a state of study and trial. The Commission has been searching for a final formula and the joint committee has been concerned with the necessity that a reliable formula be established.

The unsettled international situation has a direct effect upon the pattern of our atomic energy program. Had a satisfactory system of international control been established certain provisions of the Atomic Energy Act, in due time, would have automatically become void and many vital powers of the Commission would have been transferred to an international agency. It is now conceded, however, after nearly two years of exhaustive effort in the United Nations, that satisfactory universal agreement for reliable international control of atomic energy is presently impossible.

INFORMATION VERSUS SECRECY [5]

It might be fitting to discuss some of the things which are peculiarly the business, or headache, if you can tell the difference, of the United States Atomic Energy Commission.

One of these problems concerns the matter of information versus secrecy. The Act tells us to make progress while in effect going in two opposite directions at the same time. We must disseminate and encourage the dissemination of scientific and technical information while at the same time we must control or prevent the dissemination of data which has to do with atomic weapons, the production of fissionable material or the use of it for power. You can see the heavy burden which these requirements put on the discretion of the Commission.

It is obvious that until an international agreement, acceptable to the Congress, has been reached, we should not help potential rivals to catch up with us on atomic knowledge which might well be used for weapon development. On the other hand, such a policy if carried to the point of the utmost secrecy and complete compartmentalization of work groups one from the other, could so delay our own progress that other nations working with the scientific data which is already common knowledge, might

[5] From "Atomic Control in the American Environment," speech by Sumner T. Pike, U.S. Atomic Energy Commission, at Stamford, Connecticut, January 9, 1948.

pass us while we were sitting comfortably in front of the locked safe. It certainly doesn't need repetition before this group that there is no simple, single atomic energy secret. You almost surely also know that there are a great many tricks of technical and industrial know-how which cumulatively make up the substance of America's lead in this area. If secrecy and security were synonymous, our job as your trustees would be much simpler. I think you can easily see that they are not synonymous, and in a good many instances too much secrecy can and probably will impair real security.

Now there is always flowing from the laboratories and work shops of the Commission and its contractors a stream of information which may be classified from "Top Secret" down through the degrees "Secret," "Confidential," and "For Official Use," or which may not be restricted in any sense whatever. It is our aim, of course, to swell the stream of information open to all, while on the other hand we must by careful examination make a determination of those things which cannot at present be revealed. As times goes on, things which were originally in the restricted group can and should be released. We have, since the war released for general use by scientists over 2100 separate papers which originated from the work of the Commission's scientists and those of its contractors. The *release* of information is a pretty highly technical, complex job; the *withdrawal* of information is obviously next door to impossible. Therefore we must be very careful in our declassification process or we may be very sorry.

There is another phase of this same problem which has more grays than black or white, and which will continue to be I suppose one of the major puzzles which we have to face. This comes from the fact we need people, large numbers of people, to do the work of research, development and application of the various phases of atomic energy. The law giving paramountcy to the objective of assuring the common defense and security provides that everyone working on the project, whether or not directly for the Commission, must be thoroughly investigated by the Federal Bureau of Investigation as to his loyalty, character and associations. This is quite a departure from our normal traditional conception of individual freedom and dignity in America. However, the conditions of operation here are unusual, not to say unique.

Bill Waymack, my fellow commissioner, a few weeks ago put down a few items which he thought were some of the facts of life with which one has to live in this business. They were:

1. The world is not dependably "postured for peace." We wish it were, but as yet it isn't.

2. The present distribution of power in the world and the present location of tensions are what we all know them to be.

3. Espionage is no new thing, and neither is the existence of governmental secrets, military and diplomatic. But our American problem of dealing with these familiar realities has become more complex, difficult and dilemmic.

4. There exist in America and in other countries ostensibly domestic or national Communist parties which operate in the interests of another power.

5. Our government must protect itself against infiltration by the disloyal and against leakage of information to the disloyal on the outside. Certain agencies of the government (the more "sensitive" agencies, as they are called) must especially protect themselves. The atomic energy operation is certainly one of the most sensitive.

6. Real protection does have to go beyond merely ascertaining whether one who is to be entrusted with information of importance to the nation's security is or is not a hired spy or fanatic devotee of another nation's ideas. Real protection does have to go to such things as make up all-round dependability.

7. Scientific advance itself has produced a situation in which information that has to be protected is scattered through a pretty wide scientific and technical field, runs around in the minds of many men, and therefore as never before is dependent on qualities of personal trustworthiness.

As you can well imagine the ideas of responsible American citizens as to how this subject should be handled are as far apart as the poles. For months the Commission has wrestled with this subject, dealing with specific cases, and is yet not too happy with the results we have reached. We cannot compromise national security and yet we must not frivolously damage or destroy the careers of people who may have innocently or in a mood of curiosity been temporarily associated with movements, the leadership of which may reasonably be considered on the disloyal side. We desperately need criteria and procedures which will reconcile those apparently contradictory requirements, or if that is not completely possible, at least to defend to the highest degree our American conception of freedom of thought while protecting the national security as the statute directs.

These problems of security, both as they relate to information and personnel, were full grown when we met them on taking over from the army-directed Manhattan Engineer District. . . .

On these points and many more, the decisions may have to be made by pressure of public opinion or possibly even at the polls. I hope that this subject never gets to be a political football, but it is naive to disregard the possibility. . . .

The decisions which have to be made . . . will not be properly made if they are the result of hysterical emotional waves generated by people who have definite bills of goods to sell.

MAKING INFORMATION AVAILABLE [6]

Giving the people help in learning what is at stake, what is the fundamental nature of atomic forces—here is a high function of the press. Providing the people with information, knowledge, and an interpretation of facts and events—all ingredients in the formation of realistic public opinion—is part of the trusteeship vested in our newspapers. . . .

During the war the American people knew nothing of the atomic project; indeed public money was spent to see to it that they did not know! Over two billion dollars were spent without public knowledge or a chance by Congress to stipulate, or even examine, the manner of spending. But that was in wartime. It was not the normal situation of a federal enterprise.

[6] From "The People, the Atom, and the Press," an address by David E. Lilienthal, Chairman of the United States Atomic Energy Commission, before the Annual Convention of New York State Publishers Association, DeWitt Clinton Hotel, Albany, N.Y., Monday, January 19, 1948.

The fact is, and we must face it—that it has yet to be demonstrated that *in peacetime* the cumbersome and time-consuming normal process of our Federal Government can make a success or insure leadership, world leadership, of such a complex scientific and technical undertaking as this. But our difficulty today goes even deeper than this. . . .

Congress has forbidden public issuance of a considerable range of information. In the law this is called "restricted data"; information that might be altogether too interesting to individuals and nations who are potential enemies of the United States.

Congress has placed severe penalties on revelation of restricted data. But it is not so much the risk of incurring penalties that deters reporters, editors, broadcasters, and speakers from the use of restricted data; rather it is their genuine desire to avoid harm to the nation's defense and security.

The first problem of the press and other media is to know what is restricted data—the information that Congress has directed, in general terms, should not be published.

The press here is in an impossible situation unless it has some guidance from the Commission that under the law has been made responsible for determining from time to time just what is secret and what is not. No one can put a piece of copy or a picture or an article alongside the brief definition of restricted data in the Act and say with certainty whether it does or does not contain restricted data. Even the scientists and engineers working in the atomic energy projects cannot decide this for themselves. Therefore the Commission maintains a declassification system, originated under the Manhattan District. Working in this system, passing judgment on all copy submitted from inside or outside the project, are more than 120 high ranking scientists, engineers and technicians, each expert in one line of subject matter, each familiar with his phase of our Declassification Guide, a secret document developed by a group of the nation's top scientists saying what may be published and what must be withheld. This system is complicated, but it is rather well administered and it works more rapidly than you would expect.

So there *is* a way, a fairly precise way, for determining whether any piece of copy or picture or anything else for publication originating inside or outside the atomic energy projects contains or does not contain restricted data. The Commission will put this machinery at the disposal of any newspaper, periodical, radio broadcaster, lecturer or picture service man who wishes to have copy examined. A division called the Public and Technical Information Service will handle the copy, and give the person asking for the service the judgment of our scientific reviewers on whether it contains restricted data.

To manage both the security guidance and the positive information service for all media of public communication, the Commission maintains a small public information staff— four in Washington, one at each of the five managerial offices elsewhere in the United States. This staff, to the limits of its capacity, will help your Washington bureaus, and your home staffs, if they request help, in all possible ways.

I have emphasized somewhat this matter of security guidance—because it is a new thing under the American journalistic sun. . . . There is no scarcity of information free and open to the technical commuity—and . . . to the press and other media. . . . There is a great volume of material open already to technical and scientific men—and to the press, if it desires to use it. . . .

The Commission does not intend to undertake the popularization, for the press and other media, of this material. We are proceeding on the assumption—and correctly, I believe—that the American press wants to do its own analyzing and interpreting and reporting of public data. The Commission wants to confine itself to making the information available, and to count upon the existing informational and educational system of this nation—notably the press and radio, and the schools and universities—to do the actual reporting and teaching and interpreting.

To repeat: The Atomic Energy Commission does have a duty to provide guidance regarding security. But most of the information—and I cannot emphasize this too strongly—most of the information necessary for an understanding of the fundamentals of atomic energy and the formulation of public policy *has long since been public*, and some of it since before the war.

The Commission does have an information responsibility, but it is a limited one—and it should be kept limited. That is our firm intention. We are opposed to building up a large information staff for the dissemination and interpretation of information about atomic energy or about the work of the Commission. There is a strong and wise tradition in this country against anything in a government information operation that smacks of propaganda; or of promotion for the prestige of particular government agencies or the men who temporarily are directing them. It is of the utmost importance that under no pretext, excuse, or justification of "national security" should the Atomic Energy Commission or any other agency create information or public relations staffs beyond the minimum actually required. . . . The Commission does, of course, report regularly to the whole Congress but these reports, made semiannually, contain only nonsecret information. To insure, therefore, that as far as possible, your representatives, the representatives of the whole people, are kept "currently informed," that they have the facts including secret data, Congress established a permanent Joint Committee on Atomic Energy of nine senators and nine representatives. To this Committee, which is thus in a position to consider in an informed way the public views and those of their colleagues in the Congress, and those of the Executive Branch, the Congress looks for guidance on broad policy decisions. . . .

It will be your job, in my opinion, not only to disseminate the underlying facts, within the limits of security, but to interpret and give meaning to those facts. It will be your task to see that your public servants, legislative and executive, are held to the highest standards of performance, to see to it that atomic energy shall never become the victim of petty politics or narrow partisanship. It will be your job not simply to increase public knowledge but what is equally important, to make that knowledge effective in determining the course of the republic.

SECURITY REGULATIONS IN OPERATION [7]

The basic policies of the United States with respect to the release of scientific and technical data developed in the United States atomic energy program were outlined in the "Statement of Recommendations of Release of Atomic Project Information," issued February 4, 1946, by the Advisory Committee on Declassification.

Appointed in the fall of 1945 by Major General L. R. Groves, Commanding General of the Manhattan Engineer District, War Department atomic development agency, this Committee was headed by Dr. Richard C. Tolman, Dean of the Graduate School of the California Institute of Technology, . . . formerly vice chairman of the National Defense Research Committee and . . . scientific advisor to General Groves. . . .

In the statement published after the submission of recommendations to General Groves, the Tolman committee said:

The directive which this committee was requested to fulfill is to make recommendations as to the release of information in the interest of national welfare and of national security. In considering the problem we have not intended to minimize the supreme importance of the establishment of international controls, nor are we unaware of the fact that such controls, once established, would profoundly alter the requirements of national security.

We have, however, thought that it would be useful to make all possible progress in releasing valuable scientific and technical information even at the present time when the elaboration of international controls is in its earliest stages. Our fundamental belief is that the release of basic scientific and technical information obtained during the development of the bomb would, over a sufficiently long term, not only enhance our national welfare but actually conduce to our national safety; however, we recognize that those charged with the security of the country may be led to the conclusion that the time is inopportune for the release of certain information of a special nature.

Even so we believe that nearly everyone will agree that there is much that can be disclosed at the present time without danger to our military security. We are convinced that practicable and sound principles

[7] From "Security Regulations in the Field of Nuclear Research," by Bart J. Bok, Director of the Harvard University Observatory; Francis Friedman and Victor Weisskopf, both members of the Physics Department of the Massachusetts Institute of Technology. *Bulletin of the Atomic Scientists.* 3:321-4+. November 1947. Reprinted by permission.

can be formulated which will make it appropriate to release such information at once provided the release is carried out with circumspection
and discernment under competent and informed guidance. The needless
withholding of new developments is bound to delay progress in technical
fields, and hence to have serious consequences for our national welfare
and security, while the disclosure of a great store of new and useful
information will stimulate the growth and development of science and
industry. It is to this end that we have primarily directed our recommendations.

On the basis of the recommendations submitted by the
Tolman committee, General Groves established a procedure for
the declassification of scientific and technical information. A
"Declassification Guide" was prepared to delineate the specific
topics which the Tolman committee recommended might be
released at once. This guide, which is classified, is under
continuing review and revision in order to insure that information not essential to the security of the United States is made
available and that other information is properly safeguarded.

The Atomic Energy Act of 1946, which was signed by the
President on August 1, 1946, placed into law the responsibilities
of the operating agency—now the United States Atomic Energy
Commission—with respect to the safeguarding of "restricted
data" as defined in the Act, and with respect to the dissemination of information necessary to insure scientific progress. . . .

The intentions of the Congress with respect to information
policies appear quite clear. The Congress . . . recognized the
importance of "information to encourage scientific progress,"
but at the same time took into account the situation existing in
the world today by establishing a policy of control of information based on the principle that the withholding of certain
types of information by the United States would serve to retard specific development of atomic energy for destructive
purposes. It is this principle which guides the Commission in
carrying out the program for the control and dissemination
of information.

The Commission believes that the basic resources of the
United States in entering the intensive program for the development of atomic energy during the war were this nation's

tradition of education and aggressive industry. It further believes that freedom of the "interchange of ideas and criticisms" is the foundation of educational and industrial progress as well as being "essential to scientific progress."

The United States Atomic Energy Commission thus has a dual responsibility:

First, to withhold that information whose premature disclosure would aid in the development of, or shorten the time of development of atomic energy for destructive purposes by any nation which is not willing to pool its development effort with other nations in order to provide—in the words of Mr. Baruch—"the mechanism to assure that atomic energy is used for peaceful purposes and preclude its use in war."

Second, aggressively to disseminate that information which is necessary to the understanding by our people of the portent of atomic energy, that information which is vital to the training of the men and women on whom we must depend if we are to realize the promise of atomic energy, and that information which is essential to the development of a strong and virile atomic industry in the wake of an inspired science.

At no point and at no time are these responsibilities separable. Their application requires that restriction be placed upon the free publication of scientific papers, in the fields of both applied and fundamental research. It appears from the program of declassification that the restriction upon publication of fundamental research permits a proportionately greater dissemination of basic science. The restrictions apply wherever scientific research is performed as a part of the United States atomic energy program, both in facilities owned by the government and in contractors' facilities.

Scientists in this program are encouraged to prepare adequate reports of their work and to publish their observations and conclusions as widely as possible. Prior to publication, however, their papers must be "declassified," that is, measured against a Declassification Guide which defines the areas of information which can be released at this time without prejudice to the security of the United States according to the basic standards established by the Tolman committee and the Manhattan District.

During the first year of operation of this declassification program, more than 1200 scientific papers were cleared and authorized for publication. In each case, the author determines the manner of publication, either through his own lectures, through scientific journals, through the general press, or in book form. Those papers which are not published in a medium of general circulation are made available to the public, to scientific and educational institutions, and to industry through the Office of Technical Services of the United States Department of Commerce.

The declassification program is administered by scientific personnel entirely. The application of the established standards, or the Guide, to the information contained in scientific papers, is done entirely by scientists in accordance with principles approved by the Commission on the basis of recommendations by the committee headed by Dr. Tolman. . . .

The total volume of declassified material is gratifyingly large, especially if one keeps in mind that at the close of the war many scientists were reluctant to have appear in print their reports of investigations that were done hurriedly and under pressure, and which, to many of them, seemed uninteresting. . . .

As was customary in the years before the war, all papers reporting on research done currently at universities and other laboratories, without an AEC [Atomic Energy Commission] contract, are submitted directly by the author or the head of the laboratory to the editorial staff of the journals. Although the AEC has jurisdiction over all matters related to atomic energy, this procedure applies at present to work done on basic nuclear physics and chemistry. Scientific papers, not prepared under the auspices of the AEC are submitted to the Commission for checking only when the author or editor feels that a question of security may be involved.

At the present time the United States Army and Navy support extensive research programs, many of them in basic research, in university and industrial laboratories. Some of the support is in the field of nuclear physics. Unofficial estimates place the total expenditure at ninety million dollars for 1946. It should be pointed out that the research so supported is *not* military research. American scientists have scrutinized these contracts carefully for undesirable features, and, on several occasions, they have succeeded in eliminating possible restrictive clauses, or undesirable obligations. Maximum freedom of publication is guaranteed under the great majority of these contracts.

The official attitude toward the problem of security is illustrated by the following quotation from an article prepared by Dr. Alan T. Waterman, Chief Scientist of the Office of Naval Research, and Captain Robert D. Conrad of the United States Navy, Director of the Planning Division of the Office of Naval Research:

> The secrecy aspect is particularly vexing, since true scientific research is incompatible with any restrictions on the free flow of information. The arrangements we have found workable are as follows: The contractor is entirely free to publish the results of his work, but in his publications not to speculate upon its possible applications in naval or military developments.
>
> We expect that the scientists who are engaged on projects under naval sponsorship are as alert and as conscientious as we are to recognize the implications of their achievements, and that they are fully competent to guard the national interest. If a development emerges which should be classified, the contractor is given the option of proceeding with it under security restrictions, or having it removed from the campus to a government laboratory or to some other contractor. No one is asked to work in secret against his will. . . .

In spite of the success of the declassification program, and in spite of the sensible approach of the AEC towards the research program, there are necessarily some unpleasant aspects in the regulation of the field of atomic energy.

The control of information and research involves a cumbersome bureaucratic mechanism. With the broadest program and the greatest effort to speed declassification, the AEC can hardly eliminate the inconvenience and time lag at present apparent in the interchange of information between AEC scientists and the world. Even within the AEC information is channelized prior to the formal act of declassification, and the speed with which new ideas and new techniques spread is thus reduced still further. An artificial barrier is created between science inside and outside the AEC.

The traditional freedom of discussion of scientific work has necessarily been curtailed. This applies to some extent even after the results of research have been declassified. Declassification of a scientific paper implies approval of a certain set of statements. It cannot foresee the questions that may arise in free discussion and the members of the AEC laboratories can therefore have no assurance about the extent to which they are able to participate in a scientific discussion.

Every AEC scientist cannot become a walking encyclopedia of declassification and, at the moment that he needs to know most, the scientist may not be able to recollect whether or not he is permitted to participate in a certain phase of scientific discussion. Furthermore, a discussion may bring up points on which the formal procedure of declassification has not even been requested.

The inconvenience involved in declassification and the difficulty of participation in free discussions create further artificial barriers. It may well be that a technique of general value for research in university or industrial laboratories may remain unknown unnecessarily long to research workers outside the AEC. The danger that a technique shall be accidentally suppressed is only a particular example of the way in which beneficial cross fertilization in science is decreased. . . .

So far "the information program has followed the policies inaugurated by the War Department." It is somewhat disappointing that the Commission has not yet had the time to clarify or change these policies. Inaction by itself becomes a block to communication. If, for example, the Commission were to determine that publication in certain fields would not adversely affect the common defense and security, then more important investigations would be carried out in these fields than under the present uncertain circumstances. Declassification by fields would also remove some of the difficulties of free scientific discussion. . . . The Commission can make such a determination under . . . the Atomic Energy Act.

Another aspect of the whole problem should not be ignored. The time lag and inconvenience caused by the partial control of information is offset to some extent by large scale support in the processes of accumulating it. Also some specific attempts are being made to remedy the effects of wartime restrictions on the dissemination of knowledge in the field of nuclear research. . . .

It is still too early to judge the effect of the Atomic Energy Act on the flow of scientific information. Officially the Commission has been in operation only since the first of the year. Nevertheless, the bureaucratic obstructions and legalistic uncertainties have already worn the nerves of the scientists involved. Papers have been held up for an undue length of time. Declassification has been refused because of ill-applied and misinterpreted regulations. Necessary decisions have been lacking. It is all too obvious that scientific work is adversely affected.

There are however many things to be said in favor of the present arrangement. The scientists are no longer dominated by the military and all controls are established by a Commission of civilians, for the members of which the American scientists have the greatest personal respect. The scientists realize that this Commission is as much bound by an act of Congress as are the scientists themselves. There is no doubt in the minds of American scientists that a general easing of international tensions will result in more liberal security policies.

EFFECTIVENESS OF SECRECY

DISCUSSION

The policy of secrecy with regard to the atomic energy program has recently met with serious criticism by scientists and others. The basis of criticism stems from the conviction that the atomic secret as such does not exist. Scientists point out that any scientist worthy of his salt, knowing that atomic energy is possible, and backed by unremitting support of his government, with sufficient materials, equipment, and personnel could duplicate the American achievement in a matter of years.

They contend that secrecy and secrecy measures merely hamper scientific research, and the efficiency of scientific endeavor. They are quick to point out the fact that such a gigantic program as atomic energy inherently requires the fullest information to every level of scientific workers, in order to secure the benefit of the knowledge, the thinking, and the experience of the full scientific community.

The point is debatable. Perhaps the scientists (and General Groves) are correct in their assumption that secrecy cannot be effective. The subject certainly deserves further consideration in relation to its effect on the question "How far must secrecy extend?" If the scientists are correct, the whole secrecy program would appear of little value. The crux of the issue is not our ability to preserve secrecy, but rather whether anything is to be gained by the complex structure we have established to maintain security of information.

One of the best summations of scientific attitude toward the whole structure of secrecy is that expressed by Walter DeCew, technical editor of *Nucleonics*, in the July 1948 issue of that publication:

> Everybody realizes that the main security of the United States rests not on keeping secrets, necessary and important as this is, but even more on outstripping all other nations in the development of atomic energy on all levels, scientific, industrial, and military.

Which brings us to the question "How effective can the secrecy policy be, in carrying out the avowed principles this nation has adopted regarding atomic energy?"

PRACTICAL ASPECTS OF MILITARY SECURITY [1]

The official position of our government presently is that "the secret of the atomic bomb" must be kept. What is this supposed "secret"? The basic principles of the bomb were well known by 1940, and the only remaining question was whether such a thing was possible. The answer rested on a nice balance among various detailed properties of matter; its finding was a long and difficult job. Now everyone has the answer: the bomb dropped on Hiroshima did, in fact, go off.

In addition to that conclusive answer, the War Department issued a splendid report by Dr. H. D. Smyth, of Princeton University, on the administrative and technical history of the atomic-bomb project from 1940 on. This document omits many details, but one should not suppose that what is left out is essential to ultimate duplication of the bomb. Smyth does report our general lines of attack. Other nations possessed of skillful physicists, given only time, can duplicate the atomic bomb.

Consequently, the net effects of blanket efforts to keep the "secret" can only be harmful to the United States. They can retard our scientific progress by restricting scientific publication in the field of nuclear physics, thus crippling our future work in this vital research line. They can jeopardize our national safety by replacing our responsibility to develop an active policy to prevent an atomic-bomb war with an empty complacency deriving from a false belief that we can keep inviolate a terrible "secret."

If this unorthodox view is granted, what should our nation— the only one with machinery for the immediate manufacture of atomic bombs—do? I suggest that we remove all security bar-

[1] From "Military Security and the Atomic Bomb," by Louis N. Ridenour, physics professor, University of Pennsylvania. *Fortune*. 32:170-1+. November 1945. Reprinted by permission of the editors. Copyright by Time, Inc.

riers to the publication of basic scientific information in nuclear physics (as distinct from atomic-bomb technology). I further suggest that the various aspects of atomic-bomb technology (as distinct from basic nuclear physics) be carefully examined to determine whether continuation of our present policy of concealment is wise. Such an examination can be made only by one completely familiar with the atomic-bomb field, which I am not.

Besides being familiar with the bomb, the person making the examination must appreciate the true nature of military security; such an appreciation will illuminate the reasons behind my first recommendation. A discussion of the logical basis of military security is here attempted. Now, the word "security" carries over into its specialized military use semantic vestiges of its pleasant general meanings (stocks and bonds, a roof over one's head, etc.), so that anyone who seeks to scrutinize the basis of security policy is regarded as a dangerous character, just as a man who makes a critical survey of religion is in danger of being thought a heretic. Nevertheless, military security is a relatively recent invention in any form. Its application to science and technology began in World War I, but attained importance and nuisance value only in the war just finished. "Military security" means the denial to the enemy, during such time as it can be useful to him, of all knowledge that, in the opinion of the authority responsible for such military security, would benefit him materially.

There are two approaches to security, both indicated in our definition. One can be called security by concealment; the other, security by achievement. To take a homely industrial example, security by concealment is practiced by the manufacturers of Angostura Bitters—the label tells us that the formula is secret. Security by achievement was practiced by Henry Ford in setting out to make a low-priced motorcar. In military operations, security by concealment keeps knowledge of the place and time of an amphibious landing from everyone except the very few staff officers who must know it; security by achievement makes possible a troop advance so rapid that radio communications can be carried on without coding—enemy interception of messages could not lead to counteraction in time to be effective.

The principal aim of security in military terms is to preserve the possibility of surprise. No one can be unceasingly alert, and the chief concern of frontline troops is their uncertainty as to the strength of the enemy they are facing, and his plans. This is just as true on the offense as on the defense; the Marines who walked ashore unopposed at Okinawa were as full of foreboding and adrenaline as Wainwright's men on Corregidor.

In old-fashioned war the matters involved in military security were operational: war plans, the deployment and number of troops, the whereabouts of naval vessels, and similar information that would clearly be of use to the enemy in formulating his own plans, both strategic and tactical. As war has grown more technical, weapon technology has become subject to military security. In World War I, the initial effect of the German use of gas or of the British innovation of the tank was chiefly due to surprise. This was, in each instance, the product of the most meticulous security by concealment; and so also, perhaps, was the fact that both new weapons were used on such a small scale that the long-term result that either achieved was negligible.

This latest war has been characterized by a still fuller mobilization of scientific and technical resources for the development of "secret weapons." The jumping-off places for the design of new technical weapons invariably are familiar principles of science; and an uncritical carrying over of the notions of operational security into the field of this scientific background has unfortunate results.

Misapplications of security arise from an imperfect understanding of the different approaches suitable for the three classes of information now subject to military security: operational information, the technical design and performance of new weapons, and the scientific background for the design of new weapons.

What are the properties of operational information that require it to be safeguarded? The first property is compactness.

A few words can carry a great secret; it is therefore easy to steal. The place and approximate time of the invasion of Normandy could have been readily communicated to the Germans in a ten-word message, and the results springing from such a betrayal would have been tremendous and might have been decisive.

Second, operational information is almost universally understandable. Thus anyone can steal it; a Mata Hari can be chosen on the basis of her figure, and her ability to understand and evaluate information on troop movements and war plans may be taken for granted.

Third, operational information is arbitrary; it therefore needs to be stolen. Most important military information consists of decisions whose exact nature can scarcely be foretold even by one in possession of all the information used to make the decision. For example, the actual invasion area in Normandy was chosen largely on the basis of its improbability. The area encompassed no ports, and it was not particularly suitable for armored maneuver; therefore, it was reasoned, this choice would fool even an enemy who regarded us as military idiots.

Fourth, operational information known to the enemy is subject to change. Consisting, as it largely does, of arbitrary decisions between comparably desirable alternatives, a plan can be altered right up to the moment when forces are committed. This makes what *we* know of the *enemy's* plans and dispositions the most secret information we have.

Finally, operational information is perishable. It is, in fact, usually communicated to the enemy; for the decision as to where and in what force to make an attack is the enemy's property once the attack has begun. Since there is always a time—usually a definable and predictable moment—when the most carefully safeguarded military information is no longer of any value whatever to the enemy, even the most stringent security measures can be tolerated since they are not permanent.

Aside from a common tendency to overdo security measures, in order not to underdo them, the principles of operational security are generally understood, and one may say it is handled as reasonably as can be expected. Operational security is usually achieved by concealment, which we have seen to be suitable.

Let us now, by way of contrast, consider the application of military security to the scientific background for the design of a new weapon—scientific security, for short. Since radar employs and is based on the well-known laws of electromagnetism, a good deal of the theory worked out by Clerk Maxwell in 1875 has been safeguarded by locked doors and armed guards. Such application of security by concealment to facts of nature, often to well-known ones, looks absurd but derives directly from the uncritical transfer to scientific security of concepts reasonable and useful in operational security. What are the properties of scientific information?

First, where operational information is compact, scientific information is diffuse. The Radiation Laboratory is preparing between five and ten million words of final report to preserve the enduring values of its work on radar. While the secret formula (or philosophers' stone) is a device often met in bad fiction, it has no basis in fact. Science proceeds by putting one foot ahead of another, and the history of successive footsteps has to be recorded in detail in order that another may follow the trail blazed by a pioneer.

Second, where important operational information can be understood by almost anyone, proper interpretation and evaluation of scientific information can be guaranteed only by the employment of secret agents who are competent practicing scientists. The world of international science is compact, and most individuals who would be useful scientific secret agents are well known to their colleagues in any country. Most scientists are rather straightforward fellows, without the wiles or the charm that would fit them for a career of espionage. And Mata Hari is definitely out. It is more economical to use scientists in *doing* scientific work than to use them to steal it.

Third, while operational information is arbitrary, scientific information is imbedded in the matrix of the universe. It exists for all to find; provided that the right questions are asked of nature, she will give the same answers to all alike. Scientific information is exactly the opposite of arbitrary; therefore security by concealment loses its point and its usefulness.

Similarly, while the arbitrariness of operational information made what we knew of the enemy's operational plans the most secret information we could have, the unvarying character of scientific information means that the enemy cannot change what he has learned under any circumstances, even if he knows we have found it out.

Operational information has as its final property its perishability; scientific information, if correct, is eternal. Here is the real danger of the present situation. If we believe today, as we seem to believe, that what we know about certain workings of nature must be concealed from our peacetime "enemies," we are committed to ending the free international scientific publication that has been the chief glory and support of our present age of science.

When the dangers to civilization of rapid scientific advance are discussed, it is rarely observed that the efforts of the pure scientist are only the beginning and the basis on which the engineer builds to realize a peacetime commercial process or product, or a wartime weapon. The atomic bomb is based on a fundamental discovery published by two Germans in 1939, but a tremendous amount of further effort had to go into transition from a simple and tentative paper in the *Physikalische Zeitschrift* to a practical weapon. Further, there is no chance of making sure, by concealment or by Canute-like treaties or armament agreements, that the enemy will be kept from developing an arsenal of effective new weapons and techniques, if war be his intention.

Since it is not science but engineering—not discovery but application—that we must fear; and since we cannot hold the engineering of a potential enemy down to any agreed-upon level either by concealment or by agreement, we must apply the security of achievement instead of the security of concealment. We must encourage scientific research and discovery in every way possible. We must make sure that all basic work that has been concealed during wartime is published at once, including atomic-bomb research. The way to be prepared for enemies in a possible future war is to be ahead of them in every department; and the way to be ahead of them is to have more, cleverer, and better-informed men working harder, on the basis of more thoroughly diffused scientific information. There is no need for restricting the publication of basic science, even in the midst of a war, for the transition from science to technology spans years.

It has been relatively simple to point out that security by concealment is the most effective basis for the safeguarding of operational information, and that security by achievement is clearly demanded for scientific information (though concealment is unfortunately now widely practiced). We must now enter the difficult field of technological security. There is rarely a simple case. Security is important, of course. Achievement will ensure that we introduce new technical weapons promptly, widely, and well; concealment will ensure that their value is not negated by simple countermeasures. We must examine each specific instance to determine whether security by concealment will gain more than it loses, or vice versa.

A good example of what happens when this examination is not made concerns the identification equipment, called IFF (identification of friend or foe), used as an adjunct to radar. Here it will be sufficient to say that IFF equipment is intended to make a specific signal in reply to a specific challenge, and thus to indicate to the operator of a radar that the challenged airplane or ship is friendly. Absence of any response means uncertainty: either the plane or ship is hostile, or it is a friendly craft with an IFF equipment that is damaged or turned off. IFF is the electronic analogue of the flag on a ship or the white star on an airplane.

From the beginning, security by concealment has been practiced and applied to IFF. Its development and manufacture, surrounded by the most elaborate safeguards, have been kept apart from the main stream of development and manufacture of radar generally. The result is that IFF equipment has not shared the tremendous advances that have occurred in the wartime radar art. It is most important that IFF facilities be integrated with radar; yet the strict security surrounding IFF has, in most instances, prevented this integration from being made by the radar designers. IFF has been grafted on after the radar design was complete. This has cost us much in terms of effectiveness of the system as a whole.

We plainly could not keep from the enemy's knowledge a device that must be installed in every ship and every airplane of the United Nations. It would be as logical to try to hide the number of stars and stripes in the U.S. flag. As soon as an airplane or a ship was lost to the enemy under circumstances permitting the possibility of capture, the IFF presumably was compromised. Yet vigorous measures of security by concealment were practiced on IFF up to two years after presumed compromise, often to the extent that an outlying squadron would not have any instruction book or other materials for its IFF maintenance technicians. The ineffectiveness of IFF, conferred upon it by misguided emphasis on security by concealement, is summed up in the fact that (except for very small numbers of aircraft on certain special missions) IFF was never used in the European theatre after D-day. Concealment here did a net harm.

Let us now examine a less clear case. Confusion by "window"—long metal-foil strips tossed out of aircraft—of ground radar intended for air search and anti-aircraft fire control was practiced both by the United States and by our enemies after the British initiated it on July 24, 1943. The fact that radar could be confused in this way had been known to the British for some eighteen months before the scheme was actually used in operations. Meanwhile it was most carefully guarded by concealment on the grounds that the British had more to lose by revealing the tactic to an ignorant enemy than they could gain by its use. Of course, the idea was so simple and obvious that people kept reinventing and proposing it in entirely good faith. Such individuals had to be let into the lodge and asked to keep quiet, lest the "secret" leak out.

After the conquest of Germany, we found that the Germans had also known of this scheme for about eighteen months before the British first used it operationally. They had concealed the idea most carefully, because its revelation to the enemy might lose the Luftwaffe more than it would gain!

Now the British and the Germans cannot both have been right about this. Security by concealment cost one side or the other—it is not our province to examine which—eighteen months' use of a very effective measure. Full realization that the enemy is never completely stupid, and that a fact of nature is not arbitrary and thus cannot be successfully concealed by man, might have resulted in a careful examination of the worth of using this measure, instead of a blanket relegation of it to the secret category.

Another story: At one time our aircraft were sinking U-boats by droves, with the help of a new radar weapon. Although the German Navy knew that a new weapon was in use and its technicians could guess at its general character, they could not figure out its exact nature although they worked night and day to solve the riddle. Not until six months after the Luftwaffe had captured and studied an example of the device that was killing the submarines—though the circumstances of its capture gave no clue to this use—did the German Navy guess that this might be the device that was giving them difficulty. Three months before the Navy caught on, a full technical intelligence bulletin, which described the captured equipment in detail, had been circulated to them by the Luftwaffe as a matter of routine coordination. By that time, dozens of such equipments were in Luftwaffe hands.

The delayed take on the part of the German Navy can be explained. It was due to the carry-over into the technical field of the operational axiom that knowledge of the enemy's secrets is the biggest secret one can have. It is incredible that the German naval authorities in direct contact with the problem of fathoming our new technique could not have recognized instantly the purport of the equipment the Luftwaffe had captured, provided the German air force had permitted them a glimpse of it or the least knowledge about it. But the secrecy guarding this captured equipment was such that some other officials received the technical intelligence report and sat on it. Three months more had to pass before the information was used.

Contrary to what the Germans thought (it cost them, conservatively, a hundred submarines), it is almost never necessary to conceal from the enemy what we know of his devices. He cannot change if he would, for his commitments are too great. Any proper weapon must be duplicated many times over (or, as in the case of the atomic bomb, an enormous plant must be devoted to the manufacture of a few highly effective weapons) and thousands of people and millions of dollars are involved.

Further, it is worth remarking that the best technical weapons do not depend on secrecy or surprise for their effectiveness. The German V-2 rocket was such a weapon. Long before it was used, I sat with a committee that met many times in London to discuss countermeasures for V-2 on the basis of the quite accurate information we had of its properties. The only hopeful one we were able to think up was that of winning the war; and this was successfully applied.

The atomic bomb is another weapon that scarcely depends on surprise. All the publicity in the world would not have saved Hiroshima or Nagasaki. We must always remember that our primary purpose is not to astound our enemy but to defeat him. Surprise that contributes to his defeat is important, but surprise in and of itself is valueless. It is therefore important in every case to examine whether measures of concealment, which are always restrictive, will be worth the handicaps they entail.

In the technical field, these handicaps can be substantial. While only a few staff planners need to have the crucial details of an operational plan, literally thousands of individuals must be fully informed about any technical gadget. Concealment applied to such a device often means in the end that designers fail to encompass the entire problem, manufacturers make parts that do not quite fit together, operating crews cannot operate it effectively, maintenance men cannot fix it, and, worst of all, field commanders do not quite know what they have got or how to make use of it. We lost four cruisers, early in the Pacific fighting, under circumstances that strongly suggest that the responsible commander did not understand the properties and limitations of the radar on his ships.

Finally, in a scientific or technical field it is quite possible to apply security by concealment with such a humorless thoroughness that the broad outlines of the subject whose secret is being kept stand out as distinctly as a dark nebula shows against a luminous galactic cloud. Those guarding the secret of the atomic bomb have to date done the best job of this. The flood of papers on nuclear fission that was inundating our technical journals was cut off abruptly during 1940. A popular article on fission printed by the *Saturday Evening Post* in 1940 led to a visit from a major who wanted the names of all individuals inquiring for this particular back number. Libraries were similarly notified that something was up in connection with this harmless article. Every copy of one issue of the house organ of a contracting firm, showing some pictures of construction at Hanford, Washington, was relentlessly tracked down and retrieved, arousing great journalistic curiosity where none had existed before. Superman was denied a proposed bombardment of three-million-volt electrons from a cyclotron (though a cyclotron cannot accelerate electrons, and the device pictured was not a cyclotron). Nuclear physicists initiated into the Secret Order of the Bomb were instructed to snub their old friends on transcontinental planes and trains, thereby pointing up their connection with the project. Letters between United States citizens in the continental United States were censored. And so on.

The most important field in which scientific and technical security by concealment is still being applied uncritically and wholesale is that of the atomic bomb. If American political leaders honestly feel that they are the custodians of a permanent secret, they are deceiving themselves. They are attempting to apply security by concealment to some well-known scientific principles and to some involved but tractable engineering problems that can readily enough be solved by our peacetime enemies, with or without further help from us.

Today, our nation has the machinery for making atomic bombs —the only such machinery in the world. This, and not any "secret" is the object of our stewardship. A few years from now, anyone who wants such machinery can and will have it, with only brief delay resulting from any concealment we attempt. Our concealment of basic nuclear science is almost certainly wrong. We should examine carefully and in detail whether the delay we produce by concealment of each individual detail of atomic-bomb technology is worth the cost of such concealment to our progress. And we in the United States dare not console ourselves by thinking that security measures that aim only to conceal will do us or the world the slightest lasting good. Our

problem is not one of science, nor of security, but of statesman-
ship.

In effect, the problem of policing or of organizing the world,
if it is raised at all by the development of the atomic bomb, must
be actively and not passively solved. This must be done within
the next two or three years. Any security by concealment that
the United States attempts meanwhile can gain us little time at
best, can create unjustified illusions of national safety, and will
damage our prospects for scientific progress.

THE HANDICAPS OF SECRECY [2]

A course which many people find attractive is that of "keeping the secret." It sounds so simple and secure. "We made the
atomic bomb all by ourselves," they say, "it is ours, we alone
have the secret, all we have to do is to lock it up and to guard
the key." But what, exactly, is the secret, and how are we to
keep it? The knowledge that went into making the bomb divides
into four categories: the basic science, the technology, the design
of the bomb, and the distribution of the minerals used. So far
as the basic science is concerned, comparatively little is now
secret, and even if it were, we could not keep it secret very long,
because these secrets are not ours but mother nature's, and dear
old mother nature is not American or Russian or British, and
she reveals her secrets impartially to all who put their questions
to her with sufficient ingenuity and skill.

The technological secrets are not basic, they are merely the
kind that competing industrial plants try to keep from each
other. Any first class chemical engineering organization, given
the basic reactions for making styrene rubber, for example, and
given the time and facilities for work with pilot plants, could
design and operate a full-scale plant. We can keep these secrets,
at best, for only a few years. . . .

[2] From "How Not to Control Atomic Energy." An address before the Third
General Session of the United Nations, San Francisco, July 3, 1947, by Joel H.
Hildebrand, chemist, author, wartime consultant to the Military Planning Division,
QMC, onetime Dean of the College of Letters and Sciences, University of Cal-
ifornia. *American Library Association Bulletin.* 41:274-5. September 1, 1947.
Reprinted by permission.

There is grave danger in believing that any fancied secret can guarantee security. It is like relying upon the Maginot Line or the Chinese Wall or armored knights or the "secret" design of the B-17. Real security is not guaranteed by any single, simple, temporary measure. All of the supposed guarantees of security just mentioned rapidly become obsolete. The best security consists in keeping ahead of every potential enemy. . . .

If we go all out for secrecy, we shall be in grave danger of so restricting knowledge as to cut off the supply of scientists capable of keeping us in the lead. How can we teach the next generation of scientists if we are forbidden to discuss the basic science which is an essential part of that training? A distinguished physicist, in addressing a meeting of the American Physical Society, closed by saying, "If it were not for the Manhattan District, I could have told you something today." Such a restriction may be a temporary necessity, but it is fraught with peril in the long run. Only a small number of atomic scientists can be trained under such a system, and many will avoid subjecting themselves to the risks of innocently incurring the severe penalties of violation.

It is the duty of the scientist to help keep this nation strong. He does so primarily by his contributions to our national well-being through discoveries in basic science. The whole superstructure of applied science, industry, jobs, and material welfare has been built upon this foundation. And when our foreign policy broke down, and we were plunged into war, it was our capacity to apply our scientific knowledge to huge production that saved us, even more than our good general military strategy. And, if we can now do no better than engage in an atomic arms race, we shall need our scientists as never before. And so I plead for such treatment of scientists as will best enable them to make their contributions to the nation and to humanity. They are the ones who best know the conditions under which they can work effectively. They need not only laboratory facilities but also freedom to consult with each other; they need "free enterprise" and their own "free press" quite as much as other citizens. If you imprison them in concentration camps equipped with lie detectors under the command of men who are ignorant of science, and silence them, as nuclear physicists and chemists are even now being silenced, they will not be able even to train their successors, and the present generation of top flight ones will die off with few replacements. Is that security? I suggest that we take a lesson from the clever fisherman in the *Arabian Nights* who unwittingly released from a bottle a frightful afreet. He solved his problem by getting the afreet under control and putting him to work. We can do the same thing with atomic energy if we are sufficiently clever. We must concentrate on developing atomic energy for constructive purposes and do our best to achieve a world order in which we need not fear its destructive aspects. Today we have a temporary advantage, we have the machinery for making atomic bombs, doubtless the only such machinery in the world. Tomorrow we will not have that advantage. While we have it we should use whatever trading value it gives us.

THE MECHANICS OF INFORMATION CONTROL [3]

When the democracies embarked upon total war, the measures they felt it necessary to take in ordering science and circumscribing communication among scientists were scarcely less complete than those imposed by the Fascists. In both world wars, the scientists of the United States, of the United Kingdom and of other democratic countries had to accustom themselves to work under regulations of secrecy in an atmosphere of darkness. This fact was brought out clearly in an address before the National Academy of Science by Sir Henry Dale, former president of the Royal Society of England:

In 1918, most of the scientists, like most of the warriors, returned joyfully to normal life and normal standards with the hope that such a call would never come again. When this hope proved vain, the call was for science and scientists, as never before, to meet the new threat from an enemy who had already enlisted most of the science of his great nation in secret preparation for an attack on the world's freedom. And

[3] From "Control of Information Relating to Atomic Energy," by James R. Newman, former counsel to Senate Special Committee on Atomic Energy and member of the editorial board of *New Republic*. *Yale Law Journal*. 56:769-802. May 1947. Reprinted by permission.

to meet this menace, we free peoples found ourselves obliged to submit again to the invasion of our scientific activities by secrecy, to a degree beyond any which had so far been regarded as possible. Secrecy percolated into domains which all earlier wars had held sacred; so that we, for example, whose work was in the medical sciences found ourselves involved in an inconsistency, which still paid conventional respect to that immunity of medical equipment and personnel which a more scrupulous age had established, but compelled us, in the name of total war, to throw a veil of secrecy over the new discoveries which could make their work of mercy really effective. To all this and much more we loyally submitted. And now that science has done its part, and the war has been won, we look for the freedom that victory was to insure. Do we find it? Or do we find science still wearing its wartime fetters, in the interests of a right assumed for any nation, at peace, to make secret preparation for the destruction of its neighbors?

The melancholy observations of Sir Henry are completely justified by the information section of the Atomic Energy Act. If the Act does not restrict the liberty of scientific thought, it without question abridges freedom of scientific communication. The controls on information were deliberately designed to regulate the interchange of scientific ideas; to prescribe when and how a scientist may publish or otherwise communicate the results of his work. And the penalties for violation of these prescriptions are drastic. The data whose communication the Act seeks to regulate are not exclusively technical and military in character, nor are they necessarily data compiled by federal workers utilizing federal funds. Even those data describing the phenomena and laws of the visible universe are under interdict; and even data independently arrived at in private laboratories are subject to control.

Scientific progress depends on the free flow of ideas—assured by the freedom to publish, to communicate and to exchange views by personal contact—among scientists the world over. Every scientist builds on the achievements of his predecessors and contemporaries; more often his own work is brought to fulfillment by the work of his successors. Unique proof of the complete interdependence of all scientific activities is found in the winning of atomic energy, a scientific and technological achievement to which scientists from so many different countries contributed that it may be regarded as a prototype of international cooperation.

Laws controlling the dissemination of scientific information, however skillfully formulated, cannot be made sufficiently flexible and selective to avoid disrupting this symbiotic relationship among scientists and retarding to some extent the national growth of science. . . .

While it may be possible to safeguard information against coming into the possession of foreign scientists and thus reduce leaks to countries which may be our enemies in future wars, this cannot be achieved without restricting the free exchange of ideas among our own scientists. Is there, then, a middle way which science and national security can travel together without seriously impeding each other? Many of our leading scientists believe not.

The question remains, moreover, have information controls any value? Can they be enforced? Since this is open to serious doubt, it may be the point should have been considered at the outset. For if either we have no secrets to keep or could not keep those we have, other aspects of the matter would become more or less academic. . . .

The use of the word "secret" for the results of scientific investigations is unfortunate and misleading. A dream or an unuttered idea are examples of things which can be kept secret if their possessor does not choose to reveal them. On the other hand, if I say, "I know the critical mass of U-235 necessary to make a bomb, and I intend to keep it secret," I am using the word "secret" in an entirely different sense. I am saying to you, not that you cannot find out what I know, but that you must find it out for yourself, without my help. This may cause you to become annoyed with me, but it cannot keep you in ignorance.

This is not to say that restrictions on the disclosure of the new basic discoveries or of technical processes, such as those involved in separating the isotope U-235, may not lengthen the period required by other nations to gain this knowledge. So the question becomes, not, shall we keep the secrets of atomic energy?—that is impossible; but rather, will the control of atomic information in the United States delay other nations enough to warrant the resulting impairment of our own research and of international comity?

In reaching a judgment on this question, three factors must be taken into account. First, it is essential to recognize that once it is disclosed that a technical device has been developed in one country, even if details regarding it are withheld, the search becomes easier for other countries. The knowledge that a problem can be solved is an important aid to others seeking a solution. . . .

Second, the general principles underlying all processes are likely to be widely known, being derived usually from some discovery of basic science. For example, the successful gaseous diffusion method of separating U-235 was based on . . . principles [identical with those] enunciated by Lord Rayleigh as early as 1896. Thus, it is only the latest improvement or modification of an existing technique which can be held in camera, and then only for an indeterminate but usually brief period. Moreover, there is no likelihood whatever, with all our preeminence in technology, that the disparity between the level of our technical competence and that of other industrialized countries . . . is such that the latter would be more than at most a few years behind us. Indeed, there is abundant evidence that other nations frequently develop technological methods and processes distinctly superior to ours in a variety of fields. . . .

Finally, the cosmopolitan character of the atomic energy project should not be forgotten. This work was the product of the scientific brains of several of the allied nations, and participating scientists inevitably acquired a considerable measure of the specialized and technical knowledge required to produce the bomb. It must be assumed that any "secrets" known by these scientists, many of whom have returned to their own countries, have been disclosed to fellow-workers in nuclear physics in other parts of the world.

Congress, nevertheless, decided that the dangers of free speech in nuclear science and related technologies could not be risked And having reached this conclusion, there remained the questions: What information was to be restricted? Under what circumstances might United States scientists exchange restricted information? How should violations be punished? The answers to these questions appear in section 10 of the Atomic Energy Act. . . .

Data on atomic energy with respect to its use for industrial purposes shall not be exchanged with other nations "until Congress declares by joint resolution that effective and enforceable international safeguards against the use of atomic energy for destructive purposes have been established. . . .

The statement plainly reveals the determination of Congress to safeguard all the "secrets" of atomic energy—including those relating solely to its industrial use. Since the production of power by nuclear processes requires either the production of fissionable material or the "burning" of fissionable material as nuclear fuel, Congress appears to have adopted a reasonable position. Note, however, that the text under consideration makes no reference to the possible exchange with other nations of technical data relating to other aspects of atomic energy even *after* "effective and enforceable international safeguards" have been established. Although no undue significance should be attributed to this omission, it reemphasizes the concern of Congress with the protection of the "secrets" and its unwillingness at the time to make any commitments as to conditions under which the resumption of free scientific intercourse would be permitted. . . .

The actual mechanics of the system of controls over information established by Congress in the Act are quite simple. Certain kinds of information relating to atomic energy are denoted as "restricted data." The Commission alone determines which of the restricted data shall be removed from this category and thereafter freely disseminated. Restricted data may not be communicated or transmitted without incurring certain penalities in the event that acts of communication or transmission are perpetrated "with intent to injure the United States or with intent to secure an advantage to any foreign nation," or, in certain instances, where the perpetrator, though innocent of such intentions has "reason to believe" that injury to the United States or advantage to a foreign power will be the consequences of his action.

While the mechanics are simple, the concepts are not; nor is the interpretation and application of the several provisions free of serious difficulties and dangers. Let us proceed to examine some of the major parts of the control machinery in somewhat greater detail.

Restricted Data. Restricted data are defined as "all data concerning the manufacture or utilization of atomic weapons, the production of fissionable material or the use of fissionable material in the production of power. . . ."

Dominated by considerations of caution Congress constructed this definition so as to embrace practically all significant data relating to atomic energy. Its manifest intention was to make the term "restricted data" an all-inclusive category from which the Commission might remove classes of information on its own responsibility and in conformity with the general security standards set forth in the Act.

The first portion of the definition raises no serious problem. Information respecting the manufacture or utilization of atomic weapons is almost exclusively of military value and should obviously be subjected to strict control. The other portions of the definition, however, are not so readily disposed of.

Information as to the production of fissionable material, a very loose and broad concept, embraces much that is of general importance to fundamental as well as applied research. If private research in this area is to contribute effectively to the future development of atomic energy, it will be necessary to keep channels of communication open between the laboratories of government and those of universities and private industry. The Commission must, therefore, reconcile objectives of opposite tendency: the maintenance of secrecy and the promotion of vigorous and fruitful research. So long as the present temper prevails, the Commission will feel powerful pressures to refrain from declassifying data, until they are generally known, in part at least, as a result of publication by other countries. Tempting as this policy will prove, it is to be hoped that the Commission will reject it, for if the United States publishes little other than what is already known, other countries will follow the same course, and the rate of scientific progress will be greatly retarded.

The larger the area which is maintained as restricted, the greater will be the responsibility of the Commission to encourage the free exchange of information among our own scientists and between federal and non-federal laboratories.

The third category of restricted data encompasses "the use of fissionable material in the production of power." In the event of an agreement between nations to set up an international development authority, the information function in this, as in other categories, will be altered radically. Even in the absence of an international agreement, however, the provisions of the Act relating to the production of power and associated controls over information must be considered if the denaturing process referred to in the Acheson-Lilienthal Report can be rendered truly effective.

Insofar as the fields of atomic power and of fissionable material production overlap, restrictions on dissemination of information relating to the former are obviously justified. However, scientists who have worked in the field have repeatedly asserted that a variety of useful data on power production could be released without the revelation of significant data on the production of fissionable material. The only justification for prohibiting communication in this area, consequently, is that it relates to the nation's economic potential, and as such has economic significance. There can be no quarrel with the general proposition that economic potential is ultimately convertible into military effectiveness, but if this is the rationale for a policy restricting the dissemination of information, then clearly there are many other categories which must be included as well: coal mining, steel production, electrical engineering, automobile manufacturing, chemicals—the list could be extended indefinitely. The policy followed by the Commission in this area will thus have implications of broad significance, and it is of considerable importance that it should not appear to endorse the principle that data should be withheld merely on the grounds that it relates to the nation's general economic potential and thus, ultimately, to its military strength.

As indicated above, the three categories of restricted data are sweepingly inclusive in scope. Unfortunately, a detailed enumeration of categories of restricted information was not feasible. Such a catalog would have been unwieldly, apart from the fact that its publication would have revealed certain information which it had been decided must for the present be kept secret. That Congress intended information within the restricted categories to be released at the Commission's discretion is, of course, evident from the express language in the latter part of section 10 (b) (1): ". . . but shall not include any data which the Commission from time to time determines may be published without adversely affecting the common defense and security."

What areas of information clearly lie outside the scope of restricted data as above defined? Much fundamental information in the field of nuclear physics does not appear to be caught up in the control net. But to dispel doubts and to relieve physicists of the intolerable fear that publication of every research finding is a violation of the Act, the Commission will be well advised to publish explicit and detailed catalogues of types of data *not* included in the restricted category. . . . Having defined "restricted data" the Act proceeds to set forth the actions involving its communication, acquisition, or alteration which invoke criminal penalties. . . .

Assume the case of scientist A, working in a government laboratory, who, having gained access to restricted [material] passes the data on to B with intent to injure the United States. A will be prosecuted and may either suffer imprisonment up to twenty years, or, in the extreme case, the jury may recommend the sentence of death or life imprisonment. The penalties are severe, but they are probably justified by the nature of the crime— a treasonable act on the part of a public servant entrusted with official secrets.

But assume that A works in a private laboratory, has no official connection with the government and uses no federal funds. Assume that A independently makes a discovery and publishes results which incorporate restricted data. If on A's trial the jury find that publication was with intent to injure the United States, he may also receive the death penalty if the jury so recommends. Moreover, either the government [scientist] or the private scientist may receive a maximum of ten years' imprisonment for committing the offense *without* any specific intent to injure the United States if it appears that he had reason to believe his act would result in injury to the United States or benefit to a foreign power.

In effect, therefore, the Act abolishes to a considerable degree previous distinctions between public officials and private individuals, and between "official secrets" and data independently arrived at. . . .

Indeed the draconic sweep of all these penalties reveals Congress' obsession with the safeguarding of secrets. The unprecedented provisions which prescribe the death penalty in peacetime for such an offense as "mutilating" a "sketch" relating to research on atomic energy partially financed by federal funds can be ascribed only to superstitious dread. Terror of the atomic bomb is natural and understandable—perhaps even healthy; but terror at the loss of the "secret" is a tribal fear which, once gaining ascendancy in our minds, must inevitably weaken rather than strengthen our defensive power as a nation. Preoccupation with the "secret," instead of with the thing itself, will stifle the scientific research from which our real strength is derived, will strengthen the pernicious misconception that we have a monopoly of knowledge in the science of atomic energy, and will beguile us into embracing the fatal fallacy that we can achieve security for ourselves by keeping our knowledge from others. . . .

Certain offenses, as noted above, are punishable even if there is no evidence of intent of either type, as long as the individual unlawfully disseminating restricted data had "reason to believe such data will be utilized to injure the United States or to secure an advantage to any foreign nation." . . .

It is fair to predict that prosecutions grounded on dissemination with "reason to believe" are most likely to be directed against scientists who inadvertently publish restricted data in a journal or monograph, against journalists publishing such data in newspapers, and against anyone having the misfortune to misjudge the character, the loyalty or the discretion of another to whom he has communicated restricted data. But these, by hypothesis, are all men innocent of any deliberate intent to engage in treasonable activities. At most they may be indiscreet. It is justifiable to punish carelessness and indiscretion concerning atomic data with severity—since data so revealed is as dangerous to the national security as that given away by deliberate treason; nevertheless punishment should be limited to those who have been guilty of carelessness and indiscretion, and this guilt should be demonstrable by objective standards. . . .

A scientist engaged in private research in nuclear physics must, therefore, keep fully informed regarding all interpretations and regulations issued by the Commission pertaining to the scope of restricted data. Only by so doing can he ascertain whether or not he is free to publish the results of his research. However, since it is manifestly impossible for the Commission to list even by title each category and sub-category of information subsumed under the definition of restricted data . . . the private scientist can never be certain that the information he intends to publish lies outside the scope of restricted data. In questionable cases, therefore, he would be well advised to submit his report or monograph to the Commission for security clearance. . . . If the Commission decides the data are free of security restrictions, that ends the matter and the scientist is free to publish his findings in any way he sees fit. If on the other hand there is a ruling that the research findings contain restricted data, the scientist who has discovered the information cannot publish it. But if the matter were to end here science would soon expire for lack of circulation and interchange of life-giving ideas. The scientist in question will find it necessary to communicate his findings to colleagues in the United States who are engaged in the same work and, therefore, have a vital interest in any advances which are made. At this point he is compelled to embark on a perilous venture. For while he is not forbidden to communicate restricted data to others, he must not only avoid laying himself open to a charge of acting with intent to injure the United States or to give an advantage to any foreign nation, but he must also be careful that he is not open to a charge that he had reason to believe that these consequences might result from his acts. . . . A scientist who communicates restricted data to his colleagues must be certain that they are loyal, trustworthy, and non-subversive; that they are fully acquainted with the control of information section of the Atomic Energy Act, and with regulations relating to restricted data issued by the Commission; and that in addition to being loyal and versed in the law, they are also discreet and keep good company.

This is, unfortunately, not a neurotic caricature of what the scientist faces when in the interest of scientific progress (or for any other reason) he takes it upon himself to impart restricted information. For it is easy to see that anyone whose transmission of restricted data turns out badly, must face the possibility of prosecution for communicating with "reason to believe" that injury to the United States . . . would result. It is, in other words, insufficient to guard one's own morals; one must also judge the loyalty, patriotism and discretion of those with whom one communicates and run the risk of imprisonment if this judgment should prove erroneous. . . .

As a further means of protecting restricted data, the Act contains provisions to assure the integrity of personnel working on atomic energy matter. All contractors and licensees of the Commission are required to agree in writing not to permit any individual to have access to restricted data until an investigation of the "character, associations and loyalty of such individual" has been made by the FBI and a determination made by the Commission that access by such person will not "endanger the common defense or security." It may be noted that disregard of this clearance is only a breach of contract, not a criminal violation. . . .

For Commission employees, the Act requires an FBI investigation *before* hiring. Similar investigations for government employees are customary and are often completed before the employee reports for duty. The provision is unprecedented, however, in making prior investigation a statutory requirement. . . .

The information section of the Atomic Energy Act is principally significant as symptom and warning. So long as the terrible danger of national destruction persists, clearly we must take such measures as we can to protect against it. But we must recognize at the same time the dangers to the fundamental values of our system which are implicit in an uncritical policy of placing immediate security considerations before everything else. If we are determined to do our utmost to preserve individual freedoms, we will scrutinize all measures which purport to serve security purposes at the expense of individual liberty. . . . While we must accept the basic proposition that we should have all the controls over atomic energy which contribute to our security, this does not mean that we are not justified in asking pointed questions about the nature and probable effect of each of the specific controls proposed.

THE RADAR STORY [4]

In the radar field, we started with the same atmosphere of secrecy, the same precautions about compartmentation of information and clearance of individuals, which characterized the atomic bomb project right to the end, and still characterize it today. However, we did away with most secrecy before the end of the war. At the end of the war, the Army was publishing a magazine on radar with a circulation of over 12,000. It had become by that time apparent that secrecy cost in efficiency far more than it gained us by keeping the enemy in ignorance. . . .

Radar itself was independently invented by the Germans, the French, the British, the Japanese, and ourselves. Each of these nations kept it secret from all of the others, not knowing to what little point this was done. Microwave radar, which has played such a great role in the allied victory, was made possible by a single invention, the cavity magnetron. This is a transmitting tube which gives previously unimaginable amounts of power on wavelengths far shorter than those available to radio engineers before the war. It was invented by the British. When the British sent a scientific mission over to this country in the late summer of 1940, one of the most impressive of the secrets they had to show us was the cavity magnetron. When the radiation laboratory was first set up, an attempt was actually made to keep knowledge of the magnetron localized in one group of the laboratory, not even letting the men who were working on a modulator to energize this tube know of the tube's design. Yet,

---

[4] From the testimony of Louis N. Ridenour, professor of physics at the University of Pennsylvania, *Hearings before Special Senate Committee on Atomic Energy Pursuant to S. Res. 179*, 79th Congress, 1st Session. p. 536-8. (1945).

all this time there was in the Russian literature a paper which exactly described the cavity magnetron, and gave the results of experiments with it.

SECRECY AND AN INHIBITED PRESS [5]

A former official of the Atomic Energy Commission has deplored the alleged lack of interest by the press and the public in news of the Commission and its atomic activities. . . . We believe the assertion there is a "lack of interest" is a misstatement of the facts.

Atomic energy was born in secrecy, was nursed and weaned in secrecy. With that beginning it looked as if it would grow to full stature in secrecy and it is only comparatively recently that some aspects of atomic research, particularly in the medical fields have emerged from their hush-hush wraps. The few newspapermen who knew about the development of the atomic bomb during the war . . . thought of it mainly as a taboo subject. Except for the eye-witness accounts of atomic bomb explosions and the material released to the press after the first one went off over Japan, the bomb is still in the highly secret classification.

Obviously, newspapermen's minds have been conditioned to secrecy whenever atomic information is mentioned. Admittedly it is a rare phenomenon among newspapermen but one that has been motivated by purely patriotic motives. It is going to take some time to erase the impression among newsmen that mention of atomic subjects should be carefully scrutinized and possibly avoided for security reasons, particularly when some of it is secret and some of it isn't.

[5] From "Atomic News," editorial. *Editor & Publisher.* 81:30. August 28, 1948. Reprinted by permission.

SECRECY VERSUS FREEDOM OF THE PRESS

DISCUSSION

Strangely enough, the information security program has received few if any real criticisms in the American press. The various information media have shown apparent complete understanding of the problems and obligations imposed by the present international situation and its secrecy requirements.

The press has not been asleep, however. When President Truman attempted to install an ill advised program of peacetime censorship and classification of news in government departments, an enterprising reporter from the *Minneapolis Tribune*, Nat Finney, exposed the measure. The press opposition brought the proposal to a speedy finish before it could be put into effect.

More recently, Representative Clare Hoffman of Michigan in drafting a measure to secure information from the executive departments included a precautionary provision calling for punishment for disclosure of restricted information. The punishment was to apply to any employee of a Congressional committee or reporter or other person who used information received in confidence. The intent may have been honorable, but the press protests to Congress brought about the death of this measure as well.

With this convincing proof of the alertness of the press to any abridgment of its freedom, the various authorities responsible for carrying out information security policies have trod softly. Secretary Forrestal, reversing the customary policy of the military, asked the press to help the Office of Defense in promulgating a program of information security. The Atomic Energy Commission from its inception as a civilian agency has enlisted the support and advice of the press and other news media both as to secrecy policies and for the furthering of its information program. There is as a result no apparent threat to freedom of press, although a problem is created by the press itself through self-censorship—not publishing anything for fear of publishing "secret information."

THE CENSORSHIP ATTEMPT [1]

What was believed to be the last prop supporting "press gag" rules proposed by the Security Advisory Board has been knocked out by an agreement between the Atomic Energy Board and the American Society of Newspaper Editors to fix a border at which information to the public endangers national security.

The SAB [Security Advisory Board], comprising representatives of State, War and Navy agencies, had prepared a tentative draft of information categories which would go so far as to bar from public knowledge facts which might cause embarrassment to the administrators whose departments would be affected.

ASNE [American Society of Newspaper Editors] promptly blasted the rules, the Veterans Administration which had adopted but had not invoked them in any actual instance erased them from its regulations, and a congressional committee grilled the three SAB members. General Dwight Eisenhower expressed his opposition to peacetime censorship and proved his sincerity by immediately opening up a large treasure of World War II documents heretofore held in strict secrecy, reserving only the condition that national security must not be jeopardized by the disclosures. . . .

Because the new secrecy move stemmed from the A-Energy program, the attitude of the Atomic Energy Commission was awaited. Chairman David Lilienthal removed uncertainty by applauding the action of ASNE president N. R. Howard, in appointing an editorial committee to meet with AEC in January. Mr. Lilienthal declared it a proper function of the press to take over the circulation of knowledge—

To disseminate facts, to interpret them and give them meaning, and to hold public servants accountable for their conduct of the people's business. The Atomic Energy Commission recognizes a joint responsibility with the press to see that these facts are available to the people of the United States, with full regard for the common defense and security of the United States. . . .

[1] From "ASNE, Atomic Board Join in Security Study," by James J. Butler, *Editor & Publisher* Washington correspondent. *Editor & Publisher*. 80:10. December 6, 1947. Reprinted by permission.

SELF-CENSORSHIP [2]

Secretary of Defense James V. Forrestal is considering a new method of protecting information of a security nature. It involves the cooperation of all media in policing themselves under the guidance of the Defense Department.

The Secretary's press aide, Captain Robert Berry, has stated this "would not be a voluntary censorship in any sense of the word." There would be no Office of Censorship, there would be no code and there would be no policing ostensibly. It would be self-censorship.

There will be voices raised in protest over the possibility of a military agency deciding what should not be printed in our newspapers or magazines or broadcast over the air. But the issue must be given fair consideration.

If we believe that certain military secrets must be protected for reasons of national security, then we must also believe that some procedure for protection is desirable. If we agree to that, then newspapers and newspapermen are not compromising themselves or their freedom in admitting that the good of the nation takes precedence and they are justified in voluntarily withholding scraps of information, which otherwise might have been printed, as long as there is no legal control or coercion.

Recommendations have been made to the President that rigid censorship rules be installed in every government department to classify information according to its importance for release to the press. This publication and many others have voiced their dislike of this form of gag rule.

Forrestal's proposed plan is the least likely, of all those proposed, to infringe dangerously on the free press guarantee. It is the only one exhibiting some confidence in the patriotism of the nation's information media representatives.

Some will question whether such a self-censorship plan could be made to work in the public interest. Will all newspapers, magazines, and radio stations cooperate?

[2] From "Self-Censorship," editorial. *Editor & Publisher.* 81:34. January 24, 1948. Reprinted by permission.

Speaking only for the newspapers, we believe that when they are properly informed on the plan their patriotism will exhibit itself just as it did during the war years when they cooperated voluntarily a hundred per cent.

PLEA FOR COOPERATION OF THE PRESS [3]

I am confronted by a serious problem . . . . That problem is to prevent information which might endanger the United States from being given to any potential enemy. There is no doubt in my mind that you and I share the same feelings in regard to the importance of safeguarding highly classified information of our vital military projects. The differences which we may share would be in the safeguarding methods employed.

In time of peace, "secret" classifications are not assigned to such matters as troop movements, ship sailings, convoy routes, and assignments of general and flag officers. At the present time we are mainly concerned with the security of technical information, facts about new developments and weapons, about new military techniques, the knowledge of which would be of value to hostile or possibly hostile powers, and thus detrimental to the future security of this country.

In the two years following V-J Day, the release of information by the armed services on their activities, including research projects, was to a large extent uncorrelated, sometimes competitive, and sometimes questionable in regard to proper security precautions. In addition to information released because of different policies in the various departments of the armed services, there were unauthorized releases of information or "leaks." Information had appeared in the press and similar media revealing the existence, and in some cases the degree of success which had been attained, in many of our secret technical and scientific projects. Many of these projects, enormous in size, in addition to the military personnel require the employment of thousands

[3] From a statement of Secretary of Defense James V. Forrestal before the Voluntary Security Conference consisting of twenty-two representatives of news agencies, magazines, radio and other news media, March 3, 1948, Washington, D.C.

of civilians, some of whom quite understandably cannot appreciate the harm of security violations.

The answer to this serious problem as I see it has two major aspects:

1. Remedial action within the military establishment in regard to the prevention of "leaks," the declassification of documents whose security no longer obtains, and the establishment of a unified policy among the various armed services for the prompt release of technical information which does not endanger national security.

2. An assumption by the information media of their responsibility in voluntarily refraining from publishing information detrimental to our national security.

Both are necessary, it seems to me, for though the efforts of the military may be most sincere and painstaking, "leaks" will undoubtedly continue to occur in this vast military establishment of ours.

You gentlemen know quite well that a good reporter does not get his story from a single individual who breaks down and tells all, but builds it up, bit by bit, from the general scraps of information obtained from many sources. In addition there are sources from which he can obtain information about military projects which lie, to all practical purposes, completely outside the military jurisdiction. We need your advice, assistance and guidance on what is and what is not harmful information. We believe it is our duty to work with you in helping to determine what is harmful by presenting the military point of view.

We do not have many military secrets. The thing that is quite "secret" today and involves the national security to a high degree may be completely releasable six months from today. This country is preeminent in military skill and knowledge—"the know-how." Our ability to devise and produce superior weapons and equipment in vast quantities had a decided effect in winning World War II and is a decisive factor in maintaining our security through an era of troubled peace or in the event of another war. Our lead over possible enemies is often a matter of only a few months on the technical side, and it is extremely dangerous to sacrifice that advantage by showing our hand.

I am confident that the average American would not complain at being denied information which if disclosed to him would be disclosed at the same time to possible enemies, and so endanger his safety. The question as to how far we can go in keeping the American public uninformed about technical progress in order to safeguard our real "secrets" is a difficult one and I hope you can help me solve it.

PRESS REPLY: COOPERATION, NOT CENSORSHIP [4]

On March 3, 1948, a group representing various media of the press, radio and moving pictures met in the Pentagon Building in response to an invitation from Secretary of Defense Forrestal.

The Secretary outlined to this group the problem represented in preventing "information, which might endanger the United States, from being given to any potential enemy," his chief concern being "the security of technical information, facts about new developments and weapons, about new military techniques, the knowledge of which would be of value to hostile . . . powers and thus detrimental to the future security of this country."

His remarks were amplified in discussions off the record by Dr. Vannevar Bush, chairman of the Research and Development Board; General Omar N. Bradley, Chief of Staff of the Army; Admiral Louis E. Denfeld, Chief of Naval Operations; General Carl Spaatz, Chief of Staff of the Army Air Force, and others.

Secretary Forrestal asked for the "advice and help" of the group in deciding how far we may go in keeping the American public informed about technical progress while protecting our secret and scientific projects.

He communicated to the group, but not as recommendations of his own, three steps which had been suggested to him:

[4] Text of the report submitted by the media subcommittee appointed to discuss Secretary Forrestal's information security proposals of March 3, 1948. Released to the press, March 29, 1948, by the Office of the Secretary of Defense.

1. Remedial action within the military establishment in regard to the prevention of "leaks," the declassification of documents and the establishment of a unified policy among the various armed services for the prompt release of technical information which does not endanger national security. This is the undivided responsibility of the Military Establishment.

2. An assumption by the information media of their responsibility in voluntarily refraining from publishing information detrimental to the national security. Such assumption of responsibility might be implemented by—

A. A Security Council of approximately six members for the purpose of advising the Secretary in regard to security matters in general;

B. An Information Advisory Unit set up by the National Military Establishment in Washington that would function twenty-four hours daily to answer inquiries on certain subjects and offer guidance to the news media.

It was further suggested that the Security Advisory Council should draft the rules governing the Information Advisory Unit's operation, and that the information unit be made up of civilians of news media experience in so far as practicable. Secretary Forrestal repeated that the above suggestions were not his own, but had been received by him and were placed before the group for its consideration.

Following a general discussion the group resolved to appoint a subcommittee, with instructions to investigate the matter and to report back to the full group with recommendations within thirty days. This subcommittee met at the Pentagon Building on March 15. . . .

The subcommittee conversed with Dr. Bush in detail regarding the security problem as it appears from his point of view as chairman of the Research and Development Board, at the same time inviting comment from Major General F. L. Parks, chief of Public Information of the Department of the Army; Captain

E. M. Eller, Director of Public Information, Department of the
Navy; Stephen F. Leo, Director of Public Relations, Department
of the Air Force.

By invitation Mr. William Mathews, editor and publisher
of the Arizona *Daily Star*, and Mr. Frank Kluckhohn, serving
as Temporary Consultants to the Secretary of Defense on Public
Relations Matters, attended and took part in the discussions.

Our conversations with all these gentlemen led to these conclusions: Secretary Forrestal is making progress now in coordinating the public information branches of the three services. But
there is an obvious absence of what might be called "top level"
policy, understood and universally agreed upon between the information branches of the military services and the Research and
Development Board, on the type of information in certain fields
which should not be revealed.

There evidently are scores of highly restricted projects under-
way in all branches of the services, some of which should be declassified, others which must be protected.

It is desirable that there be well defined agreement on policy
in drawing the line between information which should be made
public, in order to stimulate the interest and inventiveness of
Americans, and that which should be closely guarded as military
secrets. Such agreement on policy is obtainable only within the
Military Establishment. But the opinion and advice of representatives of communications media may prove helpful.

Such considerations led your subcommittee to adopt the following resolution:

> To approve the suggestion for a Security Advisory Coun-
> cil with the understanding that the Council shall have no
> concern with censorship, voluntary or otherwise. It will also
> suggest to the full committee that the Secretary invite the
> following organizations each to designate a representative to
> serve on the Advisory Council: The National Association
> of Magazine Publishers; National Association of Broad-
> casters; one representative of the Associated Press, the In-
> ternational News Service and the United Press; the American
> Society of Newspaper Editors; American Book Publishers
> Council, Inc.; the Motion Picture Association; the American

Newspaper Publishers Association; one representative of the networks; National Conference of Business Paper Editors.

It was felt that such a representative committee, meeting at the call of the Secretary of Defense, might be of assistance to him and to his advisors in public relations by expressing to him the media point of view in relation to problems affecting security and public information.

It was not believed that such a committee would be helpful, either to the Secretary or to the press, radio and moving pictures, if it became identified with formal censorship of any kind. The only censorship that can be exercised in the public interest at this time, outside of the Military Establishment's own necessary protection of vital secrets, is the ever-present censorship imposed by the public responsibility and patriotism of those engaged in the publishing, radio and moving picture fields.

The subcommittee repeatedly questioned those in charge of the information branches of the three services regarding the number of cases of deliberate or careless publication of stories regarded as injurious to security. Only three were mentioned as having occurred since V-J Day.

On the other hand, testimony was received from each of the three services attesting the willingness and even anxiety of editors and reporters to obtain proper clearance before publishing stories in the "twilight zone" of security. When reporters or editors are informed of the reasons for not making certain information public, their attitude was represented as being cooperative on the whole.

The subcommittee was unable to discover any practical need for an Information Advisory Unit, made up of experienced civilians and working in the Military Establishment on a twenty-four hour basis.

The number of queries received did not justify the establishment of such machinery, it would tend to duplicate and therefore to confuse and delay the operations of the information branches in the three services; it was doubtful if men commanding the confidence of their brethren in press and radio would be obtainable for such service at this time.

Furthermore, there could be no parallel now between the operations of such a unit and the operations of the Office of Censorship under Mr. Byron Price during the war. The sanctions for enforcement of wartime, "voluntary" censorship are neither available nor desirable. Should any formal censorship machinery become necessary in the future, one war-learned lesson to be applied is that its direction should be responsible only to the President of the United States.

The subcommittee, therefore, resolved—

> To reject the Information Advisory Unit and leave it to the Defense Department to coordinate its own public relations operation.

It is the subcommittee's definite impression that Secretary Forrestal will press vigorously for necessary coordination of public relations operations within the services to the end that all information which does not involve military secrets and thus endanger the national interests will be made available to the American people.

Your subcommittee is confident that Mr. Forrestal is in thorough agreement with that principle.

We favor the adoption of the accompanying resolution.

RECOMMENDATIONS OF THE PRESS [5]

Conditions in the world today require the perfection of our national defense, an important part of which lies in the fields of scientific research and development of new military weapons.

Protection of necessary military secrecy in such fields in a country rightfully jealous of its free and uncontrolled media of communications presents a problem in national security.

We recognize the existence of such a problem.

Its wise solution is the responsibility of the National Military Establishment. But it is shared to a degree by all media of public information.

[5] Text of the resolution adopted unanimously by representatives of the various news media meeting to consider Secretary Forrestal's information security proposals. Released to the press by the Office of the Secretary of Defense, March 29, 1948.

As representatives of such media we have willingly assumed our proper part of that responsibility.

We do not believe that any type of censorship in peacetime is workable or desirable in the public interest.

If any exists, we would not be sympathetic with an intent, on the part of the Military Establishment, to propose peacetime censorship.

We do believe that consciousness of the fact that security of the nation could be compromised by careless or premeditated publication of classified military information on technical, scientific developments should impose an effective restraint on all responsible media of public information.

We commend Secretary of Defense Forrestal upon steps now being taken under his direction to coordinate Military Establishment policies designed for the quick and full release of all information to the American people compatible with the necessary protection of knowledge which should not be revealed to potential enemies.

In his formulation of means to effect policy in this respect, but without the implication of censorship machinery in any form, we suggest to the Secretary that he call upon each of the [information media] organizations . . . to designate a representative as member of a Security Advisory Council.

We recommend that these organizations respond and that the council be available to the Secretary for advice and discussion of the security problem from the viewpoint of the press, the radio and the moving picture industry. Establishment of such continuing liaison, we believe, will be mutually helpful to the information media represented and to the Secretary of Defense.

BEGINNING OF RESULTS [6]

Once the patriotic press of this country is aware of the danger to our national security involved in premature publication of vital technical and scientific information of a military nature, it will guard its columns carefully against such disclosures.

[6] From "Security Problem," editorial. *Editor & Publisher.* 81:36. April 3, 1948. Reprinted by permission.

Already the publicity given the first meeting between media representatives and the Secretary of Defense on this security problem has brought results. More and more newspaper stories in the "twilight zone" of security are being submitted to the Defense Department for proper clearance. Of course, the military branches cannot tell a newspaper what it can or cannot print. But once an editor or reporter is appraised of the security aspects of a story, he usually is eager to cooperate.

THE DANGER OF TOO MUCH COOPERATION [7]

Neither in depth nor scope is the public discussion which prevails for other government affairs even approximated in the field of atomic energy. . . . The absence of wide debate and criticism concerning the administration of this far reaching law is a phenomenon unique in the conduct of important public affairs. There are, of course, strong reasons for this peculiar situation. Some, like the requirements of secrecy, will appear obvious; others may appear more subtle. . . .

Throughout the history of this country we have rarely tolerated departure from the principle that the chief protection of society against incompetence, unfairness, and corruption in government is the unlimited opportunity for public scrutiny and protest. . . . Sixty years ago Lord Bryce observed "a healthy and watchful public opinion" as a commonplace of the American political system: "Mischief is checked in America more frequently than anywhere else by the fear of exposure or by newspaper criticism in the first stage of a bad scheme." . . .

Ordinarily there is no need to encourage criticism of large government enterprise; the danger is rather that it goes too far. . . . Even in the conduct of the war agencies, whether civilian or military, we have insisted upon this principle. . . . Nevertheless, in the case of the administration of the Atomic Energy Act critical debate has been largely absent. . . .

[7] From "The Atomic Energy Act: Public Administration without Public Debate," by Herbert S. Marks, former assistant general counsel, War Production Board, most recently General Counsel, Atomic Energy Commission. *University of Chicago Law Review*. 15:839-54. Summer, 1948. Copyright by University of Chicago. Reprinted by permission.

Nor have any adequate substitutes for the usual process of public criticism been found. The two that are sometimes referred to as assuring a measure of public accountability, the Congressional Joint Committee on Atomic Energy and the Commission's public advisory committees, are certainly of great value, but they alone are clearly insufficient. . . .

Perhaps the requirements of secrecy are such that there can be no public participation in the problem of atomic energy in any customary sense. As the question is subjected to analysis, however, this answer may appear less clear. At all events, while secrecy may seriously inhibit debate, that factor alone hardly accounts for the silence of the interests that are directly affected by the atomic energy program.

Ordinarily the reaction and response of special groups, favorable or unfavorable, to any particular government action give rise to and sustain public debate. With limited exceptions, nothing of this sort has happened in the atomic energy program. In a variety of ways the Commission's program has an important daily effect upon national life. Procurement of raw materials, letting of contracts, construction and operation of plants involving hazardous new industrial processes and hazardous industrial waste products, administration of regulatory powers—all these activities and many others in this three billion dollar enterprise are in fact affecting the public at many points.

These Commission actions fall in areas of public sensitivity which, judging by the experience of all other government agencies, should produce a vocal response from those groups which are disappointed in Commission decisions. Indeed, some decisions of the Commission occur in the most sensitive areas of public concern. The effect which Commission action has upon the press itself is the best example.

Under Section 10 of the Atomic Energy Act the Commission is given broad powers to control the dissemination of restricted data. Simply stated, practically all information relating to atomic energy is classed as restricted by the Atomic Energy Act. The Commission is authorized to remove information from this category whenever it concludes that it may be published without impairing the national security. We need not concern ourselves here with the question which is sometimes raised as to whether the law is merely an official secrets act or whether it includes broader censorship powers. The press and publishing industry have apparently accepted the principle that whether or not the Act, strictly construed, applies to unofficial as well as official secrets, they will publish nothing in the face of advice by the Commission that publication would be prejudicial to the national security. In short, for practical purposes, they seem to have accepted in the field of atomic energy an arrangement somewhat similar to the one which existed more generally during the war under the Office of Censorship.

This voluntary restraint on the part of the press and the publishing industry, and their wholehearted cooperation with the government in maintaining security, are deserving of highest praise. But what is surprising is that there has not even been any debate concerning the details of administration. How does it happen that the public bickering between press and government over the scope and details of censorship so frequently observed in connection with the war agencies does not occur here? Are we then to conclude that the Commission's "security guidance" has been so satisfactory to the press that there has never been occasion for debate concerning it or public notice of the debate? . . .

Secrecy is certainly the most important factor in accounting for public inertia in relation to the administration of the Atomic Energy Act. In the present state of world affairs, the requirements of security altogether remove from public view certain activities and certain problems of the Atomic Energy Commission. In addition, there is everywhere an air of secrecy which seems impenetrable, even when it is not. The mere mechanics of securing a pass into a Commission installation for a routine interview appear formidable, even for the visitor who knows he is entitled to the pass. The areas of information that are shut off for reasons of security inevitably seem to obscure those which are open. No matter how much the questioner may be assured that he can understand what he needs to know without access to what is hidden, he always has a lurking uneasiness that his interpretation of what is in sight will be distorted by what is unknown.

Much of the subject matter—even that which is completely open—is technically complex, and therefore hard to understand. It is not only complex, it is totally unfamiliar. . . . There is, moreover, a general frame of mind which inhibits the active curiosity without which scrutiny and debate does not take place. A taboo-like quality attaches to atomic energy, which is perhaps no more than another way of saying that the immense proportions of the new physical force, the seeming magic and real mystery connected with it, its tradition-shaking consequences, and the walls of secrecy and epic drama which surrounded it from the first, make of it a subject from which we instinctively shy away.

Also important in suppressing curiosity is the belief that to ask questions in this field is unpatriotic. We have come to feel that because it is wrong to disclose secret information it is somehow wrong and possibly illegal for the uninitiated to seek information about the subject. . . . We may hopefully agree with Mr. Lilienthal that "there is nothing in the nature of atomic energy, nor in the necessary requirements of secrecy in certain areas of knowledge that prevents the people as a whole from exercising their historic role of judging what shall be the course of public policy." But the people are not now exercising that historic role and it is plain that if they are to do so very special exertions will be required of them. . . .

Active curiosity, far from being improper or illegal, is a normal, lawful public responsibility. It has been asserted on behalf of the Commission that "by and large the sources of information on public issues are already open." And it is a fair estimate that the official material made available by and about the Commission up to the present time compares in quantity and content with the official material that is made available about other large government operations in a comparable period of operation. Here and there one will see the censor's hand in the official material concerning the Commission's activities. But such material is mainly distinguished from the information about other government agencies in that it has not been illuminated by public reaction.

It takes active curiosity on the part of the press and public to give meaning to official handouts, no matter how enlightening the government tries to make them. The official material of other government agencies is subjected to searching public analysis and questioning which uncovers and evaluates the reasons behind decisions and the consequences implicit in them. Because of security restrictions, an effort to subject the available materials about the Commission to the same treatment would sometimes be frustrating. Surprisingly often, however, the results would be illuminating.

It should be understood that the general public on the one hand and the Commission on the other have different responsibilities in respect to security. It is the duty of the Atomic Energy Commission under the law to see to it that those things are kept secret which in the interest of national security should be kept secret. It is the duty of the public to cooperate with the Commission in this effort, and this the public has been doing with remarkable effectiveness. But, as the Commission itself has repeatedly asserted, it is also a public responsibility to find out and to understand those things which need not be kept secret. This can only be accomplished through incessant questioning.

The Atomic Energy Commission is no more omniscient than any other government agency in its capacity to determine precisely what information within its vast area of nonsecret knowledge the public needs to know. It is the duty of a democratic public to direct to its government every question that its curiosity provokes. It is the Atomic Energy Commission which must bear the responsibility of deciding whether an answer to any particular question may prejudice the national security. . . .

There must also be a willingness to criticize. Partisanship that exercises a restraint upon legitimate criticism out of a fear that such criticism will aid the enemies of the McMahon Act defeats its own purposes. . . . In refraining from criticism, these groups have . . . deprived the administration of the Atomic Energy Act of . . . the strength that comes from constructive exposure of weakness and error and the opportunity thereby created for correction. . . .

The usual but never tolerable condition of a government official is one of continual harassment by a seemingly specious, unfair and unsympathetic press and public. That this condition makes officials wary and that it often makes the process of getting information from a public agency difficult is not surprising. The fear of embarrassment which the official or his agency may suffer as a result of disclosing information can be a more important factor in deciding whether or not to answer a question than the public need for an answer. . . . A party in power may assert that a strong opposition is essential to democracy; but it cannot be expected willingly to supply what might be used as ammunition by its opponents.

In the case of the Atomic Energy Commission, there is, moreover, a special hazard to the process of debate and criticism. The line between what must be secret and what can be open is not a sharp one. When areas of information involving possible embarrassment are probed, the temptation must always be present to draw the line so that embarrassment will be avoided rather than to draw the line only where the reasonable requirements of security indicate. The danger is not that the Atomic Energy Commission or its staff would thus act deliberately. The danger is rather of unconsciously confusing the needs of security with the desire for self-protection from critical comment. During the war, journalists developed a sixth sense which enabled the press to tell whether the government's releases and its response to questions were really as full and frank as security would permit. This experience may ultimately be repeated in the field of atomic energy. But it will not be repeated as long as it continues to be possible to say that only about a dozen newspaper reporters in the United States are equipped to write about atomic information accurately and with understanding.

The absence of public scrutiny and criticism which the Atomic Energy Commission has so far experienced will not last indefinitely. . . . If too long delayed, our atomic energy program will almost certainly grow so far out of touch with the American environment that when the forces of criticism finally begin to operate with their customary vigor they will produce drastic upheavals. . . . If this should happen, not only will the continuity essential to the success of the undertaking be destroyed, but the public, without the knowledge gained by prior participation in the problems of atomic energy, will not be in a position to insure the establishment of a sound administration in its place.

OBLIGATIONS OF A FREE PRESS [8]

Five months ago President Howard [of the American Society of Newspaper Editors] appointed a special committee of this Society on atomic information problems. The project grew out of informal conversation between officers of the Society and members of the newly created Atomic Energy Commission, notably the chairman of the Commission, David Lilienthal, and our long-time member and colleague who is on the Commission, W. W. Waymack.

The special committee held its first meeting in Washington, on January 12, 13 and 14. The committee was given the fullest access to appropriate information and background by the Atomic Energy Commission. Since that time subcommittees have listed the installations which are under the Commission's charge.

As the committee wrestled with the problem, a conception unfolded of the real challenge to the daily press which the field of atomic science urgently presents. It is a field which ranges to the very limits of the human problems of democratic self-government and improvement to the general welfare.

It is hardly to be expected that mankind could learn in a year or two, or in a generation, to live in an atomic era, even if all the agencies of public information and education all acquitted themselves perfectly. We have not wholly mastered, in a longer time, the much simpler problem of living with the motor car.

Nuclear fission made its spectacular debut as an instrument of destruction. Therefore, public education about atomic power,

[8] From "American Society of Newspaper Editors Reports on Atomic Information Problems," text of the report by the Special Committee of the ASNE on Atomic Information Problems. *Bulletin of the Atomic Scientists.* 4:211-12. July 1948. Reprinted by permission.

in the press as elsewhere, begins with this handicap: many people tend to avert their eyes from it, to despair of mastering it, and even to wish that this realm of science had never been entered. Such a posture of fear is general enough so that newspapers are not under public pressure in this field, as much as they are in the field of government and elsewhere, to bring information and understanding to the people. The necessary element of secrecy, which conceals many particulars about our application of atomic power, makes it easy for editors to tell themselves that their very failure to inform the public about the facts and implications of atomic power is a patriotic service.

This plight of the press is understandable enough. But it is not excusable for any longer than it takes us as editors to recognize that newspapers must go out to meet their responsibilities in this new field if they are to hope to preserve our functions in a free society.

In other words, newspapers must equip themselves to report and discuss news of science, specifically of atomic science, from every angle that will obtain wider reading for it. We must find ways to integrate it into popular thinking about government and education and economics and foreign relations. . . .

The initiative and the responsibility ought to come from outside government from the newspapers themselves. Probably the social scientists should be invited in, to listen and discuss and to explore implications; but the primary approach should be the factual one of the natural scientists, for the place to start is with tangible data, and there is danger of branching off too soon into implications. There has been too little popular mastery of the basic physical facts, and too much vague philosophizing about "one world or none," in our newspapers.

The duty of the periodical press to get into this factual field with both feet is immediate, for several reasons. One is that, in the best circumstances, it will be four or five years before all the colleges and high schools can be equipped with textbooks incorporating what is known right now, and ought to be being taught right now about nuclear fission. Newspapers have a real opportunity to serve in this breach, and to help the schools to stimulate the interest which will produce the new young scientists we need.

Another reason why the task is immediate is that public anxiety and tension are going to increase, and not diminish, as we, and presumably other nations, learn more about atomic science. As long as there is no dependable international system of inspection and control (and such a system seems remote) there will be growing apprehension about what our rivals are doing. This may well lead to the formulation of national and world policy in an atmosphere of ignorance and panic. In such a climate the newspapers must do their utmost to impart all the exact information available, in understandable form, clinically free of opinion, to a public which has been enabled to receive and appraise it.

In such a broad reportorial and editorial effort, factual errors are sure to be made. They appear now, with a frequency which appalls informed people, even in writing and speaking by persons assumed to be competent. This is a hazard which must be reduced by the kind of hard work to which David Lilienthal summons us. But it is less a hazard than the hazard of not trying aggressively to do the job, and in the right kind of collective effort truth should vastly outweigh errors.

The second field with which the committee has concerned itself is the more explicit one of the present and prospective relations between working newspapermen and those departments of government, such as the Atomic Energy Commission and the Office of National Defense, which are concerned with the national security.

The problem of where to draw the line between publication and secrecy—between protection of classified information and the printing of news vital to the sound formulation of public policy—arises at every stage in the reporting of atomic information. In the broad field of all news involving national security, it is at least possible to draw a rather sharp line between technological and what we may call political or policy information, and to be sympathetic toward protection of technical secrets while insisting that news involving policy is the public's business. But this is not so easy in the atomic field, because the technological and the political are intertwined.

The Atomic Energy Commission has a monopoly not only of the fissionable material in the United States, but of the dependable spot news about it.

The Commission is proceeding, with a sound combination of enterprise and prudence, to remove from the secret or classified list data pertaining to atomic science, as rapidly as such data can properly and safely be made available to the public. The responsibility should be on the press to examine such material, as it is declassified, for information of interest and value to the public for news stories.

The Commission is under the unusual handicap, in dealing with newspapers, of being unable to deny a story, in many cases, even when it knows it to be untrue, because a denial might be somewhere nearly as informative as a confirmation.

The sum of our atomic know-how is thousands of specific bits of knowledge. Most of these are not only embedded in documents, but are running around all over the country in thousands of memories. Innocent breaches of security may come from disclosures which seem harmless and unimportant in themselves, but which make a pattern if all the right pieces are picked out and put together.

It is essential, in the committee's opinion, that the Commission have an information unit, not only to serve the press and other agencies, but to do the job of internal information within the Commission staff and the affiliated personnel of private contractors. Governed by the atomic security act, as well as by over-all legislative policy respecting government information agencies, such a unit ought not to initiate news, beyond announcing with adequate details, spot news information about a government program heavily cloaked in security. Initiative in this field must be peculiarly the responsibility of the newspapers. The committee frankly does not know how much the Commission and its information unit can or ought to give the newspapers in the way of security guidance. In the committee's opinion the present information unit is doing a highly competent job, with careful consideration of all of the complex factors involved, and only experience on both sides can help to develop further procedural answers.

Your special committee recommends that this Society appoint a standing committee on atomic information problems to serve for the next year, to do these things:

1. To get set up regional seminars or training courses for newspaper reporters and editors on atomic science.

2. To work with the Atomic Energy Commission for—in Chairman Lilienthal's words—"that flexibility and adequacy of relations between the Commission and the press which will insure, under security conditions, the fullest possible freedom of news handling."

It is profoundly evident to your committee that there are two kinds of national security. One is security through secrecy, and it is short-range security. The other is security through knowledge, through information, through achievement, through progress, and that is long-range security. The evidence is conclusive that whatever kind of secrecy is necessary in this atomic program impedes the kind of progress that comes through sharing knowledge widely and through competing freely, the kind of progress that stimulates the flow of young scientists into atomic research.

Some secrecy we must have, but we must not put our reliance in it. In the continuing cross pull between secrecy and progress, the press must array itself on the side of security through achievement—on the side of the full measure of knowledge and understanding which produce achievement, and which it is the mission of the press to diffuse.

There always will be plenty of pressure on the side of secrecy. The danger is that, if the press defaults in its duty to knowledge, there will be too little pressure for achievement.

We believe in the American system as a product of free institutions, and we believe that a free press is one institution which has made that system great. How, then, can we *widen* the margin of our know-how in atomic science, in competition with rivals of other philosophy, instead of seeing the margin steadily narrowed by them? We can do it by following the precepts that got us first to where we are today. We can widen our margin not in the narrow sense of superiority of weapons, but in the broad sense of equipping ourselves superiorly to show the world the leadership which can direct atomic power toward the constructive uses that lie somewhere ahead.

It is fine to work for peaceful application of atomic power. The United States is doing that today—we are building the foundations for an atomic era. But the truth is that the major purpose of our atomic industry today, as a matter of the highest national policy, is still to advance the use of atomic power as a weapon. It would be a dangerous deception of the people to pretend otherwise. The surest way to get beyond that stage, in the absence of a dependable system of international inspection and control, is to widen the margin and so to enhance our security. . . .

EXISTING LEGAL RESTRICTIONS ON PRESS FREEDOM [9]

The first amendment to the Constitution, which provides that the Congress shall make no law "abridging the freedom of speech or of the press," has never and does not now mean that the individual may say, or that the press may print, everything which either desires.

An example is found in title 18 of the Code which contains provisions making it a criminal offense to exercise the right of free speech or a free press if the effect thereof be to, among other things, incite insurrection, carry on certain correspondence with foreign governments; to interfere with, impair or influence the loyalty, morale or discipline of the military forces of the United States; to advocate the overthrow of the government by force.

Chapter 4 of title 50 of the Code, sometimes known as the Espionage Act, makes it a crime to obtain unlawfully, or permit to be obtained, information affecting the national defense or to utter disloyal words in time of war.

[9] From remarks by Representative Clare E. Hoffman of Michigan, before the House of Representatives. *Congressional Record.* 94:5849-50. May 12, 1948.

If it be said these restrictions on the right of free speech and a free press apply only in time of war, other limitations of the abridgment of the right of a free press may be cited. Section 1305 of title 19 of the Code prohibits the importing of any book, pamphlet, writing, print, picture or drawing which contains information detrimental to the national welfare. It prohibits the importation of obscene books, pamphlets, papers, and so forth.

A better known example is found in the federal and state laws which prevent the disclosure of grand jury proceedings.

The statute which created the Atomic Energy Commission makes it a criminal offense to disclose certain information.

The Internal Revenue Code, which makes available to the Finance Committee of the Senate, to the House Ways and Means Committee or to a select committee of the Senate or House specially authorized to investigate returns, or to a joint committee so authorized, sitting in executive session, certain information, makes it unlawful for any employee or officer of the United States to divulge or make known certain information.

Subdivision (f) of section 55 of title 26 of the Code further provides that it shall be unlawful for any person to print or publish in any manner whatever not provided by law certain information contained in tax returns. . . .

One outstanding example will prove the point. Not long ago, the Security Advisory Board of the State-War-Navy Coordinating Committee, acting under Executive Order 9835, put out a document prescribing minimum standards for the handling and transmission of classified information in executive departments and agencies of the Federal Government. That document restricted the disclosure of, among other, "confidential" information.

Confidential information was defined as follows:

The term "confidential" as used herein applies to information, the unauthorized disclosure of which, although not endangering the national security, would be prejudicial to the interests or prestige of the nation or any governmental activity thereof, or would cause serious administrative embarrassment or difficulty, or would be of advantage to a foreign nation.

Under that definition, had it become effective, the press would have been prohibited from disclosing any information which, in the opinion of the administrator, would "cause serious administrative embarrassment."

There, permit me to say to the gentlemen of the press, was a real abridgment of a free press. . . .

The proposed restrictions were revised and finally representatives of the departments and of the press agreed upon a voluntary censorship of information which might be obtained from the departments. . . .

As every reporter knows, in his quest for news he frequently is confronted by a door closed by some subordinate in an executive department. He is politely, but firmly, told that the information sought is confidential. The door remains closed, the information is not available.

RECONCILING SECURITY WITH FREEDOM OF THE PRESS [10]

The old and vexing question of "official secrets" is again troubling Washington and the nation's agencies of public information.

The recent attempt of a security board representing the State and Defense Departments to define "classified" or confidential material, numerous restrictive incidents encountered by the press in the coverage of news and a trend—in some departments pronounced—toward "censorship at the source" have stirred up a hornets' nest. Some observers believe the flow of governmental news has been only slightly affected, but others invoke the First Amendment to the Constitution and inveigh loudly against peacetime censorship.

The truth, as usual, seems to lie somewhere between these two extremes, but there is some cause for concern in the definite trend toward more restrictions and greater and greater "security."

[10] By Hanson W. Baldwin, Special correspondent of the *New York Times*. *New York Times*. November 16, 1947. Section 4, p. 4. Reprinted by permission.

The reasons for this trend are many. One is the carry-over into peacetime of wartime security regulations; it is difficult in bureaucratic Washington to rid the government of standards and rules established during the war. Another is obviously the tense international situation and the danger, ever-present in the official mind, of Communist "boring from within" and of espionage.

A third is the technological revolution in weapons through which we are passing; the atomic bomb, long-range guided missiles, biological agents and other new devices are such terrific mass killers that secrecy about some of their details is imperative. A fourth reason is the increasing influence of the military in Washington; they probably wield today greater power than in any prior peacetime period in American history.

Most of the complaints about restrictions, censorship and "over-security consciousness" relate, indeed, to the military departments, though there have been some complaints about state and other executive agencies.

The incidents that have occurred range from the ridiculous to the dangerous. In several instances newspaper men have been questioned—though very politely—about the sources of their stories by military officers. In one case a newspaper man, who is also a Naval Reserve officer, was refused information by the Navy Department but obtained the information from public and civilian sources. The story he wrote, so the Regular Navy said, contained "confidential information" and a group in the department wanted to "punish" him through his reserve officer status.

For some time after the war information about new German submarines and other Nazi technological developments was classified and detailed information about them denied to the American public, although exactly the same type of matériel was in Russian hands. The exact disposition of Italian men-of-war has not yet been made public. German war documents are still largely classified and inaccessible to the average historian or newspaper man.

This last restriction illustrates one of the problems of the "over-security-consciousness" of today. The German documents are in the joint custody of Army, Air Force, Navy, Joint Chiefs of Staff and the British; each one of these services fears that unrestricted access to these documents might yield some important bits of specialized information of benefit to our potential enemies. The answer, of course, is official study of the documents and "selective declassification."

But joint custodianship and the normal bureaucratic processes of "declassification" have been slowed almost to a standstill by demobilization and the lack of money and personnel needed to wade through the tons of documents available.

There is no easy or general answer to preserving essential security without the imposition of non-essential censorship. The security board's attempts to find suitable definitions covering all varieties of government information cannot possibly succeed, for security and freedom cannot be thus easily pigeonholed.

There are, however, for a democracy, a few general rules that apply to the problem. One is, the less censorship or restriction of news in peacetime the better. Another is that no censorship or suppression which acts solely to protect government against criticism is justifiable.

The third is that the few secrets which can be justifiably termed "secrets"—just precisely how the atomic bomb works, for instance—should be real secrets, not subject to careless or deliberate revelations.

And the fourth is a good guiding generality: "Eternal vigilance is the price of liberty."

IMPLICATIONS OF OFFICIAL SECRECY

DISCUSSION

So far the discussion of the problem of federal security of information has been limited to the development of the atomic energy program. Little has been said about actual measures already taken to insure secrecy, which operate to protect the atomic "secrets" and other information vital to the national defense. Specifically, these measures had their origin in the Army and Navy Regulations.

Secrecy has always been an essential part of the military establishment, both in peace and war. Generally this secrecy is limited to distinctly military matters, such as weapons, operational plans, troop dispositions, etc. However, the recent war brought forth a new concept of total war, in which almost any civilian activity could properly be the concern of the military. Weather reports, crop failures, industrial bottlenecks, strikes, almost anything in wartime might be interpreted as subjects of importance to the enemy, and thereby restricted military infortion.

Generally speaking, there is little opposition to the total war concept as applied to information control by the military. The public and the press during World War II offered their fullest cooperation without question. Even today, three years later, the international situation provides sufficient concern to gain public acceptance for continued secrecy measures in areas vital to the national security.

However, there is the pronounced fear that the term "secret" is being applied to many operations of no significant importance to national defense. There is always the danger that secrecy be carried to the extreme and be utilized to cover up mistakes or inefficiency on the part of government officials. This fear became particularly acute following the issuance of the President's Loyalty Order of March 21, 1947, which included a section devoted to the establishment of rules for handling confidential documents. Such documents were defined as those "the unauthorized disclosure of which, although not endangering the national security would be prejudicial to the interests or the prestige of the nation or any governmental activity thereof or would cause unwarranted injury to an individual or would cause serious administrative embarrassment or difficulty, or would be of advantage to a foreign nation."

This went far beyond the military secrecy regulations, and would have formed the basis of a broad program of peacetime censorship. However, it was brought to a halt by public disclosure by an alert Washington correspondent, Nat Finney, who received the Pulitzer Prize in journalism. At the time, embarrassed government spokesmen denied that there was any attempt to institute governmental censorship, saying that the rules merely enunciated existing governmental practices. This merely added fuel to the fire.

Summing up the attitude of the press, George Sokolsky, noted *New York Sun* columnist told the Silurians, an organization of New York newspapermen, in a speech on May 15, 1948, that "a public official has no right to suppress news. When he does, we of the press must get the facts. We must dig and dig deeply. Let us print what we know. Let time tell if it's untrue. We have more to gain by gambling that way than with suppression."

There have been numerous charges of news suppression during the past year, but the charges have been difficult to prove. The advantage rests with the individual suppressing the news. It should be pointed out, however, that the evidence of intentional suppression is extremely limited, and that there is almost no evidence of any information being wrongfully withheld by any government official. Much of the existing evidence has a strong flavor of partisan politics, natural in an election year. This was the case with most of the charges by Congress that the executive branch was withholding vital information from the legislative branch. It would be difficult to determine the actual facts in these instances.

While undue secrecy and restricted information pose serious problems with reference to security of information, the problem is real enough on its own merits, without being obscured by political side issues.

ARMY REGULATIONS: "CLASSIFIED" MILITARY INFORMATION [1]

The War Department defines military information (including intelligence) as all information primarily under the control and jurisdiction of the War Department or of primary interest to it. This meaning rests primarily on the idea of control, jurisdiction, origin, or degree of interest, rather than on substance of the information.

Military information is of varying degrees of value to enemies and potential enemies of the United States and therefore requires corresponding degrees of protection. Official matter must be examined and, if protection is required, graded in accordance with the degree of protection necessary. . . . Classified military information is military information which requires grading to indicate the degree of precaution necessary for its safeguarding. . . .

Official matter requiring classification shall be examined, graded, and marked top secret, secret, confidential, or restricted. Top secret is a special grading given to certain secret matter . . . the security aspect of which is paramount and whose unauthorized disclosure would cause exceptionally grave damage to the nation. . . .

Documents, information, or matériel, the unauthorized disclosure of which would endanger national security, cause serious injury to the interests or prestige of the nation, or any governmental activity thereof, or would be of great advantage to a foreign nation shall be classified secret. . . .

Documents, information, or matériel, the unauthorized disclosure of which, while not endangering the national security,

[1] Excerpts from Section I, Army Regulations No. 380-5, August 15, 1946, issued by the War Department, Washington, D.C.

would be prejudicial to the interests or prestige of the nation, any governmental activity, an individual, or would cause administrative embarrassment, or difficulty, or be of advantage to a foreign nation shall be classified confidential. . . .

Documents, information, or matériel (other than top secret, secret, or confidential) which should not be published or communicated to anyone except for official purposes shall be classified restricted. . . .

The safeguarding of classified military information is the responsibility of all military personnel, civilian employees of the War Department, and of the management and employees of all commercial firms engaged in classified work or projects for the War Department. Classified military information will be disclosed only to military or civilian personnel having a legitimate interest therein. . . .

It is the obligation of all authorities to keep classified matter of current interest or continuing value constantly under review and to down grade it as soon as conditions permit. . . .

All requests from private individuals, firms, or corporations and federal or state agencies or departments for classified military information . . . are subject to policies established by the Director of Intelligence, War Department, General Staff. . . .

When classified military information is disseminated under the provisions of these regulations to persons not subject to military law, they will be informed that it affects the national defense of the United States within the meaning of the Espionage Act and that its transmission to an unauthorized person is prohibited. . . .

Either public or private discussion of classified military information with or in the presence or hearing of any person not authorized to have knowledge thereof is strictly forbidden. . . .

When a person in the military service appears before a committee of Congress and is called upon to give testimony which he knows to be confidential or restricted, he will respectfully request that his statements be taken in executive session only and not appear in the record of hearings, the *Congressional Record,* or other document open to public inspection.

When called upon to give testimony which he knows to be top secret or secret, unless he has previously been authorized by the Secretary of War to give such testimony, he will respectfully state that he is not authorized to disclose the information desired, and will inform the appropriate member of Congress that a written request for the specific information should be transmitted to the Secretary of War. Testimony of a secret nature, when authorized by the Secretary of War, will be given only in executive session. . . .

Recommendations to the War Department for legislation will be classified until released by the Secretary of War. Prior to such release, no information as to any legislative recommendation will be revealed to any individual or association not under War Department control except as may be required by law.

The nature and content of reports of the War Department on bills referred to it by committees of the Congress will not be disclosed to individuals or agencies outside the War Department.

ARMY REGULATIONS: REQUESTS FOR INFORMATION [2]

Private individuals, firms, corporations, and federal and state departments and agencies may receive classified information from the War Department and from War Department contractors subject to the availability of the information and provided War Department facilities will not be overtaxed and national security or the welfare of the Military Establishment will not be adversely affected.

ARMY REGULATIONS: SAFEGUARDING TECHNICAL INFORMATION [3]

Prior to furnishing a prospective bidder, subbidder, contractor, or subcontractor with drawings, specifications, or other pertinent information concerning any project or projects of a

[2] From the War Department Memorandum No. 380-5-2, September 10, 1946, "Military Information."

[3] From Section V, Army Regulations No. 380-5, August 15, 1946, issued by the War Department, Washington, D.C.

top secret, secret, confidential, or restricted nature and annually thereafter so long as such documents, etc., are in his custody, clearance will be obtained in accordance with separate letter instructions and a general secrecy agreement . . . will be signed by the individual or by a responsible officer on behalf of the firm or corporation concerned. . . .

The Army representatives or inspectors of the technical service are the local representatives of the War Department and will take the necessary measures to insure the safeguarding of classified information or projects in the hands of the contractors or subcontractors or in process of manufacture in their plants.

Army representatives or inspectors will advise contractors or subcontractors as to their responsibilities and the practical measures to be taken to safeguard top secret, secret, confidential, or restricted matters and will act favorably, if practicable, on any suggestion or request of the company tending to preserve secrecy. If at any time conditions at any plant, or any action of a company or its employees, jeopardize the security of classified matter pertaining to the War Department or violate the provisions of the Espionage Act, the army representative or inspector will request the contractor or subcontractor to take prompt remedial action. If adequate precautionary measures are not taken immediately, he will report promptly to the chief of the technical service concerned and, if the situation requires, to the commanding general of the army in which the item is in process of manufacture. . . .

A private individual, firm, or corporation which enters into a contract to engage in technical work for the War Department becomes responsible in matters within his or its control for the safeguarding of all top secret, secret, confidential, or restricted matters that may be disclosed or that may be developed in connection therewith. A clause to this effect will be included in such a contract, but its omission will not release the contractor from his responsibility under the Espionage Act and other pertinent laws.

Contractors are responsible that all classified projects allotted to subcontractors or agents are fully protected by a similar agreement.

Whenever for any reason a contract agreement or subcontract has been made which does not include a security clause but later is found to involve top secret, secret, confidential, or restricted matter, the technical service concerned will take the necessary steps to insure that the project or work is properly classified and that the contractor, agent, or subcontractor is informed of the classification and of his responsibility in the matter.

ARMY REGULATIONS: CORPORATE FINANCIAL REPORTS [4]

Companies engaged in war production are enjoined from publishing operating statements or other financial reports which would indicate any of the following data concerning production under classified War Department contracts: rates of production, total production, or production processes.

ARMY REGULATIONS: INFORMATION POLICIES [5]

Policies governing release of military information to the public. Popular support and understanding of the army is advanced when the public is well informed of its activities. Therefore, it is the duty of all army agencies dealing with public information to release or make available to the public, directly or through *any type of* informational media, unclassified military information which is of public interest. At the same time, such agencies must constantly guard against disclosure of information injurious to national security. . . .

Policy governing release of information concerning the activities of manufacturers engaged in work for the Department of the Army.

1. It is the responsibility of the manufacturer to protect classified military information and not to disclose the nature of classified activities to unauthorized individuals or agencies.

[4] From "Military Information; Restrictions on Publication of Operating or Financial Statements by Companies Engaged in War Production," War Department Memorandum No. 380-5-1, issued Washington, D.C., August 7, 1946.
[5] From "Release of Military Information," Memorandum No. 360-25-1, released by the Department of the Army, Washington, D.C., January 7, 1948.

2. Within bounds of security set forth above, a manufacturer may release for publication information regarding his activities. Matters of doubt will be referred to appropriate public information authority for review prior to publication

Policy governing visits of media representatives to military installations and manufacturing plants engaged in work for the Department of the Army.

1. Subject to the provisions of AR 380-5 governing visitors, visits of media representatives, including those representing national and distant media and representatives of advertisers, to military installations and plants engaged in work for the Department of the Army, may be authorized by the commanding officers and Department of the Army plant representatives concerned.

2. Review of material resulting from such visits is not required unless there is doubt as to whether it contains classified military information. . . .

There is no censorship of American press or radio or of material prepared by Army war correspondents. The responsibility for protecting classified military information is governed by paragraph 15, AR 380-5. In the interests of national security, classified information will not be released for public dissemination.

MILITARY INFORMATION CONTROL: THE SCIENTISTS' SURVEY [6]

Professor Einstein said not long ago that our nation, like so many others, was falling before a terrible illness, "the Prussian disease." The symptoms of this ailment appear in unexpected places. A recent example which is of particular interest to scientists concerns an inquiry that the Federation of Scientists began last November into the problems of security and personnel clearance and their relation to scientific research. There has been a concerted attempt on the part of the military and naval establishments, and at least one civilian agency, to block this investi-

---

[6] From "How Far Should Military Censorship Extend?" report by the Committee on Secrecy and Clearance, Federation of American Scientists. *Bulletin of the Atomic Scientists.* 4:163-5. June 1948. Reprinted by permission.

gation, and to prevent scientists from finding out just where they stand on security matters. It is such gradual encroachment upon the rights of scientists as citizens, and upon their freedom as creative scholars, the suppression of criticism, and the establishment of the official one-track mind, that is referred to here as "the Prussian disease."

The Federation's Committee on Secrecy and Clearance, composed of research scientists at Cornell University, undertook the circulation of a questionnaire to the directors of representative laboratories in industry, universities, and government departments in order to establish objective data upon which to base a report to scientists on this widespread and pressing problem. We sought to find out: (1) In how many laboratories and under what circumstances the procedure of investigating the loyalty and associations of employees has been introduced; (2) What criteria and methods were used in making decisions; (3) The extent to which loyalty investigations are required for men doing non-secret research. . . .

In connection with our survey, we have encountered a kind of opposition which seems to us to be so important to the community of science, and to the whole country, that we have prepared a separate report on this special topic. We have found that our attempts to seek what we hold to be information needed for the national welfare have been opposed by the security agencies of more than one branch of government under the rather thin claim that we have sought classified information. What was an honest attempt to get the facts has now been the target of memoranda and directives from the Army, the Navy, the Air Force, and the Research and Development Board, the successor to the OSRD [Office of Scientific Research and Development]. The use of the legitimate function of military security to suppress public discussion of administrative malpractice is not new, but it is always dangerous. . . .

We believed then, and we still believe, that the questionnaire was soundly constructed, and that its purpose is self-evident: to establish the extent to which clearance procedures are employed, especially in laboratories where nonclassified work also goes on, and to find out what procedures are employed. . . . The degree of response was high for a mail questionnaire. . . . Some of the most secret of all laboratories—such as the atomic bomb laboratory at Los Alamos—gave us a candid and complete account of their special problems. But then we found the first sign of trouble.

One of the forms was sent to the director of the David Taylor Model Basin, a Navy laboratory in Washington, D.C. The director answered, saying that he had referred our inquiry to the Chief of Naval Operations "inasmuch as all . . . government laboratories are involved and a common policy necessarily governs all such agencies." This seemed not inappropriate in the highly centralized Navy Department. We waited.

Three weeks later a letter came which rather surprised us. It was from the Office of the Chief of Naval Operations, signed by direction of Rear Admiral Inglis, Chief of Naval Intelligence. He said in part, "The answers to many of the questions posed in your questionnaire would be of a classified character and . . . the completed questionnaire cannot be returned to you." This was a surprise. We could not see what was classifiable in the answers if any reasonable care were exercised by those filling out the form.

The secretary of our Committee then wrote to Admiral Inglis, saying, "We should appreciate your answering as many questions as you can in the questionnaire, indicating those which cannot be answered because the information is classified." After four weeks, Admiral Inglis, over his own signature this time, replied, "I regret to inform you that I am unable to supply you with the information requested."

Many of the Committee members have dealt extensively with security matters and intelligence officers. We could not understand, then, nor do we see now, why any of the questions implied classified answers. More than that, we cannot see why the Chief of Naval Intelligence would not explain which questions were objectionable, so that we might reconsider them, or plan proper safeguarding of the answers, or comply with whatever procedure might be agreed upon.

The answers kept coming in; we saw no reason for further concern. Then we began to hear rumors and tales. By word of mouth at scientific meetings we heard of several universities whose scientists had been told, generally without explanation, not to answer the questionnaire. Finally we obtained a number of documents, showing a widespread concern of the military with our questions. We shall discuss a few examples.

One was from the office of an Army Ordnance District to a university administrator, who forwarded it to a university department which had no Army contract whatever, and a contract for specifically unclassified work only with the Office of Naval Research—like many other university laboratories. The communication stated that answers . . . would constitute violations of the Espionage Act, and of Army regulations. It asked persons who had answered the questionnaire to inform the Army by return mail.

Next, the Navy. This time it was a captain in the Bureau of Ships, who sent a memorandum to all contractors approved for classified electronics work. He enclosed two citations from naval regulations, one Art. 76, par. (10) (b), being especially interesting: "The disclosure of information CLASSIFIED or NON-CLASSIFIED (capitals in the original) . . . which for reasons of public policy should not be disclosed . . . is prohibited."

The captain's own letter said in part, "In order that all of the Naval Establishment . . . may live up to the spirit, as well as the letter of these regulations and laws . . . it is deemed important to request that information regarding the Navy's classified electronics material not be disclosed. . . . [Such information] is interpreted to include information regarding the percentage of such work being handled, as well as information regarding security clearance of personnel employed or to be employed on this classified material." This was a little hotter.

A captain in the Office of Naval Research also took action. In a form letter sent to a director of a completely *unclassified* ONR research project in a university, the request was made that "questionnaires originating outside the government soliciting information on such projects not be answered, but that the questionnaires be referred to this office." And then he added this remarkable sentence. "If this questionnaire concerning your

Office of Naval Research project is answered, and should this information fall into unauthorized hands, valuable intelligence information would be obtained which would be detrimental to the National Security." The project director had been operating on the assumption that unclassified research means that free discussion is permissible. The Navy captain apparently thinks otherwise.

The Air Force was not far behind. From the New York office, Air Material Command, over the signature of a colonel in command, we have a really strong memo, sent to all Air Force contractors. It quotes from a letter sent out from the Dayton headquarters, again naming answers to questions . . . of our questionnaire as violations of the Espionage Act, and the subject of immediate government action.

But the most disturbing incident came lately. It originated from the Research and Development Board, which is headed by Dr. Vannevar Bush. This agency, primarily civilian in make-up, has apparently at least some policymaking employees more military than the military. We have a memo, which was, rather ironically, sent to one of the members of our Committee in his capacity as consultant to the RDB. Its wording is so revealing of the frame of mind of the writer that we quote it in full:

RESEARCH AND DEVELOPMENT BOARD

Washington 25, D.C.
19 February, 1948

MEMORANDUM TO: Expert Consultants, Research and Development Board

Information has reached the Research and Development Board that certain organizations are circulating to scientists in industry, questionnaires asking for information regarding investigation and clearance procedure used by government agencies in connection with those scientists who are rendering part-time service to the United States Government. These questionnaires are so comprehensive in detail as to create doubt concerning their goal or objective.

There are in existence today a large number of organizations whose objective is to gather such information and later use it as material for propaganda and "smear" programs in an attempt to discredit the United States form of government.

It is therefore requested that if any questionnaires of this type, or any other questioning the methods of the United States Government, are received in the future, that they be referred to this office for appraisal before any answer is given.

Any information you may be able to give the Research and Development Board regarding any such questionnaire which you may have filled out in the past will be very greatly appreciated.

(signed) F. H. Richardson
Deputy Executive Secretary

This is surely intolerable. It contains the very "smear" it speaks against. It operates wholly by innuendo, naming no names, citing no questions. It implies that our questionnaire is to be used as material for an attempt to discredit the United States form of government.

It asked for approval by the RDB of *any* questionnaire which questions the methods of the United States Government. Any methods, in all fields? We presume so. Is the Condon scandal to be criticized? Only after the RDB has appraised the criticism and satisfied itself as to the motives of the critics. The RDB does not even pretend to worry about the Espionage Act, and military security. It puts interest and concern squarely upon the basis of preventing "propaganda and 'smear' programs" against the United States Government. When an objective questionnaire tries to elicit information concerning the degree to which the requirements of clearance are affecting the conditions of work and the ordinary civil rights of scientists, it is dubious to the RDB. We would be less than candid if we did not admit that we are concerned and critical about the methods of several government agencies. But we will not surrender our right of criticism to the RDB. It is they, and not we, who "attempt to discredit the United States form of government." We conceive that we are attempting to defend it.

Was military security at all involved in the attack upon our questionnaire? We still do not believe so. It is debatable perhaps that the amount of work which is classified in a university laboratory is itself a classified fact. (Although it hardly seems that whether a laboratory does all, none, or half of its work under government contract is secret.) But not once were we ourselves told that this was held to be the case. An explicit request for advice from the Chief of Naval Intelligence went unanswered.

We might have arranged to keep the answers to those questions unpublished or we could have come easily to some other agreement about them. It is not likely that a Committee like ours, operating publicly, open to the inquiry or the scrutiny of anyone, and composed of academic people, most of whom are themselves veterans of many a secret project, is a cover for espionage.

More likely, the real intent is that indicated by the letter from the RDB. They are worried frankly not about any military security but about criticism, criticism of the often arbitrary and alreay-much-criticized procedures of clearance. And we had not yet even criticized. Our questionnaire was simply an effort to get the facts.

We have told this story of the response to our questionnaire as a sign of "the Prussian disease." We are confident, if others are not, that the cure for this illness is a free and open discussion of the methods of some agencies of our government, and a real attempt to defend the principles upon which our democracy stands.

MILITARY INFORMATION CONTROL: THE XS-1 CASE [7]

Capital newsmen are awaiting Department of Justice and Air Forces guidance as to how far they may go in describing military weapons developed in peacetime.

The latest round of conjectures was set in motion when *Aviation Week* magazine published an article, December 22, [1947] telling of the faster-than-sound flight that had been completed. On the same day, a story carrying somewhat similar facts appeared in the *Los Angeles Times*.

Raised immediately were questions whether the publications had disclosed forbidden information, had associated parts of allowable information to put together a story that revealed something the military arms preferred to keep hidden, had published

[7] From "Justice Department Studies 'Break' on Speed Plane," newsstory. *Editor & Publisher*. 81:8. January 10, 1948. Reprinted by permission.

matter of current information properly at their disposal—or had used "old stuff."

The Air Forces and the Department of Justice swung into action, but both declined to say what the objective was, other than "study."

The only statement the Air Forces would make is: "It is Air Forces opinion that the XS-1 project was classified information and publication of the story was a security violation. Having no facilities for prosecution of such a matter, the Air Forces turned the matter over to the Department of Justice for information and whatever action might be needed."

Although a picture of the XS-1 was released by the Army a year ago, the Air Forces claim that only performance is restricted information.

Robert H. Wood, editor of *Aviation Week*, said he was under the impression that the Air Forces would release the story later, which was the reason for running it December 22.

THE DANGERS OF MILITARY CENSORSHIP [8]

Three quite different censorships of the press were operating in the present war: (1) compulsory censorship at the border, (2) voluntary restraints inside the country administered by the civilian Office of Censorship, and (3) rigid compulsory controls outside the country enforced by the Army and Navy.

Censorship ought to stop with the shooting. There is no danger of giving information to the enemy when the enemy is already licked. Consequently, the first two kinds of censorship, like the Office which took care of them, have virtually ceased to function. As to the third type, military censorship, much more doubt exists. I do not know how far the situation abroad before December 7, 1941, has been restored. After the Armistice in 1918, the British and French continued their censorship, and the effect of this on the Versailles Peace Conference was bad. . . .

[8] From *Government and Mass Communications, A Report from the Commission on Freedom of the Press*, Vol. I, by Zechariah Chafee, Jr, professor of law, Harvard University, and vice chairman of the Commission. p. 464-8. University of Chicago Press. Chicago. 1947. Reprinted by permission.

In spite of the cessation of hostilities in the present war, the prolonged occupation of enemy territory and the possible perpetuation of the draft in some form or other will naturally incline many Army and Navy officials to think that the retention of their powers of censoring is necessary to national safety. There is a tendency for military people to extend their great wartime powers of censorship (a) into areas of politics during war, and (b) beyond the period of hostilities. Inasmuch as the war organization must now persist through a long occupational period, war censorship inevitably has great political consequences for several years to come. Without knowing the actual amount of American military censorship at the moment in European and Pacific areas, I think that it will be useful to make the assumption that it is considerable and then inquire about the effects of such a hypothetical situation upon the need of American citizens to know essential facts.

Mr. Price . . . was very careful to distinguish between military facts and political facts. Regardless of his success, censorship by the Army and Navy is something quite different. Military censorship has always tended to exceed its bounds and go into political censorship. One of the numerous unfortunate consequences of modern methods of warfare is that the area of military concern is constantly widening. Almost every activity becomes a part of national defense. . . .

It is a very difficult problem, which is bound to become increasingly frequent as the range of governmental activities increases. We have to realize that in the governmental hierarchy, both in the armed services and in civilian offices in Washington, there are all sorts of inhibitions against free discussion. . . .

Thus wartime habits have created new barriers between American citizens and the truth.

CIVILIAN CONTROLS: WARTIME SECURITY MEASURES [9]

The necessity for a uniform practice within the government with regard to the security of information has become a matter

[9] From "OWI Regulation No. 4," issued by Elmer Davis, Director of the Office of War Information, to the heads of all governmental departments and agencies, September 28, 1942.

of some urgency. Practice has differed markedly among the departments, with the result that some documents which should have been treated as secret have been permitted too free a circulation, while others which were in no sense secret or confidential have been improperly classified in these categories.

In order to further uniformity in this regard, I have issued the attached regulations. It is to be noted that these regulations provide only a minimum standard. It would be advisable for each agency to adopt such additional regulation as would:

a. Make more specific the general regulations of the Office of War Information in accordance with the requirements of the agency; and

b. Provide for appropriate handling and safeguarding of classified information in accordance with the particular organization and routines of the agency.

I believe that the security of information would be considerably advanced if each agency having classified information were to designate a trusted official as a security officer. May I ask you to be good enough to make such a designation within your own agency?

This Office stands ready to offer such assistance as is possible in facilitating the operations of your security officer.

OWI REGULATION No. 4

In order to provide uniform safeguards over information which might prove of aid or comfort to the enemy and to prevent undue restriction of information which may appropriately be made available to the public, the following regulations are hereby issued by virtue of the authority vested in me by Executive Order 9182.

1. DEFINITIONS

a. The term "information" as used herein shall include documents, maps, charts, blueprints, photographs, models or other materials which convey information relating to national defense, as well as copies thereof obtained by any means of reproduction or transcription.

b. The term "classified information" shall designate information relating to national defense requiring special provision for safeguarding. Information which needs no safeguarding shall be referred to as unclassified information.

c. There shall be three categories of classified information as follows:

Secret Information is information the disclosure of which might endanger national security, or cause serious injury to the interest or prestige of the nation or any governmental activity thereof.

Confidential Information is information the disclosure of which although not endangering the national security would be prejudicial to the interests or prestige of the nation or to a governmental activity thereof.

Restricted Information is information the disclosure of which should be limited for reasons of administrative privacy, or is information not classified as confidential because the benefits to be gained by a lower classification, such as permitting wider dissemination where necessary to effect the expeditious accomplishment of a particular project, outweigh the value of the additional security obtainable from the higher classification.

d. Documents such as books or pamphlets, the pages of which are permanently and securely fastened together, shall receive the most restrictive classification, if any, which is attached to any of the material contained therein.

2. AUTHORITY TO CLASSIFY

The head of each Federal agency of his designated representative shall classify information as secret, confidential, or restricted if the character of the information indicates the need for such classification. . . .

3. OVERCLASSIFICATION

Documents or materials requiring classification shall be assigned the least restrictive classification consistent with the proper safeguarding of the information or material. Care should be taken to avoid overclassification, particularly in cases where undue restriction may prevent dissemination of information which should properly be disclosed to the public or to Congress. . . .

5. DISSEMINATION OF CLASSIFIED INFORMATION

a. No person is entitled solely by virtue of his office or position to knowledge or possession of classified information. Except as provided by subsections d(3) and d(4) below, such information is entrusted only to those individuals whose official duties require such information.

b. The head of each agency, or his duly authorized representative, shall maintain lists of persons receiving secret information and lists of persons receiving confidential information from that agency.

c. The head of each agency may, by regulation, provide for the registration of secret or confidential information.

d. (1) The distribution of secret matter shall be held to the absolute minimum.

(2) Confidential information shall be disclosed only to those persons in the service of the United States whose duties require that they have such knowledge, except as hereinafter provided.

(3) Restricted information may be given, when for the good of the Federal service, to any person known to be in that service, provided that the consent of the originating agency is secured; but shall not be released or communicated to the public, the press or any other agency through which information may be disseminated to the public.

(4) Under unusual circumstances classified information may be entrusted to persons not in the employ of the Federal Government whose special services to the United States require such information for the more effective rendering of such service, provided that the consent of the originating agency is secured.

(5) Classified matters shall not be discussed in personal correspondence. Secret matters shall not be discussed over the telephone. Necessary references made

to confidential matters over the telephone shall be held to the lowest practicable minimum.

(6) No secret or confidential information shall be sent in clear over leased or private wire, whether telephone, telegraph or teletype, or in clear over any scrambling device unless the design and installation have been approved by the Signal Corps of the United States Army, or other appropriate authority.

6. RESPONSIBILITY

Each agency shall accord to matter classified by any other agency the type and degree of care in handling that is required by the classification marked thereon. The safeguarding of classified information is the responsibility of all employees of the Federal Government. Classified information shall be discussed by persons having access thereto only with other persons authorized to have access to the same information. . . .

8. REGULATIONS TO BE ISSUED

The head of each agency shall issue such further regulations as he may deem necessary to enforce the provisions of this order and shall assume responsibility for its enforcement.

9. ESPIONAGE ACT

Attention is directed to the following extract from the Espionage Act concerning unlawful disclosures of military information through willful action or gross negligence:

Whoever . . . being entrusted with any document . . . relating to the national defense, willfully communicates . . . the same to any person not entitled to receive it, or willfully . . . fails to deliver it on demand to the officer or employee of the United States entitled to receive it; or . . . through gross negligence permits the same to be removed from its proper place of custody . . . shall be punished by imprisonment for not more than ten years and may, in the discretion of the court, be fined not more than $10,000.

10. EFFECT AND DURATION

a. Subject to these regulations and such further regulations as may be issued by the Director of the Office of War Information, the classification and publication of

statistical information shall be in accordance with determinations made by the Director of the Bureau of the
Budget as provided in Executive Order 9103.

b. These regulations shall take effect immediately and
shall remain in effect until further notice.

Editor's Note: OWI Regulation Number 4 was amended March
13, 1944, to provide for a category of "Top Secret" information "the
security aspect of which is paramount and whose unauthorized disclosure
would cause exceptionally grave danger to the nation." Such Top
Secret matter was to be handled in accordance with a letter of instructions
"to be issued to certain personnel of agencies designated to handle"
such matter. "Top secret documents will be of such nature that only
specifically designated individuals will handle them or originate them."
This is presumably the basis of the secrecy structure called for under
the President's Loyalty Order of March 21, 1947, about which government officials later said that it merely enunciated "existing practices."
There is no evidence, however, that the regulations established under
OWI Regulation Number 4 have been abandoned since the war, but
neither is there any evidence to prove that such regulations are still in
effect, other than generally unsubstantiated charges of individual Congressmen and some Washington correspondents.

THE EXTENT OF OFFICIAL SECRECY TODAY [10]

Throughout the entire executive branch there is, and long
has been, an increasing tendency on the part of officials to conduct their affairs in secret, and to regard information as something
to be withheld from the public, the press, and the Congress of
the United States, including both Houses. Only those who work
in Washington and whose daily task requires a free access to
information, can grasp the length to which this obsession for
executive secrecy has gone. . . .

If the Congress does not meet this situation head on, and
press the issue until it is resolved, then the future of free, representative government is dark indeed. People must be able to trust
their government. In some way the facts must be available to
the public. Somehow the truth must be told. And the truth
is not being told now.

[10] From "The Iron Curtain at Home," remarks of Senator Homer Ferguson
of Michigan before the United States Senate. *Congressional Record*. 94:10272-7.
August 7, 1948.

How is it possible that suppression of information on such a wide scale can be accomplished? The reason is the enormous accretion of power in the executive branch. Let me show briefly how this came about.

More than a generation ago, Congress began delegating power to independent agencies. . . . In many instances . . . Congress sought to perpetuate the system of checks and balances by making direct report by the agencies to Congress a statutory obligation.

Then came the crash of 1929 and the depression. The emergency was so acute . . . that grants of power and great sums of money were voted to the Executive simply because somebody had to act, and act quickly. Large sums of money were appropriated directly to the President, so that he might use them without any record whatever.

Now began the era . . . when executive agencies multiplied. . . .

Now comes the first obstruction to information. A sizable contingent of the New Dealers were committed from the start to the idea of a planned economy . . . and they did not want to answer any more questions than they had to—either to Congress or anybody else. Coincidental with this development came the installation of public relations and publicity men on an enormous scale, for the agencies had made the obvious discovery that secretaries for information were just as useful for twisting information and keeping it back as they were for giving it out. . . . Gone were the days when a cub reporter could buttonhole anybody in sight. All sorts of mazes and catch-alls for news and information were set up, and it took an experienced and industrious reporter to master the bypaths in this labyrinth.

In the wake of the first New Dealers came people with every sort of panacea and program, the Communists included. . . .

Gradually, here a little, there a little, now a big chunk, now a small piece, this great power was built up. As the power grows, the question becomes more pressing on the Executive. How much shall Congress and the people be told?

At this stage, after the middle 1930's, the picture in Washington began to be colored by the situation abroad. . . . Because opposition to Mr. Roosevelt was so intense, he adopted a devious course in carrying out his objectives in his foreign policy. Many of his supporters freely admit this now but maintain that he had no other choice . . . that he saw what the country must do where others could not see it, and that, because of their obtuseness, he had to work his will by strategem and maneuver. So the practice of withholding vital information grew. This policy of concealment was maintained consistently up to Pearl Harbor. Then, with our entry into the war, secrecy in many things became military necessity. . . .

The addition of the special war powers and the constitutional power of the Commander in Chief sufficed to turn the White House into the GHQ of the world. . . . The result was that a sort of political-military hierachy was built up, an entirely new bureaucracy that tended to bypass many of the executive agencies and center itself in the White House, the State Department and Military Establishment. The Bureau of the Budget was taken from the Treasury in 1939 and attached to the White House. It became a master planner of new types of executive machinery. The State-War-Navy Coordinating Committee served to bind foreign policy and the military ever more closely to the President and an ever-increasing number of confidential agents and functionaries, of whom Mr. Harry Hopkins was the chief, made their headquarters and did their daily work in the White House. What these people said and did was secret, to be revealed to Congress, the press, and the people only if it seemed expedient.

Suddenly, in April 1945, President Roosevelt died and Mr. Truman succeeded him. Four months later the fighting stopped. Some people supposed that the era of secrecy would end with the fighting. But it just did not. Undertaken in peace and consolidated in war, the concentration of power and the secrecy to protect it remained. Mr. Truman, while a Senator, had been intensely critical of this secrecy. I have some personal knowledge of that, having served on the War Investigating Committee. I knew how he felt about it. But when he became President he became the willing prisoner and mouthpiece of this power clique. The hierarchy which had carried out the decisions made in the White House were still in their jobs and they did not propose that either their actions or those of the President should be looked at or scrutinized.

The perfect illustration of this was the congressional investigation of Pearl Harbor which began in the autumn of 1945 after the fighting was over. I was a member of that investigating committee and I shall never forget the experience nor the roadblocks that were put in our way. Hearings were held for seventy days and a record of ten million words was accumulated, but from beginning to end vital documents were withheld, crucial witnesses declined to appear and, under pressure, other witnesses altered their testimony—everywhere secrecy and suppression.

Presently, when the soft policy toward Russia was abandoned and the get-tough policy adopted, the arguments for secrecy were reenforced. A strange picture. There stood this political-military hierarchy, centered in the White House, there was the labyrinth of agencies with all the functionaries, Communists, and fellow travelers included, using information for their own purposes, keeping it from others.

Mr. President, let me show you a piece of this labyrinth. I have spoken of the State-War-Navy Coordinating Committee. Back in November 1944, Secretary of War Stimson complained to Secretary Hull that State Department officials were going directly to the Joint Chiefs of Staff on questions with military implications. Mr. Stimson thought such matters should be handled through the War and Navy Department offices. Mr. Hull suggested that the three secretaries get up a committee and a staff to handle these matters. This was the genesis of the State-War-Navy Coordinating Committee and, with the addition of Air Force representation it exists today. It has been a powerful policy arm. One of its creations was the Security Advisory Board, an office now housed in the State Department. A little over a year ago this Security Advisory Board became involved in an attempt to impose the most elaborate rules of secrecy this government has ever known.

Early in 1947 a young man named Hamilton Robinson was appointed chairman of this Security Advisory Board. Who was Robinson? He was a young Wall Street lawyer with a most socially correct background of education at Princeton and the

Yale Law School. During the war he rose to the rank of colonel as a management engineer under General Somervell. After the war was over, Robinson looked around, as he said, for something constructive to do. He found this constructive work in the State Department and was promptly made chairman of the Security Advisory Board and put to work in the administration of the loyalty order. Now, I want to show you how constructive Mr. Robinson could be in systematizing the suppression of information.

President Truman issued the loyalty order on March 21, 1947. Buried down in the order is a section labeled "Miscellaneous." Let me read it to you:

The Security Advisory Board of the State-War-Navy Coordinating Committee shall draft rules applicable to the handling and transmission of confidential documents and other documents which should not be publicly disclosed and upon approval by the President such rules shall constitute the minimum standards for the handling and transmission of such documents and information and shall be applicable to all—

Observe the phrase, to all—

departments and agencies of the executive branch.

The statute on which the President based the loyalty order is the Civil Service Act which permits him to draw up rules for determining the fitness of candidates for civil service jobs. You will search the statute and the Constitution in vain for any clause or phrase which permits the President to initiate a censorship, yet that is exactly what he did.

Robinson was assisted in his task of drawing up censorship regulations by two men from the Military Establishment. Colonel Charles Blakeney of Army Intelligence, and Commander Lichliter, of Navy Intelligence. In making a draft of rules for secrecy the collaborators drew heavily on already existent service regulations for the handling of confidential matter. In other words, the instructions which are supposed to guide a military commander in keeping military secrets were turned to civilian use.

Eventually an elaborate code was drawn up and distributed to the heads of the more than fifty executive departments and agencies. Let me read the heading. It is very explicit:

Preliminary draft: Minimum standards for the handling and transmission of classified information in executive departments and agencies of the Federal Government. (Issued pursuant to Executive Order 9835.) Purpose: These rules constitute minimum standards for the handling and transmission of confidential documents and other documents and information which should not be publicly disclosed and are applicable to all departments and agencies of the executive branch.

Permit me to read one more section, the most remarkable of all:

The term "confidential" as used herein applies to information the unauthorized disclosure of which, although not endangering the national security—

I want to stress those words—

would be prejudicial to the interests or prestige of the nation or any governmental activity thereof—

Mark you, Mr. President, I am reading these words from that order—

or would cause unwarranted injury to an individual or would cause serious administrative embarrassment or difficulty, or would be of advantage to a foreign nation.

Administrative embarrassment. What a prospect for a bureaucrat. Every executive employee, from the humblest clerk to the most powerful administrator, would be free thereafter from any fear of prying or discovery. At long last the executive branch would be impregnably buttressed against Congress and the people.

I have found no record of any department or agency entering a protest at this "constructive work" of Mr. Robinson's. I can find no record anywhere of any official suggestion that, if certain documents had to be kept confidential, the problem be taken to Congress and there thrashed out. No intimation of any kind was made public, save for the original publication of the President's order in the Federal Register. No one knew anything about it until early in October last year, 1947. Then a reporter named Nat Finney, of the Washington bureau of the *Minneapolis Tribune*, overhead some employees of the Veterans' Administration discussing a censorship order which had just been imposed in their agency. Finney followed up the lead, discovered Robinson, and asked for a copy of the censorship rules. Robinson refused to give it. Finney got hold of a copy elsewhere, wrote a series of stories and published them.

This exploded the works. Undersecretary of State Robert Lovett authorized the publication of a memorandum saying that "these standards merely represent a codification of existing practices." This could only mean that by a sort of unofficial understanding a censorship was already in force. The State Department's "Directory of Committees," which listed Robinson and his board, a manual seemingly as innocuous as a phone book was labeled "Restricted."

Right at this point Representative Keating wrote to President Truman about the press exposure and asked for details. The President made a strange reply. "I have seen the article to which you refer," he wrote, "but have never heard of the program to which the article refers." In other words, the President all but denied that he had ever read the Executive order which he had signed. It also revealed a strange lapse of memory in the White House offices, if Mr. Finney's testimony at the investigation by the House Committee on Expenditures in the Executive Departments is to be taken seriously.

My first feeling [said Mr. Finney] about what I uncovered was that it was the result of the misguided zeal of relatively subordinate members of the administration. With that in mind, I took the information I had, documents and all, to Mr. Charles G. Ross, the President's press secretary, and Mr. Ross agreed to call the matter to Mr. Truman's attention. Mr. Ross told me that, so far as he knew, the President had no close knowledge of the matter. I sent Mr. Ross a one-page memorandum, presumably for the President's attention, stating the objections to the proposal. Frankly I expected that Mr. Truman would put a stop to the thing and that would be the end of it.

But it was not the end of it. When the question was put to the President at a press conference last November, he was enraged. What did reporters mean, he asked, by taking fragmentary bits of information to build straw men and then knock them down?

Last Thursday the President denounced the congressional investigation into loyalty as a "red herring," and he allowed himself to be quoted, to distract people's attention, and said that "The public hearings now under way serve no useful purpose." But he will not surrender the records that would give the answer "Yes" or "No." Nine months ago he pushed aside all questions of his censorship scheme. That was a straw man. Now, another instance is a "red herring." Who thought up the idea of this streamlined gag rule? We do not know. What is the true reason for withholding the records in the loyalty investigation? We do not know.

Mr. Robinson was summoned to testify before the House committee. His testimony was far from clear. Mr. Finney, the reporter who testified later on March 10, 1948, observed this fact.

I note [said Mr. Finney] that he says he did not say that public officials should have the power to decide what the public was to be told and what it was not to be told. He did not tell the truth about this on your record. He plainly said to me that he believed public officials should have such power to give or withhold information, deciding what the public should be told, and what it should not be told, and that the formal establishment of such power for public officials was the purpose of the so-called minimum standards by the Security Advisory Board.

The Board maintained that the draft had been distributed for inspection and suggestion only. It was said that the phrase about administrative embarrassment had been struck out and that, anyhow, the censorship could not be in force until the President approved the final draft. Why then did Mr. Lovett say that the draft merely codified existing practice?

Under these rules of secrecy who, outside, could tell what was secret and what was not? No one, no Senator, no Member of Congress, nor any reporter could know all the types and kinds of information the agency might have. By a stroke of magnificent irony, Mr. Robinson found it expedient to resign from the State Department, so great was the storm of disapproval, while Mr. Finney was awarded the Pulitzer Prize for his fine scoop, but these developments do not solve the mystery nor the threat of this censorship. The Secretary of the Security Advisory Board assured the House Committee that action on the investigation was complete. The Eightieth Congress is about to adjourn: the

House investigation is over. Are those rules now in force? Has
the President approved the draft? We do not know, nor will
we know until some problem arises in Congress and needed
information is withheld or until some reporter comes up against
a blank wall in his search for facts.

What is at the bottom of all this? Within the space of thirty
days Dr. Studebaker, the recently resigned Commissioner of
Education, has declared—and it is now in the official record of
the Senate and the Congress—that pressure was put on him to
tone down a speech on communism. Almost simultaneously
Luther Evans, Head of the Library of Congress, wrathfully told
the National Association of State Librarians that the Government
was trying to dragoon him into restricting library material heretofore free to all.

Dr. Evans said:

> There seems to be a tendency among bureaucrats, particularly
> bureaucrats who are concerned with the armed services, to keep away
> from the public, and even scholars, information which might in any
> way be misconstrued if published, or which might by any chance make
> it more difficult to have their way free of the annoyances of public opin-
> ion or the constituted representatives of the people in Congress.

Secrecy, suppression, restriction on every hand. The Executive withholds from Congress FBI reports on Communists in
government while the Library of Congress is urged not to let
the Russians have access to what everybody else can see.

The attempt to impose a censorship on a wholesale basis has
been underscored again and again by secrecy and censorship in
individual instances. This was the case with the renewal of the
President's authority to make reciprocal trade agreements.

Before an agreement with any country is made the President
must give public notice of what he is about to do so that any
interested American businessman, manufacturer, or exporter
whose interests are affected shall have a chance to present his
figures and plead his case.

A committee appointed by the President analyzes the testimony given by these businessmen and then makes recommendations to the President. This committee keeps a record of its discussions in a secret minute book.

Now in the past the authority to make tariff revisions has been limited to terms of three years. At the end of such a term the President must come back to Congress for a renewal of the power. The three-year term expired this year and a few weeks ago, in May 1948, a bill for renewal came before the Finance Committee of the Senate.

While deliberating on the case the chairman of the Finance Committee asked Mr. Clayton, the special adviser to the Secretary of State, to produce the minute book—that is the minute book of this committee. He refused. Why? Because, said Mr. Clayton, these minutes "have considerable confidential material in them, which business interests furnished on the understanding that the material would be kept confidential because it is private information which they do not wish their competitors to see."

Well, could the clerk of the Senate Finance Committee see the minute book? "I don't think so," said Mr. Clayton. Could the Chairman of the Senate Finance Committee see the minute book? "I am not authorized to make it available," said Mr. Clayton.

Well, why not? Mr. Clayton wrote a letter on May 5 saying why not. "The President," said Mr. Clayton, "is the one responsible for decisions on tariffs under the act and is entitled to the opinions of his advisers expressed fully and freely without the constraint which would inevitably come from the knowledge that they might be made public."

The President's committee may hear in confidence something which the President refuses to let the Senate committee know in confidence, yet this same Senate committee must pass upon the question as to whether the President shall have the authority to make any tariff concessions at all. . . .

Where, then, are we heading?

If every Communist and fellow traveler were discovered and expelled from the government today, we would still have this problem of executive secrecy on our hands tomorrow. Where the power is, there will secrecy be also.

There has been an attempt to impose a censorship on every single department and agency in the executive branch. The Military Establishment has attempted to get the press, the radio and the movies to deliberately censor themselves. American newspapermen in foreign countries have been dragooned at the behest of their own government. The Library of Congress has been tampered with. Congress has been thwarted in its effort to get information on Pearl Harbor, on appointees to the Atomic Energy Commission, on reciprocal trade operations and now on the loyalty program affecting the vital security of the nation. . . .

In all these instances the President has taken the position that the specified information sought by congressional committees are matters confidential to the President in his conduct of the executive department and that the executive officials cannot divulge them without his approval.

He relies upon the prerogatives of his high office, the constitutional powers vested in him, the principle of separation of powers, and upon historical precedents supporting his position on one or more of these grounds. The general ground of the President's refusal to give papers and information to congressional committees is that it would not serve the public interest. In specific cases he has maintained that to divulge such information would either violate the confidence in which he acquired the information or hinder his agents in the future acquisition of confidential information necessary to the proper exercise of the public business. What Presidents have claimed as sacred and secret in their own persons as the Chief Executive they have also sought to extend to all subordinate officers in the executive department. . . .

In sum, the President claims the right to don the cloak of absolute executive immunity whenever in his sole discretion he desires to do so, and to extend it as he pleases to cover all other officers and operations of the executive branch. . . .

By modern conditions, the Federal Government now extends its concern to every detail of national life and to almost every crossroad of the world. It would be strange indeed, if at this juncture of affairs, Congress was blocked in its legislative function by the iron curtain of Executive refusal to supply Congress with the facts on which it must legislate.

Moreover, the nature of one of the dangers to our security forces Congress as a representative of the people to be far more

alert to conditions in the executive department than was necessary in the days of narrowly limited Federal Government. The
Communist menace today is not that governments will be seized
by forcible means. It is that they will be undermined and taken
over by the insidious infiltration of Communists into high government offices.

Congress, no less than the President, is charged with the
security of our government and our national life. Congress, no
less than the President, must meet the new methods of subversion
in our governmental household. Congress is charged with the
responsibility of protecting the security of our people through
legislation. But if, when it tries to do so, the President can
deny to Congress the information it needs to legislate intelligently, then the President has gone beyond the prerogatives of
his office and threatens the very foundations of representative
government.

DEFENSE FOR SECRECY CONTROLS [11]

It would be most presumptuous for a congressional committee with one piece of information before it . . . to pass judgment upon whether the public interest requires that information,
or some part thereof, to be held confidential. The information
in the hands of the committee may on its face and to the un-
suspecting appear completely innocuous. The President, the
Secretary of Defense, or some other officer in the executive
branch might, on the other hand, have good reason to know that
public disclosure of the apparently innocuous information, because of its relationship to other pieces of information, is contrary to the public interest or to the national security. Intelligence
officers, those of foreign powers as well as ours, know full well
the value of picking up and fitting together a number of pieces
of information, each by itself apparently innocuous.

The President is charged with the defense of the United
States, both in terms of internal and external security. Under the

[11] From remarks before the House of Representatives by Representative J.
Percy Priest of Tennessee. *Congressional Record*. 94:5963. May 13, 1948.

President, the Congress has specifically provided that various aspects of that defense are to be maintained by specified officers and agencies in the executive branch, for example, the Secretary of Defense, the Director of the Central Intelligence Agency, the Atomic Energy Commission, the Federal Bureau of Investigation, and others. To say . . . that these officers and agencies, and others of like national importance, are to be required, at the request of any committee of the Congress, to disclose information to that committee, despite the fact that the particular officer knows that such a disclosure will impair the national security, is to say that these officers and agencies can no longer be responsible for that security. Responsibility for the national security must carry with it the authority, the unquestioned authority, to decide what information may and what may not be disclosed.

THE NEED FOR MORE INFORMATION [12]

There is no more urgent problem facing this Congress than the problem of bolstering our armed forces in a manner which will give us national security, not only during this present critical period in international relations, but during the long years ahead.

There is an almost complete unanimity among the members that the bolstering process shall take place. Unfortunately, there is almost as complete a disagreement as to how we shall go about the job. . . .

It is apparent that the confusion over what we shall do stems from a basic confusion over what we are trying to accomplish. It stems from the failure of the administration to define a clear-cut objective, and for that purpose, to make intelligent use of the machinery furnished to it by this Congress. The confusion of Congress in regard to national security stems from the confusion inherent in the administration's attempt to implement policy without first having disclosed the nature of that policy. . . .

What are the recommendations of the National Security Council? What is the considered judgment of our highest rank-

[12] From remarks on the floor of the House of Representatives by Representative John W. Byrnes of Wisconsin. *Congressional Record.* 94:5339-41. May 3, 1948.

ing and best informed civilian policy makers in the field of national security—makers of military, foreign, and domestic policy—acting in concert and compromising their differences of opinion in an integrated policy satisfactory to all?

The reports and recommendations of this Council are not public property. They are the "property" of the President of the United States. He receives, under the act, such reports and recommendations as the Council deems appropriate or as the President may require. The President, under the act, has the implied power to do as he sees fit with the recommendations of this highest level policy-recommending body.

I do not question the President's power to keep such recommendations and reports secret, as he may see fit, but I seriously question the wisdom, at this particular time, of keeping under cover the specific recommendations of the National Security Council concerning the dilemma which confronts Congress and the people as a result of the conflicting requests of the Secretaries of our armed branches. If, as seems illogical, the Council has made no recommendations as to our objective and the methods necessary to attain that objective, then they should be requested by the President to do so immediately, and their recommendations should forthwith be presented to the people and the Congress. . . .

The point is that we do not know who, if anyone, is championing the considered views of a deliberative body which represents the highest levels of all elements concerning our national security picture. Nor do we even know whether an integrated policy with clearly defined objectives has ever been enunciated by this body.

It may be said that the President's decisions represent the recommendations of the Council. What are the President's decisions? We do not know, except as they are hinted at in press conferences following presidential audiences with one of the various secretaries involved in the national defense controversy. We have been given no concrete estimate of the situation, no declaration of short or long term policy. The President, by failing to specify our objective, is preventing Congress from intelligently providing means and methods supported by enlightened public opinion. The formation of a cohesive national defense policy with which to back up our foreign commitments is seriously endangered. . . .

We should neither be lulled into a false sense of security, as happened prior to the last war, nor panicked into taking ill-considered or hit-and-miss action through ignorance of the whole situation, as we appear about to do. We should be given the facts, and those facts should come from the source best equipped to obtain them.

If the people and their Congress are presented with the considered judgment of a group which it has specifically charged with the formulation of a national security policy, a group which has the specific mission of integrating our domestic, foreign, and military policy and of bringing about cooperation between the elements in our national defense setup, is there any reason why we cannot approach this whole problem with a clear insight into our total requirements?

SECRECY HANDICAPS IN ANTITRUST TRIAL [13]

Atomic energy has caught up with the courts. For the first time, an important case has been vitally affected because secret information cannot be brought out in open court under security rules.

The case is the government antitrust action against Union Carbide and Carbon Corporation and other producers and processors of vanadium. This indictment, charging price fixing and monopolization of the world supply of vanadium, an important alloying metal, has been hanging fire for nearly two years. The original indictment was in June 1946.

Now the Antitrust Division of the Department of Justice has dismissed it with the permission of Federal District Judge J. Foster Symes in Denver, and has brought an "information" instead against some of the defendants.

[13] From "Atom Secrets Tie Antitrust Case in Knot," by Roscoe Fleming, special correspondent for the *Christian Science Monitor*. *Christian Science Monitor*. 40:1. September 11, 1948. Reprinted by permission.

The vital point is that vanadium and uranium come from the same ores, the carnotites of western Colorado and Utah. Under the original indictment, which charged the defendants with using their position as government agents during the war to get a monopoly on the supply of vanadium, it would have been impossible either to attack or defend without citing production figures. No machinery exists to try such cases in secret.

Peter J. Donoghue, new head of the antitrust division for the Rocky Mountain states, and his principal assistant, Gerald McAuliffe, explained that they had sought for a long time to find out from the Atomic Energy Commission just how far they could go. Finding it impossible to present full testimony without the possibility of infringing on national security, they have decided to reshape the case.

Lawyers for the defendant corporations complain too. They sought several months ago to have Judge Symes dismiss the case on the ground of nonprosecution. Judge Symes denied this motion.

Now, according to Morrison Shafroth, attorney for some of the defendants, they also are handicapped, because they claim everything they did was in cooperation with the Manhattan District to win the war and they cannot show full evidence of this under the new situation.

The new information charges monopoly of the supply of vanadium and its products, and continues to charge collusion to fix prices on the ores. But no mention is made of monopolizing the ore supply.

The government's charge is, basically, that the companies used their preferred position as government agents to drive out independent buyers and mills.

One aspect of the situation that aroused great interest in Colorado but never did get [into] the case because of security, if for no other reason, is that mine operators charged after the war that the companies went right on buying the ores from them on the sole basis of the value of the vanadium contained therein, obtaining free from the miners the uranium content which the government was so eagerly buying.

The Atomic Energy Commission has now taken over established ore-buying depots, laboratories, and other means in western
Colorado, and has set a scale of prices based on uranium content.

The original indictment was brought against six corporations
and five individuals: Union Carbide and Carbon Corporation
Electro Metallurgical Company, Electro Metallurgical Sales Corporation, United States Vanadium Corporation, and Electro Metallurgical Company of Canada, Ltd., and Vanadium Corporation
of America, and five individuals, all officials of one or more companies. The new information leaves out the individuals and
Electro Metallurgical Company of Canada.

EFFECTS OF SECRECY ON ATOMIC ENERGY
LEGISLATION [14]

Until August 5, 1945, when the first atomic bomb was
dropped on Hiroshima, neither Congress nor the public knew
that an instrument of such vast destructive possibilities was even
contemplated. Only the scientists, the military leadership of the
Manhattan Project, and the very highest echelon of the Administration knew of the work and of its almost limitless consequences should a bomb be successfuly produced. Thus, the secrecy
surrounding the project gave these two groups, the scientists
and the military, an enormous head start over the rest of the
country (and the world) in anticipating the problems created
by the release of atomic energy and in developing techniques for
meeting these problems.

As early as 1943 the scientists began writing and circulating
papers covering such topics as the destructive capacity of the
bomb, possible national and international political consequences
of its use, and possible peacetime uses of atomic energy. . . .
By the end of 1944, however, they had settled upon the need
for quick dissemination throughout the world of the few basic
facts which would permit an unprepared public to understand

[14] From "A Law Is Passed—The Atomic Energy Act of 1946," by Byron S.
Miller, formerly associate general counsel of the Office of War Mobilization and
Reconversion; now Midwest Director, Commission on Law and Social Action,
American Jewish Congress. *University of Chicago Law Review.* 15:799-821.
Summer, 1948. Copyright by University of Chicago. Reprinted by permission.

the new problems presented by atomic energy. In February 1945, the formation of an organization of atomic scientists was considered but security rules of course precluded action at the time. . . .

Despite contrary assurances from the War Department, no adequate informational measures had been prepared to enable the public to form an intelligent understanding of the significance of the atomic bomb. First reports about the bomb created mental chaos; the few carefully prepared articles were no match for the fanciful speculations put forth by writers, broadcasters, and speakers all over the country. The scientists attempted to fill the information void, but without preparation, without experience in the workings of our mass communications systems, and without adequate resources or freedom to reach the bulk of the people before misleading, even harmful, first impressions had been formed. Indeed, it is hard to conceive how any system short of mass censorship during distribution of prepared material could possibly have transmitted the story of the atomic bomb without creating the very first impressions which have since caused so much harm—the notion of "secrets"; the confident expectation of a defense against the bomb; and the assumption that other nations will be incapable of atomic warfare for almost a generation.

During these months legislation was being drafted under the supervision of the Interim Committee, behind locked doors and subject to severe security precautions, by General Royall, then Special Assistant to the Undersecretary of War, and William L. Marbury, a well-known private attorney. There is some indication that this secrecy was continued even after Hiroshima; hence the scientists were caught unawares when President Truman sent a special message to Congress on October 3, followed the same day by introduction of the Interim Committee bill in the House by Representative May and in the Senate by Senator Johnson—the May-Johnson bill. There can be no question that the bill reached Congress in unorthodox fashion, since it was not cleared through the Bureau of the Budget, or by the Bureau with other departments and agencies as is customary. . . .

From the standpoint of the May-Johnson bill's backers such haste was well advised. No sooner was the bill introduced than there rose from atomic scientists throughout the nation an avalanche of outraged criticism that could only have been spontaneous and deeply felt.

In late October the President began to have misgivings about some aspects of the bill. . . . He had no notion that scientists would have any serious objection to the proposed law. His concern was echoed by men then occupying key posts under him. . . . Newspapers, magazines, and broadcasters throughout the country were charging that the bill was being railroaded through without giving the public a chance to form an opinion on the issues. . . .

The Senate voted to establish a Special Committee on Atomic Energy . . . to study the entire field of atomic energy and to prepare alternative legislation. The heat was off; there was time for the scientists, the public, and the government to settle down to the more difficult task of developing constructive suggestions for the content of atomic energy legislation. . . . The result was a superior piece of legislation, a testimonial to the latent capacities of free discussion. . . .

From the time of the President's first offhand statements about preserving our monopoly of the "secrets" of the atomic bomb, the majority of the public, as shown by public opinion polls, accepted the simple notion of "secrets," perhaps subconsciously hoping that preserving these "secrets" would protect us against all danger of atomic warfare. Though later polls showed that most people accepted the intellectual proposition that we could not retain our monopoly, nevertheless their emotional dependence on the concept of "secrets" was probably not seriously affected by the logical inconsistency of such a position.

In this respect members of Congress followed the public pattern. From the early questioning of witnesses on the general subject of atomic energy, there was no question but that the law would contain some provision to preserve the "secrets." Indeed, an early propaganda coup was scored when the words "security" and "secrecy" became interchangeable in this field. Hence, from the outset, few scientists publicly advocated a policy of complete declassification, although many were apprehensive of the evils that had been and could continue to be committed in the name of secrecy. . . .

The bill moved into conference . . . [and after much] violent opposition . . . was approved . . . in the House. Approved by the Senate the same afternoon, it was sent to the President for signature. On August 1, the Atomic Energy Act of 1946 became law.

NEED FOR SECRECY: THE MOSCOW TALKS [15]

A lid of secrecy, tighter than anything else Washington has seen since World War II ended, has been officially clamped on the momentous Kremlin conversations.

This in itself is considered of the greatest significance, for informed observers here interpret it as evidence that the negotiations are in a very fluid state.

Secretary of State George C. Marshall gave emphasis to this interpretation in the only remark he permitted himself to make on the Moscow talks at his weekly press conference.

He warned the press that even speculation as to what was going on could be harmful. Any sign that Washington, London, or Paris—or Moscow, for that matter—was leaking information, he suggested, could destroy whatever progress had been made.

NEED FOR SECRECY: EXPORTS TO RUSSIA [16]

The State Department has clamped the lid on release of Commerce Department information about United States export licenses to Russia and its satellites. Secretary Sawyer wanted to make public a list of goods recently licensed for export, but after several phone calls from the State Department and a personal visit from Secretary Marshall he agreed to withhold the data. Marshall feared Soviet propaganda might twist the figures into charges that the United States is boycotting all but ERP countries. The proposed release, all copies of which were de-

[15] From "Kremlin Talks: Top Secret," newsstory. *Christian Science Monitor.* 40:1. August 5, 1948. Reprinted by permission.

[16] From "Exports to Russia," newsstory, from Periscope section of *Newsweek. Newsweek.* 32:16. June 21, 1948. Reprinted by permission.

stroyed, showed that United States exports to Iron Curtain countries in the three months since March 1, when the restrictive policy was adopted, were off 75 per cent from the February rate, those to Russia dwindling to a tenth.

SECRET VERSUS OPEN DIPLOMACY [17]

The water pipes of diplomacy may have "sweated" a little in this hot spell of East-West relations marked by the Moscow meetings, but there have been no major leaks.

In place of "off the record" information which diplomats have given the press of their own countries during earlier "secret" meetings, foreign correspondents have had to get along mainly with semiofficial speculation offered at great distance from Moscow. And at Washington, London, and Paris even this has been scarce and contradictory.

In the circumstances, it is natural that the battle of the two diplomacies—"open" and "secret"—should be revived. Woodrow Wilson's dream of "open covenants openly arrived at" seems far from fulfillment in such negotiations as are under way at Moscow and Berlin. Yet these private discussions appear to be yielding results not attainable in publicized meetings. One reason for this is that in open discussions the statesmen often talk to be heard at home rather than to be listened to by their opposite numbers in the conference.

Two questions are being asked about the current diplomatic dealing. Does it prove the superiority of secret to open diplomacy? Is it, indeed, secret diplomacy? The answer to both questions is No.

The world's experience with secret diplomacy is one big reason why other means for international adjustment—the League of Nations, the United Nations—have been sought.

The twentieth century's emphasis on open diplomacy reflects general dissatisfaction with the results of nineteenth century secrecy—the worst of which was World War I. This emphasis is a warning against secret clauses in alliances, or secret alliances

[17] From " 'Secret' vs. 'Open' Diplomacy," editorial. *Christian Science Monitor.* 40:14. September 3, 1948. Reprinted by permission.

which do not seek the advantage of peoples involved but only of ruling coteries or special interests.

Still there are few champions of open diplomacy who would urge that discussion of international problems be publicized at every step and debated even in their most delicate phases in public. Citizens of democracies do not demand that much openness of their legislators who work in an area fortunately free from threat of force and from pressures of national pride and prestige.

The Moscow meetings fall into better perspective when classified as the international equivalent of "cloakroom" discussions, say, by American Senators. What the public has a right to know about these "confabs" is what they really produce. There can be no secrets in the law; none should be hidden in international agreements.

The results of the Moscow talks will soon be general knowledge—of that there can be little doubt. They will probably lead to other conferences, the works of which will have to stand judgment before the world. This is hardly "secret" diplomacy.

Nor is it likely, indeed, that the methods of secret diplomacy could be effective in the East-West impasse. For the contest between East and West is more than a race to acquire military allies among governments. It is a rivalry for allies among peoples everywhere. The enlistment of popular sympathies cannot be arranged in a huddle of striped-trousered diplomats (and there are few such today, in any case) but must be won by broad appeals of word and action, policy and deed. What has been going on in Moscow is not secret diplomacy but private negotiation—a necessary phase of democratic procedure on the international as on the national level.

DANGER OF INCREASED DIPLOMATIC CENSORSHIP [18]

There is genuine danger today that the world's international sparring match is leading to increased censorship, less news, and

[18] From "Censorship Censured: News Blackouts Cast Shadow on West," by William H. Stringer, chief of the London News Bureau of the *Christian Science Monitor*. *Christian Science Monitor*. 40:II:9. August 26, 1948. Reprinted by permission.

more blocking of the usual avenues of journalistic information along the western diplomatic front.

Just now the world's public has willingly for three weeks gone without an official report on the tense four-power deliberations at Moscow. Newspapers have accepted this temporary censorship, because they have felt these critical talks could proceed more constructively away from black headlines and the temptation to propagandize. But the peril lies not in these brief blackouts but in the quiet, gradual attempts to shut off news accesses, to withhold and censor information on the grounds that American or British security—usually American—is being jeopardized.

For instance, Washington's State and War Departments were recently quite annoyed because one of the most peripatetic and assiduous American journalists in London produced a news story to the effect that the United States was pressing to have the Brussels Pact enlarged into an Atlantic pact, by the inclusion of the United States and Canada. If the story was true, it is well to ask oneself: Should or should not the American people have been apprised of the proposal? The defense chiefs must have feared publicity would jeopardize negotiations. But does or does not such an attitude mean that the American public is informed of the pact only when it has become an accomplished fact, too late for alteration, and [that we are] back in days of Tallyrand and secret diplomacy?

To tighten notoriously loose security regulations of the State Department, security officers from the Army and Navy and the Justice Department have been lent to Washington and embassies abroad. In many instances, this represents a conscientious effort to keep secret the genuinely highly "classified" data and effectively to muzzle those officials who, unlike their opposite numbers in the British Foreign Office, have exceedingly loose tongues.

But on another day a curtain of censorship mysteriously, for no assigned reason, descended over the London discussions of the Big Four deputies for foreign ministers who were negotiating the future of Italy's former colonies. A spokesman who had previously briefed correspondents disclosed he had been forbidden not only to state what nation or nations had requested the blackout but also to specify why secrecy had been imposed.

No newspaper wants to commit in today's precarious peace any such security breach as happened once during the last war, when a journal revealed in effect that the United States had broken the Japanese secret code.

But such bad faith can be prevented without going to extremes. Correspondents often encounter some small difficulty in getting past the British Foreign Office information officers to talk with diplomatic officials who actually are making and are responsible for policy, but the door is never quite closed, and it never should be in any British—or American—chancellery.

This is hardly the same caliber of journalistic responsibility which was displayed by American press chiefs in Washington under wartime voluntary censorship. It is well known that bureau chiefs then met regularly with some highest military officials who felt free to discuss with them all but the most secret expending military operations. The system worked because "off the record" meant off the record, but newsmen had an invaluable background of this inside information to guide them in handling what could be published.

Now the world is no longer at war, but it is in a twilight zone, where undeniably there is need for a strict prohibition on the publication of certain military information. There also is a need for the State Department to tighten its own security regulations, to close possible avenues to espionage. But it is well to recognize that some of the present pressure for restricting journalistic information is coming not from, say, the House Un-American Activities Committee but from military authorities— from the same authorities who, for instance, were not particularly happy to have newspapers disclose the entirely nonsecurity fact that General Lucius D. Clay at Berlin has far more authority to act without consulting the State Department than has his opposite number, General Sir Bryan Robertson, to act without consulting the British Foreign Office.

A free press is vital to a free people. The right of people to know is basic to the development of a civilian foreign policy which civilians will support. Except in instances of the very critical negotiations with Russia and in cases where military security is involved, there is no justification for drawing a veil between the people and a knowledge not merely of what the government has done last week but what it intends and proposes to do next week.

It is a risky business to shut off these avenues of enterprising and independent journalistic research. It can perilously restrict a nation's knowledge of what its own diplomats are up to.

On the other hand, it is easy to understand the chagrin of top officials at very occasional and half-baked stories which reach some home offices from Europe.

It also is an unhappy fact that newsmen have come to regard the specification "off the record" in off-the-record press conferences given by one high American official this side of the Atlantic as meaning simply, "You can print it, but just don't attribute it."

NEED FOR MORE FOREIGN POLICY INFORMATION [19]

The apparent failure of government officials to provide for a territorial corridor into Berlin has precipitated a serious crisis. The American people did not make that mistake. It was caused by the lack of judgment on the part of representatives charged with the responsibility of protecting American interests abroad. Furthermore, the American people were not aware of this development because the executive branch had failed to advise them of facts and circumstances surrounding agreements with Russia. To what extent other Berlin crises have developed at the present time is not known because the American people do not have adequate information.

This is not the time to withhold facts from the American people. When the President called the special session of Congress, that was the appropriate time to discuss frankly with the representatives of the people the activities in relation to our foreign policy. . . .

Although the question of maintaining a sound domestic economy and the problem of the rising cost of living are paramount issues, they cannot be separated from our foreign policy.

[19] From remarks before the House of Representatives by Representative Edward H. Rees of Kansas. *Congressional Record.* 94:5502-3. August 17, 1948.

Living costs are influenced by our foreign policy. The tremendous amount of food and other goods shipped to foreign countries and paid for from our funds to some extent is bound to influence the economy of this country.

The impact of the foreign-aid program upon our economy makes it important for us to know more about our foreign relations and commitments so that American farmers, businessmen, and the laboring people can estimate the extent to which goods and services will be required abroad in the future. The Economic Cooperation Administration charged with the responsibility of administering our foreign-aid program has been in operation since April 1948. The American people are entitled to a report concerning its operations and accomplishments.

The people of the United States are entitled to frankness from the Chief Executive and the Secretary of State. The most serious aspect of the foreign situation at the present time is that no one outside of the Chief Executive and his most confidential advisers knows anything about it. We Americans receive rumors and hints as to developments, but we have no official statements or facts upon which to base our conclusions.

The domestic economies of the democracies of the world have been shaken, some beyond repair. Only the United States remains as the last hope for the freedom-loving peoples of the world. In our efforts to work out solutions to the common problems of these democracies against totalitarian governments, we must be informed as to the progress and developments in our foreign relations. The so-called bipartisan foreign policy must not be used as a cloak behind which to conceal pertinent facts from our people. . . . In wartime there may be reasons for withholding certain facts, but in peacetime the people and the Congress ought to be informed with regard to negotiations and agreements that are made on their behalf.

Let me not be misunderstood. I recognize the difficulties involved in dealing with a nation such as Soviet Russia. However, it is my belief that the wisdom of the American people should not be underestimated, nor should the Chief Executive assume that the American people do not have sufficient intelligence to understand facts if they are presented properly.

I have a deep and abiding faith in the ability of our countrymen to work out the solutions to our many grave national and international problems. However, without sufficient facts and information from those to whom such knowledge is available, we cannot achieve success. If America is to maintain its place of leadership among the democracies of the world, its people must have all available facts and information upon which to determine their decisions.

THE EXTENT OF COMMUNIST INFILTRATION

DISCUSSION

The essence of the entire program of federal security of information is the fear that the secret of the atom bomb might be "lost"—accidentally through careless release of information or new "leaks"; or deliberately through disloyalty on the part of persons having access to the secret.

The various information controls serve to prevent careless leakage of vital information, but their success is based upon the loyalty of federal employees having access to secret information. The "cold war" with Russia emphasized the need for preserving the atomic secrets, and the Canadian spy trial emphasized likewise the need for proof of loyalty of all persons in "sensitive" departments and agencies.

For the first time, the American public expressed concern over the possibilities of "fifth column" activities within the government itself, going on record favoring strong control measures.

Once the opinion polls showed the trend of public opinion, Congress intensified its search for evidence of Communist infiltration. The House Committee on Un-American Activities published a resume of its ten-year experience, listing arguments to prove the connection between the American Communists and their Soviet counterparts. The "Communists in government" theme had been the basis of much New Deal opposition and its exponents now came forth with new probes and the search for Communists in the government became one of the most popular Congressional activities of 1948, supplying considerable ammunition for the political campaign.

Regardless of the motives of some of the investigators, the sum total of "evidence" produced gives rise to considerable speculation. The House Committee on Un-American Activities produced sensational evidence of the existence of widespread spy rings. The Taber committee and others found "proof" of Communist infiltration in the State Department. Various individual cases were reported, both in government and in the atomic energy program.

It is impossible to judge the validity of the data produced in light of the political implications of the investigations. However, some of the more important findings are reported here chiefly to show their influence on the government's loyalty program.

These are by no means all the cases discovered, and a number have been deliberately omitted, such as those cases where information security was not involved in any way or where political aspects were obvious.

The most important individual case, of course, was that of Dr. Condon, which aroused scientific and public disapproval more than any other. His case, too, was exceedingly important in focusing public attention on the federal loyalty program and the problems surrounding it.

THE COMMUNIST THREAT [1]

What is communism? "It is an evil and malignant way of life," says J. Edgar Hoover, Director of the FBI. It is based on brute force, fear and terror. Communists have infiltrated every activity of American life. They are traitors to our country and wolves in sheep's clothing.

Nearly twenty years ago Russia gave notice, and I quote:

The worldwide nature of our program is not mere talk but an all-embracing and blood-soaked reality. Our ultimate aim is worldwide communism.

When a neighbor gives you notice that he intends to destroy you, your home and family, your religious belief, and your government, and do it with force and bloodshed, you are an exception if you do not take measures to resist that threat, even unto death. You have no choice. . . .

[1] From remarks before the House of Representatives by Representative George A. Dondero of Michigan. *Congressional Record*. 94:6169-70. May 18, 1948.

The Committee on Un-American Activities has found that the Communist movement in the United States is foreign-controlled and that its activities are carried on by secret and conspiratorial methods. They claim that they are a political party; we know they are not. Political parties in the United States are not controlled by foreign governments. We have a right under our Constitution to protect ourselves. . . .

I said at the beginning that Communists and other subversive elements had infiltrated into every activity of America. Not even the churches and schools have been immune from their attack. The Federal Government here in Washington has been especially fertile soil for planting their seed. Their presence in key positions and influential posts has been particularly galling to loyal citizens everywhere. Members of Congress have protested with some effect.

For a number of years, I have exerted every effort to turn the spotlight on these termites and remove them from the government. My efforts have been rewarded with some success.

The extent to which Communists and Communist sympathizers got into the very heart of our nation is evidenced by the fact that they were able not only to obtain secret and highly confidential information from the records of our government in time of war but were able to actually steal the records and transport them to a distant city.

The story of the Russian spy ring as it operated in Canada during the war and at a time when Canada was the friend and ally of Russia is undisputed evidence of the treachery of the Moscow government. It demonstrates the ruthlessness of godless and unprincipled communism.

So clever are some of these agents of the Kremlin that they have been able to hoodwink and deceive loyalty boards and the Civil Service Commission into giving them a clean bill of health for employment within our government. . . .

That "eternal vigilance is the price of liberty" may be a trite saying; but, not since the founding of our Republic, has liberty been so seriously threatened as it is today.

THE MODE OF OPERATION [2]

We are now engaged in defending our country and ourselves against Russian aggression, which has created, supported and used Communist parties and "front" organizations in other lands to assist and spearhead its efforts to undermine and seize governments through other means than the free electoral choice of the peoples concerned. Although "sedition" is an ancient evil, the Soviet-Communist use of seditious organizations as a "fifth column" against governments in other countries is of comparatively recent origin. "Sedition" is used in this paper to describe advocacy of the overthrow of our federal or state governments by force and violence if need be. It is intended to mean what is sometimes called "peacetime treason"; the use of the word "treason" does not convey what is meant in view of its restricted constitutional definition and requirements. [Under the constitutional definition adopted for historical reasons, treason consists only in levying war against the United States, or in adhering to its enemies, giving them aid and comfort, and requires proof by two witnesses of overt act.—ED.]

"Sedition," as thus used here, does not include mere criticism or libels of government or public officials, which were forbidden by the obnoxious Sedition Act of 1798. The terms have to be taken in their modern connotations, in the light of the revelations as to Communist organizations, methods, and objectives.

Marx and Engels began teaching communism in 1848, a hundred years ago. The objectives of this seditious philosophy, as consistently stated by all of its interpreters from Marx to Stalin, have been the overthrow of capitalism throughout the world by violence, the establishment of the dictatorship of the proletariat; and by the extinction of the bourgeoisie, the attainment of a so-called "classless society," in which the state will eventually wither away.

[2] From "Communism vs. the Constitution: The Power to Protect Our Free Institutions," an address before the Maryland State Bar Association, June 26, 1948, by Frank B. Ober, chairman of the Maryland Commission on Subversive Activities. *American Bar Association Journal*. 34:645-8+. August 1948. Reprinted by permission.

This sinister, corroding doctrine makes its chief appeal to those in such poverty that they have nothing to lose by a change. Revolution inevitably feeds on distress. It also attracts political opportunists, gullible mystics or so-called intelligentsia, whose theories have never been tested by the hard facts of reality.

Although the doctrine of communism has been taught for a century, it achieved its first *practical* success in the bloody Russian revolution of thirty years ago. It thus changed from an abstract international philosophy to a weapon of nationalist aggression. The comintern was then formed in Moscow, with sections in each country, to further Russian aims.

The American Communist party was formed as a section of the comintern in 1919, in response to the directions of its president Zinoviev. Absolute obedience to the comintern was required of its branch parties in other countries. Leaders of the American party, such as Browder and Foster, have been members of the Executive Committee of the comintern, making frequent trips to Moscow for instructions, and the Executive Committee itself is under the complete domination of the Kremlin. . . .

While the formation of Communist parties in other countries under the domination of the comintern manifested her ultimate aggressive intent against other nations, Russia was for more than twenty years too occupied with her own revolutions, famine and experiments, to constitute an imminent threat to the rest of the world. This long period of inactivity lulled the rest of the world into a false feeling of security.

Meanwhile, as pointed out by Mr. Churchill, communism had begotten fascism and the more murderously efficient nazism through which Hitler came to power. It was Hitler who perfected and improved the weapon which the Communists had forged, the seditious fifth column, to aid him in his conquests of other countries. In Austria, in the critical year 1938, and in Czechoslovakia and Norway later, Nazi parties and local Quislings aided his armies. The Communists, then temporarily allied with Hitler, also contributed largely to the fall of France. Russian communism commenced its expansion, successfully using seditious fifth columns in conquering, between 1939 and 1948, ten Eastern European nations, with a population of 93,000,000 and an area of some 629,000 square miles. The pattern of the Communist method is clear: (1) organization of a strongly disciplined Communist party with members who are individually pledged to carry out the mandates of their leaders, who, as history abundantly shows, slavishly follow the Party line, irrespective of their own national interests—the opposition to war during the temporary Russian alliance with Hitler and subsequent support thereof is perhaps the most dramatic example out of a multitude of instances of goose-stepping to Kremlin music; (2) infiltration of labor unions to stir up industrial strife for political ends; (3) espionage and sabotage; (4) planting of Communists in key government positions; particularly in police and army posts; (5) forcible overthrow of the existing government by the minority Communist party at some psychological moment of political or economic crisis, and usually with the presence or threat of the Red Army; (6) elimination of all opposition parties and the liquidation of their leaders; and (7) finally, the formalization of the conquest through so-called democratic elections, at which 100 per cent of the electors are frightened into voting for the Communist party and the local Quislings selected by Moscow.

The "cold war" in other countries is in full swing. Finland is in process of absorption, and a third or more of the voters in France and Italy vote the Communist ticket, though their recent bids for power were unsuccessful. In China, the Communists, with Russian support, control a large part of the country.

There are likewise strong Communist parties in most of the countries in the Western Hemisphere, as the Canadian spy trials and recent violent events in Chile, Brazil, Colombia, and Costa Rica have warned. In our country the party is credited with less than a hundred thousand members, yet, as pointed out by J. Edgar Hoover, we should not be lulled into a false complacency, because, as the Communists boast, for every one who is an active member there are ten ready to follow the Communist line. They have so cleverly maneuvered themselves into strategic positions that never in history did so few control the thoughts and actions of so many.

We have but recently been reminded by Mr. Churchill of the almost incredible mistake of the democratic countries in permitting Germany to rearm after World War I, which led inevitably to World War II. Warfare is no longer preceded by formal declarations. "Cold" warfare is waged during intervals of peace, or the armed truce which is so often blindly mistaken for peace. We have just proved again that, under our Constitution and given sufficient time and protection by allies to prepare, a war can be magnificently won. But once again we see the danger signals of another war and the establishment of beachheads in the form of seditious parties.

NEED FOR INVESTIGATION [3]

It is now definitely established that during the late war and since then, there have been numerous Communist espionage rings at work in our executive agencies which have worked with and through the American Communist party and its agents to relay to Russia vital information essential to our national defense and security. Russian Communists have worked hand in hand with American Communists in these espionage activities.

It is established beyond doubt that there is grave need for vigorous, persistent and courageous continued investigation to determine the identity of those guilty of past offenses, the methods employed in the past and at present to move carefully selected Communist agents and their sympathizers into key positions of government, and to break up all Communist espionage conspiracies and activities prevailing at this time.

These situations should command and receive the most diligent attention of this committee, of the Attorney General's office and the grand jury proceedings under his authority, and of the Federal Bureau of Investigation. They should proceed without partisanship and without prejudice. It would be greatly in the public interest if they could receive the support of the White House rather than to be obstructed by it.

This committee believes the eradication of espionage from the Federal Government should command the same cooperation

[3] From "Summary of Report on Spy Inquiry," the interim report by the House Committee on Un-American Activities on its recent investigation into Communist activities. *New York Times.* 98:3. August 29, 1948. Reprinted by permission.

between the White House and the Congress and between the two major American political parties as has been utilized in the formation and implementation of our bipartisan foreign policy.

As evidence of this committee's sincerity in desiring to co-operate fully with the executive agencies in the ferreting out of all disloyal and un-American practices in government during our committee's existence, we have opened our files to the security officers and loyalty board representatives of the executive departments. . . .

Contrariwise, under the President's executive order, the files and records of the executive departments on all matters of loyalty and security have been firmly closed, not only to our committee but to all committees of Congress and to the general public. We hold that this is an unwholesome, an unwise, and an unsafe situation. . . .

During the course of these hearings our committee was shocked to have before it witnesses who hold reserve commissions in our armed forces and who refuse to answer under oath whether or not they were, are, or ever have been members of the Communist party. It was equally shocking to have former high officials of the Federal Government take such a position. The committee therefore recommends that the armed services revoke the commission of any officer who refuses to answer this question. . . . The committee further recommends that any official or employee of the government who will refuse to state under oath whether or not he is a member of the Communist party should be removed, and his name "flagged" against any future government service.

SPY PROBE: UN-AMERICAN ACTIVITIES COMMITTEE REPORT [4]

After three weeks of probing atomic espionage, the House Un-American Activities Committee suddenly canceled its proposed public hearings . . . and instead released . . . a thirty-six-page written report of its conclusions. The key findings:

[4] From "Spy Probe: The Finger Points," newsstory. *Newsweek.* 32:24. October 4, 1948. Reprinted by permission.

During the war, diplomatic representatives of the Russian government in the United States organized and directed several espionage groups made up of American Communists for the purpose of obtaining secret information concerning the development of the atomic bomb.

These espionage groups were successful in placing some of their members in highly strategic positions in various atomic-bomb installations, where they had access to the most secret and confidential information.

These groups were successful in obtaining and transmitting secret information concerning the atomic bomb to diplomatic representatives and espionage agents of the Russian Government.

The committee cannot accurately evaluate the importance or volume of the information thus transmitted. It has been established, however, that . . . this information has been and will be of assistance to the Russians in the development of the atomic bomb.

The failure to prosecute those who were engaged in this conspiracy is completely inexcusable . . . The committee must point out that it has conducted its investigation only under the greatest handicaps. The lack of cooperation by the administrative branch of the government has amounted practically to obstruction of the committee in conducting its investigation. . . .

The Thomas committee was no less forthright when it came to personalities. Revealing that it had uncovered three separate acts of wartime treachery, the committee charged four persons, including two American scientists and a Communist party official, with attempting to steal this nation's atomic secrets for Russia. . . .

In conclusion, the Un-American Activities Committee reiterated that the full story of wartime espionage cannot be told because of the presidential directive which denies Congress access to files in the executive branch of the government.

"MARY" AND THE SPY RING [5]

The tall, thin blonde was of old American stock and full of the idealism which had flowered at Walden Pond and Brook Farm. For her in the mid-30's, there were evil forces to be

[5] From "The Case of Mary and the Spy Ring Shrinks to the Case Against the Reds," newsstory. *Newsweek*. 32:22-3. August 2, 1948. Reprinted by permission.

conquered: In Europe fascism was on the grim ascendant, in America one third of the nation was underprivileged. A desire to do something about this took her into the underground stream of Communist espionage. . . .

She became a Communist in 1936, taking the party name "Mary." . . . She was given small errands to run, letters to deliver, confidential packages to pick up, people to contact. She was made to feel that this secret and exciting business was all part of a great idealistic world movement. If there was something slightly shady about it all, it was for the eventual good of her own country.

When the time was ripe, after Germany invaded Russia, "Mary" was introduced to a shadowy figure named "John." She soon learned that in reality this introduction was her debut into the "Apparat," the party underground. From then on she was an agent of one of the spy rings which systematically milked the United States of political, economic, scientific, and military information. "John" was nominally an executive in a war relief agency. But this was merely a front for activities which, unknown to the agency's prominent backers, were infinitely more important than food and clothing packages. "John" made her his sweetheart and his courier.

"Mary's" run was between Washington and New York. The government officials who acted as agents would meet her on street corners and casually hand her envelopes. Or she would pick up other envelopes from a well patronized photo studio in the basement of what was later called "the House in Washington." The material she gathered would go back to New York to Soviet officials or to "John," who would put a few blueprints among relief shipments of old clothes.

As courier for "John," she met the secretary of a prominent Southern "liberal" senator, with a high official of the Treasury, with a personal adviser to President Roosevelt, and with important Office of Strategic Services men. From numerous Federal departments, and agencies, party cells poured their information. By accident, "Mary" learned that there were other Communist rings operating as busily as hers in Washington.

The apparatus which "John" led had specific missions: to get blueprints of the new B-29 bombers, to collect information on American activities in China, to assemble scientific weather data, to get complete data on the plastic explosive R-D-X, and to keep tabs on OSS operations in France. So skillfully did the ring work that no member was ever caught, even though some were on FBI "unreliable" lists. And so well had the party prepared the ground that its agents in the government got not a cent for their work and, in fact, continued to pay their party dues.

But the conscience which had involved "Mary" in the movement began to backfire. When "John" died in 1944 and this one strictly personal loyalty no longer existed, her doubts overcame her Communist training. In a move which took both physical and intellectual courage, she decided to break with the Apparat and reveal her work to the FBI.

To FBI officials the outline of her story was not news. But the names she earnestly mentioned staggered them. Even to men whose work was counterespionage, her story was unbelievable. Warily fearful that she might be a "plant" or worse, a double agent, they refused to take her seriously. . . . But she persisted. As her information began to check with independently gathered facts, the FBI finally became convinced of her sincerity.

It was now a question of getting evidence that would stand up in court. Against her wishes, they prevailed upon "Mary" to return to her job and to continue her activities—but with a difference. From that moment on, there was always an FBI shadow following her as she made the rounds, photographing the people she dealt with, tapping important telephone wires. But one vital element was lacking: With the death of "John," the party had broken up his ring. Most of her assignments were now semi-legitimate party work.

Nevertheless, the FBI and the Justice Department went ahead. A federal grand jury was impaneled in New York on March 22, 1947, to hear the woman's story and to question the people she named. If one of these principals could be made to crack on the witness stand, the case would break wide open.

The jury began meeting for a few hours a week, hearing a parade of witnesses. But attempts to make the witnesses go beyond a routine description of their government jobs were met in several instances by a firm refusal based on the constitutional ground that it would be "self-incriminatory."

Among the more than a hundred witnesses who appeared before the jury was an array of top New Deal talent. It included a member of the "little cabinet," a White House adviser, a State Department employee, and a White House employee.

Confronted with evidence that they had visited "the House in Washington," all of the witnesses implicated stoutly maintained that they had gone there merely to have their pictures taken—and these photographs were produced.

What little percolated out of the grand-jury room now began to assume a pessimistic tone. From New York and Washington came "inside" stories that the jury would be dismissed without handing down an indictment, that the espionage case was washed up.

Simultaneously there were strong hints in many quarters that the espionage case reached so high that it was politically "too hot" to pursue. Government officials denied this, maintaining that what stymied the case was the lack of documentary and other testimony to clinch "Mary's" story. The fact remained that the grand jury had been in session for more than a year investigating this case alone, and had not found an indictment.

"MARY'S" SPY RING PERSONNEL [6]

New England-born and reared Elizabeth T. Bentley . . . was "Mary." As courier for the spy ring headed by the late Jacob Golos, she frequently had turned over information to "Al," . . . Anatoli B. Gromoff, first secretary of the Soviet Embassy in Washington from September 1944 until February 1946.

If true, Miss Bentley's story was easily the most significant development yet in the House committee's investigation of Russian espionage in the United States. If true, it provided the missing link between the Golos ring and the Kremlin, proving

    [6] From "Investigation: Truth, Half-Truth, Untruth," newsstory. *Newsweek*. 32:20-1. August 23, 1948. Reprinted by permission.

conclusively that any government official who may have offered information to Golos actually had served a foreign power, the Soviet Union, wittingly or unwittingly.

Nor could there be much doubt that this part of Miss Bentley's story was true. Although the FBI would not confirm it publicly, it did so off the record in detail. FBI agents on several occasions had trailed Miss Bentley and Gromoff. They had even taken motion pictures of them. They still had the $2,000 which Miss Bentley had turned over to them.

But if Miss Bentley's testimony on Gromoff was unassailable, much of the rest of her story still rested only on her word. She previously had named more than thirty government officials—some Communists, some fellow travelers, and some evidently just dupes—as men who supplied the Golos ring with the information which it had turned over to Russia. Whittaker Chambers, a longtime Communist party member, subsequently an editor of *Time*, had given testimony circumstantially backing her charges against several of them. Last week the House committee started giving them an opportunity to answer the charges.

The result: Some balked at the committee's questions. Some answered them freely—but categorically denied almost everything Miss Bentley and Chambers had said.

The witnesses who refused to answer questions based their refusal on constitutional grounds. Over and over again, they repeated that any reply might serve to incriminate or degrade them.

Victor Perlo, a former War Production Board official who had been named by Miss Bentley as a key figure in the spy ring, was asked whether he was or ever had been a member of the Communist party. He declined to answer. He was asked: "Have you ever given Miss Elizabeth T. Bentley confidential government information?" He sighed: "I refuse to answer the question on the grounds . . ."

William Ludwig Ullman, a reserve Army major who had been named by Miss Bentley as the chief photographer for the ring, likewise refused to say whether he ever had been a Communist. He was asked: "While you were in the Air Corps did you have any information relating to the B-29?" He replied quickly. "I refuse to answer that question on the grounds. . . ."

Henry H. Collins, Jr., a former Military Government officer, was faced with Chambers's charge that he once was a member of the Communist party. "I refuse to answer . . . ," he said. He was asked whether he knew Chambers. He said he did not. He was asked whether he knew a man named "Carl," which had been Chambers's party name. "I refuse to answer," he said, "on the grounds. . . ."

A. George Silverman, a former War Department employee, and Charles Kramer, former aide to Senator Claude Pepper of Florida, refused to say whether they were Communists "on constitutional grounds." Had they ever known Miss Bentley? Again they refused to answer—again "on constitutional grounds."
. . .

Exasperating as these refusals to answer might be, the committee at least had one consolation: By citing the constitutional provision against self-incrimination, the witnesses had at least lent some air of authenticity to previous testimony by Miss Bentley and Chambers.

But the witnesses who point-blank denied the charges left the committee in complete bewilderment, which the members made no effort to hide. They had been noticeably impressed by Miss Bentley and Chambers. The stories sounded convincing. But the denials sounded convincing too. Someone was lying. But who?

Duncan Lee, an ex-lieutenant colonel in the OSS, denied that he was a Communist or had ever been one. He denied that Miss Bentley had ever collected party dues from him. He denied that he ever gave her OSS information. He admitted, however, that he knew Miss Bentley, saying that she had fastened herself on him and his wife, becoming "a personal nuisance."

Lauchlin Currie, a former executive assistant to Franklin D. Roosevelt, was equally sweeping in his denials. He never gave any unauthorized person any information about China, he said, nor about codes. As for Miss Bentley's charge that he conspired to keep N. Gregory Silvermaster, whom she described as "probably an NKVD agent," in the Board of Economic Warfare, he said he merely had referred Silvermaster's case to Undersecretary of War Robert P. Patterson for review.

Others who flatly characterized the Bentley and Chambers charges as false were Harry D. White, former assistant secretary of the Treasury; Donald Hiss, former State Department employee; Dr. and Mrs. Bela Gold of Pittsburgh; and Frank Coe, secretary of the International Monetary Fund. . . .

Just to increase the committee's bewilderment, the secret witness on whom it had been counting to fill the gaps in the story of Russian espionage refused even to say whether he ever visited Niagara Falls. He was Alexander Koral, an engineer for the New York City Board of Education. The committee had reason to believe that he had succeeded Miss Bentley as the spy-ring courier after she broke with the Communist party.

Like the others who balked at the committee's questions, Koral's refusal to answer lent weight to the Bentley-Chambers testimony. . . . If Koral talked, committee spokesmen said, he could "break the spy ring story wide open." But all he would say was "I refuse to answer . . ."

COMMUNIST INFLUENCE ON FOREIGN POLICY [7]

State Department officials who wanted to tighten up American policy toward Soviet Russia before the end of World War II were balked by Alger Hiss and others.

Testimony to this effect has been put into the record of the House Un-American Activities Committee by Adolph A. Berle, Jr., former Assistant Secretary of State, one of those "trimmed" by the pro-Russian group. . . .

He admitted he had been "worried" about Mr. Hiss ever since Mr. Chambers came to him in 1939 and described Alger Hiss, his brother Donald, Nathan Witt, and Lee Pressman as government officials who were "sympathetic to the general Communist point of view and to whom they might have access and perhaps a sympathetic approach in case anybody brought a request."

[7] From "Berle Links Hiss to 'Pro-Soviets,' " newsstory. *Christian Science Monitor.* 40:5. September 2, 1948. Reprinted by permission.

At the time, Mr. Hiss was given blanket endorsement by Felix Frankfurter, Associate Justice of the United States Supreme Court, and Dean Acheson, Assistant Secretary of State.

Mr. Berle's open break with the Acheson-Hiss group came in the fall of 1944 when a difference of opinion on Russian policy developed in the State Department.

> I felt that the Russians were not going to be sympathetic and cooperative [Mr. Berle explained]. Victory was then assured, though not complete, and the intelligence reports which were in my charge indicated a very aggressive policy not at all in line with the kind of cooperation everyone was hoping for.
>
> I was pressing for a pretty clean-cut showdown then when our position was strongest.
>
> The opposite group in the State Department was Mr. Acheson's group, of course, with Mr. Hiss as his principal assistant in the matter. Whether that was a difference on foreign policy—and the question could be argued both ways—was a problem, but at that time Mr. Hiss did take what we would call today the pro-Russian point of view.
>
> Now that was a reason for worry. It was not necessarily a reason to draw the conclusion that he was a disloyal man. Many people who were quite loyal, including a good many of the army officers, felt the Russian army would be of importance in case of an invasion of Japan and that by consequence it was desirable not to raise any issues until later.
>
> I say that in Mr. Hiss's defense, although I got trimmed in that fight, and as a result went to Brazil and that ended my diplomatic career. I mention that, because I did have a biased view.

Mr. Berle described Mr. Chambers when he came to his home in 1939 as appearing to be "in fear of some sort of reprisal" and "obviously under some emotional strain." But as a result of his warnings about the Hisses, Mr. Berle said he established

closer liaison between the department and the FBI, promoted the writing of the Foreign Registration Act, and helped establish a group in the department's European division to study the foreign intelligence in the hope of establishing any link between the Communist group here and the Russian Government.

He also took special care, he said, to protect the department's codes. "We didn't let them run around," he said. "This was not," he added, "any fixed suspicion but just the theory, if there is any chance, let's not take it."

Mr. Berle also disclosed that he suspected Mr. Hiss's office for breaks in news that got into the newspaper column of Drew Pearson before the department knew about it. "Other people besides Mr. Hiss could give leaks to Washington columnists, so I don't know as you could allege that as a fatal crime," he said, "but it just meant you were a little cautious."

The committee has not queried Mr. Hiss about his differences with Mr. Berle but, on his first appearance to deny the Chambers charges early in August, they delved into his attitude toward Russia when he was helping write the United Nations charter.

He disclosed then that he favored the veto that the Soviet Union has come to use so frequently because he was convinced the United States Congress would not have approved the charter without a veto for possible American use.

He said he had not personally favored giving Soviet Russia three votes, including those for Byelorussia and the Ukraine, instead of only one vote.

REPORT ON THE STATE DEPARTMENT [8]

Congressional leaders are determined that any doubts in connection with employment of personnel in the State Department should be resolved in favor of the United States rather than the employee.

Most Republicans and Democrats will accept the views expressed by Representative Karl Stefan (Republican, Nebraska), chairman of the State Department Appropriations Subcommittee in its report to the House recently:

Officers or employees who are suspected in the slightest degree should be encouraged to resign.

[8] From "Solon Assails Risks in State Department," the eighth in a special series by Gustaf A. Nordin, Washington correspondent for the *St. Paul Pioneer Press and Dispatch*, April 25, 1948. Quoted in the *Congressional Record*. 94: A2822-3. May 3, 1948. Reprinted by permission of the *St. Paul Pioneer Press and Dispatch*.

That is a mild approach in comparison with the views of others who cannot understand the continued employment of men and women whose loyalty or association with poor security risks is tolerated.

The Stefan report to Congress discussed briefly the extensive hearings held on the security phase of the State Department "and the employment of individuals who were considered poor risks from the security angle."

Committee investigators disclosed in these hearings, reports on 108 former, present, and prospective State Department employees.

The committee does not feel that the Department has been as diligent as it might have been in the selection of its personnel and has not sufficiently exercised the prerogative given it under the so-called McCarran rider, contained in appropriation acts for this Department for the past several years [Stefan reported].

The official report, which summarizes the employment history of the 108, is still being held by the House Appropriations Committee. Representative John Taber (Republican, New York) ... is chairman of the committee. . . .

The fundamental issue involved is whether these employees are security risks. A cloud will hang over the State Department as long as such reports as gathered by the Taber committee are in existence and not brought into the open for explanation.

Representative Taber declared on the floor of the House that the investigations made by the special agents

demonstrate beyond any question that the first thing for the United States to do is to clean up the State Department and get rid of those whose incompetency and disloyalty is a menace to the United States and to the successful prosecution of any type of foreign policy. . . .

The State Department officials in charge say that the evidence is insufficient to warrant dismissal.

Congressional leaders, clamoring for action under pressure of a United States-Soviet war of nerves, claim that the connections of these employees make it imperative that the interests of the country supersede the protection of the employee.

Hamilton Robinson, in charge of the State Department's Office of Controls, prepared an order in which he defined who constitutes a security risk. The first point is:

A person who engages in, supports, or advocates treason, sub-version, or sedition, or who is a member of, affiliated with, or in sym-pathetic association with the Communist, Nazi, or Fascist parties, or of any foreign or domestic party, organization, movement, group, or combination of persons who seek to alter the form of government of the United States by unconstitutional means or whose policy is to advocate or approve the commission of acts of force or violence to deny other persons their right under the Constitution of the United States; or a person who consistently believes in or supports the ideolo-gies and policies of such a party, organization, movement, group, or combination of persons.

Participation in one or more of such parties or organizations, or their "fronts," contribution of funds, attendance at meetings, registration to vote in such parties, or signing election petitions for party members, are major factors, according to Robinson's order. He said the department also would consider written evi-dence or oral expressions by speeches or otherwise, of political, economic or social views, which throw a light on the security chances this country is taking with such employees.

The information filed with the Taber committee in this secret report exposes practically all of the 108 employees investigated. If the investigations were objective and are factual, few, if any of the 108, should have been retained in employment or, in the case of job applicants, should not be considered as proper State Department risks. Taber tells his colleagues:

I just want to tell you that I do not go off half-cocked. The in-vestigations of the committee indicated a very large number of Com-munists on the rolls of the State Department. The very least that they have there now is fourteen, and those cases instead of resulting in immediate dismissal as the interests of the United States required, have been dragged on and on for six, eight, and ten months.

I do not know whether anyone is entitled to wonder whether we are getting American representation in the State Department.

Most of the findings of the special agents appear to support Representative Taber's charges of communism in the Depart-ment.

STATE DEPARTMENT INFILTRATION [9]

The mysterious House committee report dealing with alleged State Department negligence in retaining employees considered "poor security risks" wraps together a puzzling story which, on the face of it, either means the government has been successfully invaded by Communists and fellow travelers or overzealous investigations are being made by federal security agents.

This document has not been released for publication. It reveals, however, that some of the vital sections of American foreign policy have been laid bare to the inquisitive eyes of individuals suspected to be bad risks—so bad that in some cases as many as a dozen separate investigations have been made.

The guarded report provides 40,000 words of startling reading on 108 State Department employees. They represent only a fraction of the total 20,000 on the pay roll, yet enough to do serious damage to American foreign policy if the allegations in the report are reasonably accurate. A clean bill of health appears to have been granted a few involved in the report.

At least ten of the employees were formerly employed by the important wartime branch of OSS—Office of Strategic Services. A number of them were with the Office of War Information and transferred to the State Department when OWI went out of business.

A few are held poor risks because of morals; at least one for an alleged criminal record. Three have connections in various ways with the Soviet Embassy in Washington; one is a former employee of the Embassy; another was working for the Soviet Purchasing Commission when employed by the State Department. Several were recommended highly by Professor Harold L. Laski, of England, left-wing Laborite.

Five are known to have signed Communist election petitions. Twelve are listed as being close associates or having connections in some way with suspected Soviet espionage agents. One is

[9] From "Inquiry Hints Red Invasion of United States Pay Roll," third in a series of articles by Gustaf A. Nordin, Washington correspondent for the *St. Paul Pioneer Press and Dispatch*, April 20, 1948. Quoted in the *Congressional Record*. 94:A2628. April 26, 1948. Reprinted by permission of the *St. Paul Pioneer Press and Dispatch*.

listed as pro-German during the war years, while in the Department. Practically all of them are suspected as members of the Communist party or as having communistic leanings. Two were questionable employees because they had twice attempted to commit suicide. Another was employed even though listed as a psychopathic case.

A study of the report reveals that the employees involved are scattered through every branch of the service. The heaviest infiltration has taken place in the Office of Research and Intelligence, foreign service, and Office of Information and Education, the latter, especially in New York City.

If the employees are as questionable risks as painted in the report, they have managed to step into the right departments. Fifteen are reported in the Office of Intelligence Research. Its official duties are:

Has the responsibility . . . for planning, developing, and implementing an integrated intelligence-research program for the Department and for coordinating it with those of other federal agencies, in order to provide the Department with the foreign intelligence necessary for the formulation and execution of American foreign policy and to provide the National Intelligence Authority and the Central Intelligence Agency with studies pertinent to the national security.

Twenty-three are in the Office of Information and Educational Exchange, whose duties are:

Has responsibility for the promotion among foreign peoples of a better understanding of the aims, policies, and institutions of the United States; the coordination of policy and action for programs of the United States in the field of international information and cultural affairs; the dissemination abroad of information about the United States; the promotion of freedom of information among peoples, etc.

The Office of Foreign Service has seven on the committee list. This service has responsibility for the administrative leadership, management, and direction of the Foreign Service.

Others on the list are recorded as being with the Division of Map Intelligence Research in the Far East, Financial and Development Policy Division, International Exchange of Persons, policy information specialists, Internal Security Division, International Labor, Health and Social Affairs, Division of Central

Services, Biographical Information Division. One is listed as a secretary to an American ambassador abroad, two others are attached to an Assistant Secretary of State office, and two are in high ranking diplomatic posts. One employee was formerly attached with the Russian Embassy in Turkey.

It seems to me that it is about time we gird ourselves for the fight against communism from within, before we attempt to blot it out from abroad.

SILVERMASTER AND OTHERS [10]

The nation's attention has been directed to allegations that during the war certain federal employees carried on subversive activities and furnished Russian agents with confidential or restricted material. In view of these and other recent developments in the foreign situation, I think it is well to review the record and determine whether government officials now employed approved such persons for appointments with the knowledge that there was a reasonable doubt as to their loyalty. The American people are also entitled to know whether the present loyalty policy of the executive branch is designed adequately to protect our national security. . . .

In testimony before the House Un-American Activities Committee, Elizabeth T. Bentley mentioned Nathan Gregory Silvermaster as leader of the largest group of alleged disloyal government employees. . . . Silvermaster was a former employee of the Maritime Labor Board, Department of Agriculture, Board of Economic Warfare, Treasury Department, Reconstruction Finance Corporation, and War Assets Administration. On April 3, 1942, he applied for a position with the Board of Economic Warfare, subject to the approval of the Civil Service Commission, which is the agency charged with the responsibility of determining the loyalty of applicants for federal positions. Exhaustive investigations were conducted by the Federal Bureau of Investigation and the Civil Service Commission. Evidence submitted

[10] From remarks by Representative Edward H. Rees of Kansas before the House of Representatives. *Congressional Record.* 94:9935-9. August 4, 1948.

in the Commission's investigation covered several hundred pages.
. . . On May 22, 1942, an official of the Civil Service Commission, after reviewing the reports of the investigation, made
the following recommendations:

> It is my conclusion that Silvermaster is definitely either an active
> member of the Communist party or so directly aligned with their leaders
> and interests in the San Francisco Bay area, if not on a national scale,
> as to color and affect his service for the Federal Government. It is
> felt that by reason of these attachments, his continued employment in
> his present capacity or at all by the Federal Government can only serve
> to advance the cause of the Communist party in its ultimate design to
> disrupt America's political and economic texture.

The investigation of Silvermaster covered a period from
1916, when he entered the United States from Russia, up to the
year 1942. Scores of competent witnesses were interviewed at
a half dozen places in the United States. Almost without exception those who themselves were not Communists or identified
with Communist front organizations stated that he was an en-
thusiastic supporter of the Soviet Communist order. . . .

His close friends and acquaintances, including his lawyers
and doctors, according to the investigation, were either known
Communists or known to be active in organizations labeled by
the Attorney General as subversive. He made several material
incorrect statements on his application designed to conceal his
activities. This is only a part of the evidence reported in the
investigation, but that which reflected on Silvermaster's questionable loyalty is documented and the testimony well corroborated.
On July 1, 1940, he transferred to the Department of Agriculture
from the Maritime Labor Board. The confidential files of the
Agriculture Department during his employment there contained
correspondence between officials of the Resettlement Administration and officials of the San Francisco section of the American
Legion.

The American Legion reported that Silvermaster had close
associations with Sam Darcy, West Coast Communist functionary.
Further, that he was a member of the Fillmore section of the
Communist party. Also that he was active in protesting the discharge of California State employees who had been dismissed

because of radical activities. The Legion reported that many of his associates are of doubtful loyalty and that one of the American Legion officials had reviewed Mr. Silvermaster's doctoral thesis and found it to be extremely pro-Soviet. . . .

While the Commission's investigation was in progress, Military Intelligence investigated Silvermaster who was then on detail from the Department of Agriculture to the Board of Economic Warfare. G-2 was interested in Silvermaster because of his access to confidential information which the Board of Economic Warfare received from the Military Establishment. After its investigation, G-2 recommended the Board of Economic Warfare to remove Silvermaster from their offices. Officials in the BEW handed G-2's investigation to Silvermaster to answer, and then advised G-2 that the charges against Silvermaster were unfounded. Meanwhile, Silvermaster was called before the Civil Service Commission to explain his activities which had been uncovered during the investigation. Much of the evidence he admitted.

At this point the investigation was dropped. Silvermaster remained at the Agriculture Department. Later, however, in December of 1944 top officials presently employed in the Civil Service Commission, over the objections of subordinate officials, approved Silvermaster's transfer to the Treasury Department because, in the words of the Commission:

There was no reasonable doubt as to his loyalty to the United States.

From here on Silvermaster transferred from one agency to another with relative ease, and his salary rapidly increased from $6,500 per annum to $10,000 a year at the War Assets Administration, from which he finally resigned voluntarily in November 1946. In all, Silvermaster worked for the Federal Government approximately eleven years, for which the people of the United States paid him more than $50,000. At retirement age he will be eligible to receive from the government an annuity of approximately $500 a year.

This Silvermaster case is typical of many of those employees mentioned before congressional committees recently. For all the good these investigations did, they might as well have not been conducted. I do not care how much evidence of disloyalty is obtained by our government investigators, if the policy-making officials and appointing officers do not have the courage to remove or refuse to employ persons about whom there is a reasonable doubt as to their loyalty, such investigations are a farce and the hundreds of millions of dollars spent for them by the American people have been wasted. . . .

I have talked with many persons who appear to be surprised to learn that William W. Remington, an employee of the Commerce Department, could be considered for, or actually transferred to, other strategic positions in the Federal Government while under investigation by the Federal Bureau of Investigation for subversive activities.

This has been the policy ever since the Federal Employees' Loyalty Program began in 1939, and exists at the present time. . . .

Testimony before the Civil Service subcommittee in July 1946 showed that employees remained for years in strategic, confidential, and responsible government positions although their loyalty was seriously questioned.

Time and time again these matters have been brought to the attention of the executive branch. Beginning in 1944, I repeatedly urged the then chairman of the House Civil Service Committee to investigate derelictions of duty by officials in the executive branch in employing persons of doubtful loyalty. Finally, in the summer of 1946, a three-man subcommittee was appointed to study the federal employees' loyalty program. I was designated as a minority member of this subcommittee. Hearings were rushed and secret, evidence was glossed over, testimony of some competent witnesses ignored, and a rather superficial report was made, to which I took strong exception.

These hearings were made available to the Department of Justice. Competent witnesses mentioned critically government top-level handling and clearing of many federal employees, some of whom were then on the federal pay-roll. At the time of the hearing in July 1946, at which a representative of the Department of Justice was present, witnesses testified that Nathan

Gregory Silvermaster was still employed by the Federal Government, and that he had been appointed over the objections of officials of the Civil Service Commission, whose conclusions had been based upon the evidence I have mentioned above. One witness stated that Mr. Silvermaster insisted upon an investigation of his suitability prior to his transfer from the Department of Agriculture. It was pointed out that if the Civil Service Commission cleared him, he could transfer without losing his position with the Department of Agriculture. However, even if a strong loyalty case were made against him and he stayed with the Department of Agriculture, the Commission would have no authority to remove him. Since Silvermaster appeared to be satisfactory to the officials of the Department of Agriculture he could probably remain there as long as he desired. It happened, however, that his precautions were unnecessary. The Civil Service Commission cleared Silvermaster and he was at liberty to transfer to any department or agency of the government.

On the basis of these hearings the President appointed a committee to study the problems of federal employees' loyalty. . . .

The committee filed its report which stated in effect that everything was fine. The American people could rest easy. There were no employees of doubtful loyalty on the federal pay roll. The Canadian Government spy case could never happen in the United States.

In March 1947 the President issued his Federal Employees' Loyalty Executive Order. The only·new feature was the creation of a host of loyalty boards within the agencies. Also, a Loyalty Review Board was created. Was it a strong independent board? Was its existence based on legislation outlining congressional policy? No; it was to be under the Civil Service Commission and its officials, whose do-little-or-nothing policy on federal employment loyalty matters prompted the first congressional investigation back in 1946. We were right back where we had started. . . .

This is the record. These are the facts which have been withheld from the American people and more recently been denied the Congress through a presidential directive ordering the departments and agencies to refuse congressional requests regarding reports, records, and files relating to the loyalty of federal employees and prospective employees. With or without charges of espionage and spy rings the performance to date is one of which the American people cannot be proud.

With the foreign situation in a highly inflammable state, we can ill afford the luxury of employees of doubtful loyalty on the federal pay roll, and we can less afford a policy in the executive branch which I have demonstrated has existed for the past several years.

On the other hand, we must not become hysterical and discharge everyone who has had a liberal thought or who has talked with a Communist or who has been seen with a Communist, but certainly we must not turn our faces away from the facts. Government employment is a trust and privilege. We must give more than lip service to the principle that American people are entitled above all to have in government service only those loyal to the United States with doubts resolved in favor of the government. . . .

The real answer to these federal employee-loyalty problems is both an effective removal procedure in the case of employees of doubtful loyalty and adequate means of preventing the initial employment of such persons.

Let me not be misunderstood. I realize this is a serious matter. I am in favor of seeing to it that every person suspected of subversive activities or views, is given adequate consideration. No one would deny them every right to which they are entitled. On the other hand the hundreds of thousands of loyal employees in the Federal Government, as well as the American people to whom all government employees are responsible for their services, are entitled to protection against any and all persons of doubtful loyalties and subversive views.

THE FEDERAL LOYALTY PROGRAM

DISCUSSION

In response to the deeply felt need to block possible Communist infiltration into government inner circles, a federal loyalty program was adopted in March of 1947. Basically it was merely an extension to all federal employees of the loyalty checks established in the Atomic Energy Act of 1946. But from the outset, the program was attacked on all sides.

Liberals charged that the program was a violation of civil rights; conservatives felt that the government enforcement of the program was ineffectual.

In spite of repeated attacks, the loyalty checks continued. Most of the opposition came from within Congress, with the press generally accepting the opinion of the Administration that the loyalty program was achieving its purposes. At the end of the first year, the record showed only a small percentage of government employees in the disloyal column, which brought forth renewed attacks on the program. Its opponents charged that this proved that agencies and departments were ignoring the evidence gathered by the FBI, while the Administration used it as proof that Communist infiltration was not as widespread as the public had been led to believe.

In view of the extremely controversial character of these conclusions, it would be well to examine the machinery and operation of the loyalty program, before examining the charges against it.

THE LOYALTY PROGRAM IN REVIEW [1]

Since the promulgation on March 21, 1947, of Executive Order 9835 "prescribing procedures for the administration of an

[1] From "The Federal Loyalty Program: Background and Problems," by Roger S. Abbott, University of Michigan. *American Political Science Review*. 42:486-99. June 1948. Reprinted by permission.

employees' loyalty program in the executive branch of the government," there has been widespread discussion concerning the nature of disloyalty, its probable extent in the federal service, and the desirability of the loyalty program.

One point of view, among some members of Congress and elsewhere, is that this loyalty program does not go far enough to meet what is regarded as the serious menace of foreign (that is, Russian) directed or inspired subversives in the government. A sharply contrasting attitude, also voiced by a few Congressmen and by others, is that the menace is exaggerated for various reasons and that the program constitutes a "witch hunt" aimed at liberals generally and a dangerous attack upon civil liberties. Between these two extremes are gradations of opinion accepting the principle of the program but with reservations of varying intensity as to some of its standards and procedures, and with a watchful eye on its operation and on its effect within the federal service and outside.

Why has this issue of employee loyalty become so prominent? What are the main features and problems of the loyalty program and its possible consequences? Basic to a consideration of these questions is an understanding of the program's background.

While the Executive Order of 1947 inaugurated the first service-wide loyalty check in the Federal Government, disloyalty as a ground for dismissal is not an entirely new concept. It may be said generally to have been introduced in 1939 in a more restricted sense in the Hatch Act, in which membership in any organization advocating the overthrow of the constitutional form of government in the United States was made a ground for removal. Before that time, Civil Service Rule I of 1884, prohibiting questions concerning political or religious opinions or affiliations, was deemed to preclude a loyalty inquiry.

In 1940, the Civil Service Commission stated its policy not to certify for employment the name of a member of the Communist party, the German-American Bund, or any other Communist or Nazi organization. Similar language in appropriation acts, beginning in 1941, prohibited expenditures for salaries of such persons. Violations of these provisions by individuals were difficult to establish; the membership records of such groups generally did not exist or were kept secret.

A further congressional step was the appropriation of $100,000 to the Federal Bureau of Investigation in 1941 to investigate federal employees alleged to be "members of subversive organizations or to advocate the overthrow the Federal Government." The findings were to be reported to Congress. The FBI reports (without recommendations) were sent to the agency heads concerned, who exercised their discretion as to what administrative action, if any, to take. To advise the agencies in interpreting these complex reports and in developing procedures for handling the cases, the Attorney General, in April 1942, created an interdepartmental committee of four officials, aided by Justice Department staff.

The vague term "subversive organizations" not having been defined by Congress, Attorney General Biddle interpreted it to include not only groups advocating forcible overthrow of the government, but also those with Communist backgrounds or affiliations and Fascist, Nazi, Italian, and Japanese organizations. The list was not published, but descriptive memoranda concerning the groups were transmitted to employing agencies for confidential use. Significantly, the agencies were cautioned that none of the organizations were denounced as subversive *per se,* except for the Communist party and its affiliates, the German-American Bund, and "certain enemy-dominated organizations." With respect to the others, it was pointed out that there were circumstances requiring their inclusion within the scope of the inquiry, but that it would be "grossly unfair" to the persons charged with participating in them to place them arbitrarily in the same category with the Communist party and the Bund. Furthermore, the objective test of membership in a "front" organization was declared to be "thoroughly unsatisfactory" and to fail completely "where the purposes of the organization are so stated as to make membership in most circumstances consistent with loyalty." Activity, rather than membership, was to be stressed, and even this was to be but one of many matters to be considered. These qualifications are worth noting in the light of later developments in 1947.

The investigation of complaints against employees revealed, according to the Attorney General, that the "overwhelming majority" had been involved because their names had appeared on the active indices of Communist "front" organizations, in most instances for solicitation or mailing list purposes without their knowledge. This lead proved to be "utterly worthless" in "all but a small residuum of the cases." It was concluded on the basis of the inter-departmental committee's report that results were "utterly disproportionate to resources expended," and that the "futility and harmful character of a broad personnel inquiry have been too amply demonstrated." It was recommended that future investigations be limited to matters "clearly pertinent to the vital problem of internal security."

Nevertheless, a similar investigation was required in the appropriation act of July 2, 1942, for the Justice Department. This produced comparably negative results. No provision was made for subsequent inquiries, possibly due in part to the known reluctance of FBI Director Hoover to have his limited investigative resources diverted from other tasks at the height of the war. In any case, the statutory provisions proscribing the employment of "subversive" persons continued in force. Furthermore, the second interdepartmental committee, created in 1943 during the course of the second investigation by the Justice Department, continued to exist and to provide one of the legal means for processing loyalty cases. In the period July 1, 1942, to June 3, 1945, 6,193 cases under these provisions were referred to the FBI for investigation, culminating in 101 dismissals, 75 other administrative actions, and 21 resignations during the probe.

To complete this picture of actions on grounds of disloyalty prior to the loyalty program in 1947, brief reference may be made to applicants and appointees (prior to certification) concerning whose acceptance or rejection the Civil Service Commission has final authority. The Commission had a broader frame of reference than did employing agencies with reference to permanent employees. Its regulations permitted it to find applicants or appointees ineligible if there existed "reasonable doubt" as to loyalty.

During the period from July 1, 1940, to March 31, 1947, there were only 1,313 rulings of ineligibility where disloyalty was a major factor, out of a total of 43,811 ratings for all causes.

This tabulation, however, was qualified by the fact that the Commission had resources during this period to investigate only 395,000 out of a total of 7,000,000 placements.

Notwithstanding these efforts by the executive branch to keep out or remove disloyal persons, concern was expressed in Congress as to the lack of uniformity of procedures for handling loyalty cases and the absence of central responsibility for action. Despite favorable developments in the war to 1946, this criticism increased and resulted in House approval of a general study of the problem, and in hearings by a subcommittee of the House Civil Service Committee from January to July 1946. The committee's report led to the creation in November 1946 of the President's Temporary Commission on Employee Loyalty, composed of six leading executive officials and instructed to inquire into the standards and procedures for investigating employees and applicants and for removing or disqualifying any "disloyal or subversive" person.

After receiving written responses to special letters sent to the FBI and the military intelligence services, and to general letters directed to fifty executive agencies, and after hearing statements in executive session by the Attorney General, the Assistant Director of the FBI and the chairman of the Interdepartmental Committee on Loyalty Investigations, this Commission prepared a report with recommendations dealing with general standards for ascertaining disloyalty and with procedures for investigating the employees in the executive branch and for handling cases. These recommendations were incorporated directly in Executive Order 9835.

With reference to the earlier efforts, the Commission concluded that they were well intended but were "ineffective in dealing with subversive activities which employ subterfuge, propaganda, infiltration, and deception." It expressed its belief, however that "the vast majority of federal employees are loyal," but that "some" are subversive or disloyal. The number of these was difficult to assess "because of the secretive manner and method of their operation." It concluded that "whatever their number, the internal security of the government demands continuous screening . . . of present and prospective employees.

The presence . . . of *any* disloyal . . . persons . . . presents a problem of such importance that it must be dealt with vigorously and effectively."

The facts presented to the Commission did not enable it to determine the extent of such a threat to our system of government. Nevertheless, it believed that the recent Canadian espionage exposé, the Communist party line activities of some of the leaders and members of a government employee organization, and current disclosures of disloyal employees provided "sufficient evidence to convince a fairminded person that a threat exists."

To provide adequate protection for the security of the government, the Commission suggested two mutually dependent lines of attack. Unless both were carried out, this basic objective could not be achieved. The first was described as "the counter-espionage phase of counter-intelligence . . . designed to protect our government from all types of espionage infiltration by the penetration of enemy and subversive networks." The second was identified as the barring of disloyal persons from the government— "counter-intelligence in its defensive rather than offensive aspect."

Although the Commission especially stressed the first approach and warned against a "disproportionate preoccupation with the question of employee loyalty alone," it did not consider means for its implementation, since the Commission's frame of reference had not included that question. The subsequent loyalty program appears to have been designed mainly in terms of the second approach.

The broad purpose of the loyalty program enunciated by the Commission and adopted in the preamble of the Executive Order is twofold: not only to afford "maximum protection . . . [to] the United States against infiltration of disloyal persons into the ranks of its employees," but also to afford "equal protection from unfounded accusations of disloyalty . . . [to] the loyal employees of the government." To this second official objective may be added, think some observers, the assumption that the program was undertaken in part to forestall more drastic action against employees by Congress.

Whether or not this belief is correct, the sweeping accusation sometimes heard that the loyalty order is an intentional attack upon the employees' civil liberties appears untenable. Actually, the order proposed the first general and fairly orderly procedure, with provision for appeal, made mandatory as a prerequisite to dismissal on grounds of disloyalty. The possible unintended effects of the program on civil liberties and the quality of the federal service present another question, examined briefly at the conclusion of this article.

The standard of disloyalty set forth in the order consists of the general test that "on all the evidence, reasonable grounds exist for belief that the person involved is disloyal to the government of the United States." Six "activities and associations" may be considered. In brief, these are (1) sabotage and espionage; (2) treason or sedition or advocacy thereof; (3) advocacy of revolution or force to alter the constitutional form of government of the United States; (4) intentional, unauthorized disclosure of confidential documents under circumstances indicating disloyalty; (5) acting so as to serve the interests of another government in preference to the interests of the United States; (6) "membership in, affiliation with, or sympathic association with any foreign or domestic organization [or] association . . . designated by the Attorney General as totalitarian, Fascist, Communist, or subversive. . . ."

This part of the order has evoked considerable criticism largely focused on the sixth point. Some questions have been raised about the wording of other points which could lead to undesirable and probably unintended interpretation, but limitations of space preclude their analysis here. The opposition to the sixth point has generally centered on the vagueness of the terms, the possible implication of "guilt by association," and the seemingly unrestricted authority assigned to the Attorney General.

The indefiniteness of the words used is undeniable, and it may be doubted whether specific and completely satisfactory definitions could be evolved for them. A further potential difficulty was seen in the order's failure to indicate that the "sympathetic association" must be with the portion of the organization's program making it "subversive," assuming that some of its objectives might be worthy. Although the language of the order would not necessarily preclude a violation of the fundamental American legal doctrine of punishment only for personal guilt, subsequent official assurances have been given in this connection.

Discussion of the power (or onerous duty) given to the Attorney General concerning organizations has emphasized that they were not granted open hearings with an opportunity to defend themselves, and that no provision was made for publication of the list of organizations so designated, so as to permit employees to be fully informed as to the government's attitude concerning them.

The former criticism has received no official rebuttal or explanation other than the statement that the executive order contains no authorization for hearings. The latter question has been answered. After months of study of voluminous files on more than three hundred organizations by a staff of Justice Department lawyers said to number as many as thirty, Attorney General Clark finally on November 24, 1947, transmitted a list of designated organizations, as required by the executive order, to the chairman of the Loyalty Review Board, who published it on December 4. The Attorney General explained that the FBI investigative reports were correlated and that memoranda on each organization were prepared and reviewed by the Solicitor General, the Assistant Attorney General, and Assistant Solicitor General, and by himself.

Notwithstanding this screening process, and the Attorney General's qualification that it is possible that many loyal persons belong to the groups, the list received considerable comment, some finding it too restricted or too inclusive. The list included forty-seven groups named in 1943 for reference only by executive agencies; thirty-three newly designated organizations (including several affiliates of the Communist party and of the Civil Rights Congress) ; and eleven schools, said to be adjuncts of the Communist party. The accompanying letter noted that the list was neither complete nor final. A number of small and local groups were not included; many were not added because the available information was insufficient. Others, innocuous at the time, might become dangerously infiltrated, and new ones might be formed.

The first legal challenge to this action was made by one of the designated organizations, the Joint Anti-Fascist Refugee Committee. Mr. O. John Rogge filed suit in its behalf in a federal district court in Washington, D.C., in February 1948, charging that the executive order violated due process by depriving the organization of a hearing. It was alleged that the Committee had suffered such damages as loss of tax-exempt status, financial backers, and friends.

The operation and procedures of the loyalty program may now be outlined. The program was not actually started until August 1947. Additional funds were sought in May after a Budget Bureau study, but Congress did not act on the request until late July. One reason for the delay was the consideration of a bill introduced by Representative Rees to replace the executive program. This measure adopted substantially the same standards as the executive order, but altered the procedures in such a way as to arouse doubt by executive officials as to its administrative feasibility and its probable cost. It was passed by the House, but not reported from committee in the Senate.

At the end of July, the executive program was granted $11,000,000, and in August it was begun. The preliminary servicewide check required each of the approximately two million employees to be finger-printed and to answer a short questionnaire, designed only for identification purposes. Contrary to popular impression, it did not involve any attesting of loyalty or disclosure of membership in political organizations. The occasional highlighted refusal to answer has represented, not an attempt at concealment, but a general protest against the program.

The next step was the transmission of these completed questionnaires to the FBI for a file check to determine the existence of "derogatory information." If none is found, there is no further investigation, and the form is returned with such notation to the Civil Service Commission and then forwarded to the employing agency. However, if some data or allegations which might have relevancy to loyalty are revealed, the Bureau then undertakes a "full field investigation" of the individual.

At the outset of the program, it was estimated that approximately two per cent of the names would produce such a question.

On March 16, 1948, however, FBI Director Hoover announced that 1,005,944 names had been cleared and that only 777 full investigations had been instituted. Of these, 170 had been completed, resulting in 33 determinations of loyalty and 94 adverse findings.

After such an investigation has been made, the agent's report is subjected to review at several levels within the FBI. If there is an adverse finding and it is approved by the Bureau, the report is sent to the appropriate agency loyalty board, composed of not fewer than three persons. If this board's examination of the report, possibly supplemented by information obtained from the employee, results in an adverse determination, a letter of charges is sent to the employee. This document contains the charges in factual detail "so far as security considerations will permit" and a statement of the employee's right to answer them in writing within ten days and of his right to have an administrative hearing, in which he may appear, be represented by counsel, and present evidence. The hearing is private, and a copy of the transcript of proceedings is furnished to him.

If the finding after hearing is adverse, the employee may be suspended, but he then has the right of further appeal within ten days to the agency head. The latter, or his designee, may fix the scope and extent of the hearing. A third appeal within twenty days after receipt of final decision may be carried to the central Loyalty Review Board. The membership of this Board, authorized by the executive order, was announced on November 8, 1947, by the Civil Service Commission after the list of twenty members had been approved by the President. The members are private citizens, meeting from time to time and serving without compensation. The membership was subsequently increased to twenty-three, with a potential total of twenty-five. The Board is representative of a broad cross section of the public and includes several prominent professors of political science, lawyers, and others. The Board held its first meeting on December 3, resulting in the development of a statement of principles and procedures for itself and for the agency and regional boards, which was issued on December 17.

Appeal to this Board may also be made by an applicant for federal employment after he has had recourse to the appropriate regional loyalty board, created and staffed by the Civil Service Commission in fourteen regions. The procedures are similar to those followed by the agency boards. The name check, instituted for all applicants after September 30, 1947, is conducted by the Civil Service Commission and is required, by the executive order, to be made against not only the files of the FBI and of the Commission, but also those of the military intelligence agencies, the House Committee on Un-American Activities, local law enforcement agencies, schools and colleges of the applicant, his former employers, reference given by him, and other appropriate sources.

If "derogatory information" is produced by this check of an estimated 500,000 applicants per year—which might occur in 2.6 per cent of the cases, according to an early Commission estimate—a "full field investigation" is made by the FBI.

The time which will probably be required for adjudication and appeal of such cases is uncertain. With reference to employee appeals, assuming that they are carried to the central board, the maximum time for an individual case has been estimated at ninety days. The handling of all appealed employee cases should be completed by October 1949. It is believed, however, that few cases—perhaps 20 per cent at the most of those in which there are original adverse determinations—will reach the top level. A large proportion of the cases will probably be "washed out" by the agency boards or heads—that is, the persons will either be cleared or the charges against them may be so convincing that they will not appeal. Thus the major work load may fall on the agency boards. The relatively few cases reaching the top board will be assigned to hearing panels whose decisions may be reviewed by the full board at its discretion.

The central Loyalty Review Board, however, is expected to set the general tone of the loyalty program and, in the words of its chairman, to "do its utmost to see that justice is done, that individual rights are protected as fully as may be." A basic dilemma was presented to it in the fact that the FBI report is vital to the entire program and that the Bureau has stated that if confidential sources are involved, their disclosure would greatly reduce the Bureau's resources. Director Hoover has declared that his agency is charged "more primarily with the security of the country from espionage or sabotage," and that it is necessary to have certain informants who will furnish data of very secret character whose disclosure would be detrimental to such security. Such sources he will not identify. Two other types of informants, he has stated, can be revealed. These are the "contact type" (who may be a lawyer, Congressman, or prominent business man) and the "next-door neighbor or fellow employee." Even in such instances, however, the informants' identity could be revealed only upon the basis of their previous consent. If such were sought, he doubts whether much information could be obtained. Nevertheless, the possibility of personal grudges and malicious rumor should be considered.

According to the original view of the chairman of the Board, it will probably not be practicable to permit cross examination "in the great majority of cases." On the other hand, it is said that a FBI representative will be available to evaluate for the hearing board the reliability of the confidential source. Furthermore, the disadvantage to the employee of non-confrontation of witnesses will be considered in the adjudication. An additionally stated justification of this policy is that, legally, the government is entitled to discharge any employee for reasons which seem sufficient to it and without granting any hearing.

Although technically the constitutional guarantee of confrontation in criminal prosecutions does not apply, the case for its use presented "grave considerations" to the Board. Serious critics, while accepting the FBI explanation, have suggested that although confidential informants may be used in the investigation, the record used by the board could be restricted to the testimony of those who could be confronted and examined—a procedure somewhat comparable to that necessarily used in some narcotics, sedition, and immigration prosecutions, even though conviction may be rendered more difficult.

A more fundamental rebuttal is made to the point that government employment is a privilege rather than right. The possible consequences of a finding of "disloyalty," or perhaps even of an unfounded allegation thereof, on the individual's future employment prospects—private as well as public—and on his reputation cannot be overemphasized.

This problem has been underlined with reference to a segment of the loyalty question outside the scope of the program instituted by Executive Order 9835. The State, War, and Navy Departments have the statutory power to remove summarily any employee "in the interest of national security." This was given to the two military agencies in 1942 and extended to the State Department in 1946 on the assumption that these are more sensitive to the destructive influence of disloyal persons.

The severe consequences potentially inherent in the use of this authority became clear in the highly publicized instance of the dismissal of ten State Department employees as "security risks" on June 23, 1947. The charges were not specified, on the ground that they were based upon highly classified material. Following the establishment of formal appeal precedures with the Department in July and review of the cases, three were permitted to resign without prejudice. After considerable press criticism, an appeal in their behalf by three prominent former administrative officials, and a determination that the newly created Loyalty Review Board did not have jurisdiction in the matter, the Department on November 17 allowed the other seven to take similar action. Its statement recognized the factor of a "possible injustice" to them (in terms of employment opportunity) if such were not done.

An appraisal of the validity of the State Department's position in this entire situation will not be attempted; nor is it feasible to examine here the confused and seemingly partial statistical picture of dismissals made under this authority by the military agencies. While more recent developments seem to indicate that appeal to the Loyalty Review Board may be granted in such cases, and that the accused will be informed generally of the charges—except perhaps in "extreme" cases—a problem appears to remain. The wisdom of the use of the very inclusive term "security risk" has been seriously questioned. In defining this phrase on October 7, 1947, the State Department lumped together loyalty considerations with character weaknesses, such as habitual drunkenness.

It has been asked whether it is just, or even necessary, to remove an employee from a "security" position by means of such a charge if there is no imputation of disloyalty, certainly a more serious blot than some more common character weakness. The necessity of such a method of removal, even assuming that the dismissal may be essential where a "security" position is involved, has been doubted, in view of the already established legal basis for discharging such persons. Whatever may be the technical considerations, the expression "security risk" seems to imply in the public mind, a basic element of disloyalty. At the least, the two labels should be clearly distinguished.

A final and perhaps most fundamental problem arising from the entire loyalty program is the effect it might have on the freedom of expression and the caliber of the federal service. This psychological factor is intangible and perhaps immeasurable. However, it has been emphasized that we live in difficult times and need bold, imaginative persons in government. In the field of atomic and other scientific research—to cite merely one area of governmental responsibility—it has been said that we need the free-thinking scientist, sometimes tending to be unorthodox. Although unquestionably loyal, he might be deterred from public service because of the risk of being misunderstood or branded.

The ultimate hope for preventing such an atmosphere may lie in the Loyalty Review Board. Demoralization, apprehension, and encouragement of negativism and mediocrity in government can be checked only if there is confidence in the fairness, courage, and broadmindedness of those who have final responsibility for administering the loyalty program.

LOYALTY REVIEW BOARD [2]

Once the sensational headlines of the congressional spy probe have faded, the inquiry is expected to result in more effective application of the Federal Government's loyalty review check.

A report just made public by the Loyalty Review Board, headed by Seth Richardson, Assistant Attorney General under

[2] From "Loyalty Checks Enhance Stature at Spy Trials," newsstory. *Christian Science Monitor.* 40:10. August 7, 1948. Reprinted by permission.

former President Hoover, shows that the board, set up last October, has already declared fifty-four persons subversive and had caught up with the two persons still employed who were named by Elizabeth T. Bentley as having furnished information to a wartime Communist spy ring.

Nevertheless, the investigation has indicated that some agency chiefs have been too "soft" in dealing with employees whom the FBI and even the Loyalty Review Board have accused of having ties with Communist or Communist-front organizations. They are likely to pay more attention to disloyalty charges in the future and not put suspected persons in jobs where they handle secret information or make policy.

The Loyalty Review Board report, placed in evidence before the Ferguson subcommittee of the Senate, investigating the case of William W. Remington, suspended Commerce Department employee, shows that the board was active in all but eleven federal agencies during the month of July. Its greatest activity was in the Navy Department where fifty persons were declared subversive and fifty-three resigned while under investigation. Thirteen of the fifty appealed to the Secretary of the Navy. In four cases the loyalty board recommendation was not accepted, but in nine it was.

Out of approximately 2,000,000 federal employees in all parts of the country, 3,177 have had charges of disloyalty laid against them by the FBI. Of these, 2,449 have been forwarded to agency and regional review boards by the President's board, Lawrence V. Meloy, the Board's executive secretary told the Senate committee.

Altogether niney-eight persons have resigned from the Federal Government while under investigation. Next to the navy, the bulk of resignations were in the Federal Security Agency.

A new term has come into use in the capital to differentiate between agencies where loyalty investigation is of priority importance. Such agencies are described as "sensitive" agencies. Hereafter, it is expected that federal chiefs will be especially careful to see that persons of questioned loyalty are not put in "sensitive" jobs.

During July, the Loyalty Review Board was active in all but eleven federal agencies. These were the Civil Aeronautics Board, Council of Economic Advisers, Export-Import Bank, Federal Deposit Insurance Corporation, Federal Mediation and Conciliation Service, Federal Power Commission, General Accounting Office, National Capital Housing Authority, Office of Defense Transportation, Office of Selective Service Records, and the National Capital Parks and Planning Commission.

The procedure followed by the Loyalty Review Board is this:

An accused employee first comes before an agency loyalty board appointed by the head of his department. He is served with written notice of the nature of the charges in sufficient detail to enable him to prepare his defense. If the agency board recommends his removal, he is entitled to appeal to the head of his department. If the department head accepts the board's recommendation, the employee can appeal to the Loyalty Review Board. The Loyalty Review Board, on completion of its hearing, makes an appropriate recommendation to the department head.

The House Un-American Activities Committee in which the most startling spy disclosures have been made was in recess after hearing Alger Hiss, president of the Carnegie Endowment for International Peace and former State Department official, deny that he has ever been a Communist.

Acting Chairman Karl E. Mundt [Republican] of South Dakota, heightened the excitement that has wreathed Capitol Hill recently by announcing that a "mystery witness" has been contacted who will "break wide open" the story of the wartime Communist spy ring in a public hearing very soon. A strict blackout was imposed on the movements of committee investigators who are contacting the man who is expected to corroborate much of the testimony given the committee by Miss Bentley and Whittaker Chambers, a senior editor of *Time* magazine.

EFFECT OF CONGESSIONAL INVESTIGATIONS [8]

Rules for checking loyalty of federal employees have been tightened as the result of recent congressional investigations.

[8] From "Congress Probes Tighten Tests for Employee Loyalty," by Mary Hornaday, staff correspondent for the *Christian Science Monitor*. *Christian Science Monitor*. 40:1. August 28, 1948. Reprinted by permission.

The changes make it certain that a newly hired federal employee can be removed from the government pay roll with maximum speed if loyalty board investigation discloses that there is serious question about his loyalty.

In its inquiry into the case of William W. Remington, Commerce Department employee, accused by Miss Elizabeth T. Bentley of furnishing information to a wartime Communist espionage ring, the Ferguson committee of the senate has expressed amazement that an employee under Federal Bureau of Investigation suspicion could get the key job in the export division that Mr. Remington had.

Mr. Remington was only suspended by his chief after the Senate committee began to investigate him.

Under the new rule, each agency will be given a copy of the FBI report on its new employees as soon as the FBI completes its investigation. Heretofore, agencies have not been given FBI reports and employees have remained on the pay roll until the regional loyalty board reached a final decision on their loyalty.

On the basis of the report, the agency can take one of four courses:

It can retain the employee, if it feels the report shows him clearly loyal.

It can assign him to new duties, with less responsibility, pending a final determination of his loyalty.

It can send him home on annual leave.

Or it can suspend him.

Meantime, the Loyalty Review Board will continue with its investigation and make a final report to the agency on the employee's loyalty. . . .

The loyalty board never has pretended that it follows judicial procedure to the letter. For one thing, it does not allow the accused to see the transcript of charges made against him. The attitude of the Civil Service Commission has been all along that government employment is not a right, but a privilege to be extended only to persons of unquestioned loyalty. It insists that where reasonable doubt exists, the doubt must be resolved in favor of the government.

Statutory authority to exclude from the Federal Government all persons who advocate revolutionary overthrow of the government was not given by Congress until it passed the Hatch Act, which become law in 1939.

THE FBI PROCEDURE [4]

Among the rights an American citizen most cherishes are freedom of speech, including the freedom to criitcize his own government, and freedom to work for orderly progress and change. But along with his rights and freedoms he has certain responsibilities. His citizenship means personal observance of law and order, and adherence to the constitutional form of government above any other.

The thing that divides us most sharply from the totalitarians is this: the Communist, the Nazi, and the Fascist advocate and practice change by violence. Nobody can be loyal both to America and to one of those systems. With us, progress and change must be brought about by constitutional means.

Loyalty to America is something that cannot be imposed by laws prohibiting a list of specified acts. It comes from within, and springs from a sense of decency. There are certain tests for loyalty, however! The President's loyalty order applies only to government employees and applicants for government jobs.

The loyalty of federal employees is of the utmost importance. The Communist party . . . highly prizes members and fellow travelers when they are able to secure key government jobs. They would be in a strategic position to carry on espionage, influence policies, spread propaganda, recruit followers, and get other Reds into the federal service.

Among the first loyalty tests are these: Has the person engaged or tried to engage in sabotage or espionage, or knowingly associated with spies or saboteurs? Has he advocated or engaged in treason or sedition? Has he advocated revolution or force or violence to alter the constitutional form of our government?

[4] From "How the FBI Finds Disloyal Government Workers," by J. Edgar Hoover as told to Stacy V. Jones. *Liberty*. 25:14+ March 1948. Reprinted by permission.

As a federal employee, has he intentionally and without authority disclosed confidential information in circumstances indicating disloyalty? Or in performing his duties, has he put interests of another government above those of the United States?

Another consideration is a man's associations. Does he belong to or associate sympathetically with known subversive groups? Among the organizations designated by the Attorney General under the order are the Communist party, U.S.A., the Ku Klux Klan, and the Columbians.

The President's program is designed to eliminate disloyal persons now in the service and to keep others from getting in. Under the order, the Federal Bureau of Investigation is checking the names and fingerprints of all employees in the executive branch of the government against its files. The great majority, as was expected, show no unfavorable record. The names of several thousand government workers are being examined and cleared each day. Some evidences of disloyalty are being found. The number of disloyalty investigations is bound to reach a substantial figure by the time the survey covers the two million persons on the federal pay roll.

If its files indicate disloyal activities by any federal employee, the FBI makes a full field investigation, going deeply enough to establish the truth or falsity of the allegations, and reports the facts to the government department employing the person for such action as it cares to take. The facts may justify the employing agency in firing the worker, or establish that he is entirely innocent and has been the victim of gossip or mistaken identity.

Responsibility for employee loyalty rests with the various departments, and the FBI merely does the investigating. Each department and agency is required to have a loyalty board from whose decision the employee may appeal first to the department head and then to the Civil Service Commission's Loyalty Review Board. Special legislation has also given the "sensitive agencies" —State, Army, Navy, Air Force and Atomic Energy Commission—authority to dismiss disloyal employees summarily.

The case of Miss A shows the damage Communists can do. In 1945 and 1946 she was assigned to duties that gave her a chance to interview veterans returning from service. She told them they didn't know what they had been fighting for, that they weren't returning to a bed of roses, and that they were in for a surprise if they expected good jobs and pay. She was so rabid that her friends cautioned her. The FBI inquiry proved that she was a Communist party member. When interviewed, Miss A denied party membership, or indeed any Communist activity. She did admit having heard of the Communist party, and finally acknowledged that she was a member of American Youth for Democracy, which is successor to the Young Communist League.

Formally charged with Communist party membership and activities, she refused to face the loyalty board in her department and submitted her resignation. This document was a harangue typical of the Communist line.

> I refuse to continue any employment that levels charges against me [she wrote]. I will therefore not appear before the loyalty board because I know that under the presidential order a person is guilty unless he can prove to the board he is innocent. I know of nothing in the Constitution of the United States which allows such a procedure.

The Communist party is not a political party, but an international conspiracy, and its active members place alien ways of life above their citizenship obligations to the United States. Naturally they and their sympathizers were the first to raise cries of "witch hunt" and "Red baiting," and are doing their best to block the loyalty program. Some sincere citizens, too, are afraid that the loyalty order and its administration are threatening civil liberties.

A government job is a matter of privilege and not of right. Misunderstanding of this point has led to much of the current nonsense voiced about the program. The late Justice Oliver Wendell Holmes put it very neatly in 1891 when he was a member of the Massachusetts Supreme Court. A New Bedford policeman, discharged for prohibited political activity, had petitioned for reinstatement. In turning down the application, Justice Holmes remarked that "the petitioner may have a constitutional right to talk politics, but he has no constitutional right to be a policeman."

The FBI takes great care not to violate personal liberties. The special agents are instructed that their mission is neither to "get" nor to "whitewash" anybody. They make every effort to avoid throwing suspicion on innocent persons. The Bureau is strictly a fact-finding agency. It makes no recommendations or conclusions, and does not prosecute. The agents don't accept unsupported charges. One suspicious citizen reported that he was sure a neighbor of his, a government employee, was a Communist. Asked his reasons for believing so, he said that whenever the man left his apartment he deliberately walked on the grass, although a sign said plainly "Keep Off the Grass." The most dangerous Communists in positions of trust conduct themselves with propriety in small things, and are smart enough not to invite attention by breaking ordinances.

The mere fact that a federal worker once joined an organization that has turned out to be subversive is not of itself proof of disloyalty. Many Communist fronts publicly espouse aims with which nobody can quarrel, and carry in their titles words like "American," "Democratic" and "Peace," so that many innocent persons are led to join.

For example, in checking the names we ran across that of Miss B, who had been a delegate to the national convention of the American Youth Congress, which was declared subversive by the Attorney General under the Hatch Act in 1941. She had indeed attended the convention, the investigation showed, but throughout her whole life there was no evidence of any subversive activity, and the FBI presented facts to her employing agency that thoroughly established her loyalty.

Continued and knowing association with such groups, "flip-flopping" to follow the Communist party line, and open activity, like distributing literature, have given questionable background in many other cases.

The process of weeding out disloyal persons in the government begins when a questionnaire is made out for each worker on the pay roll. This lists his present government connection, personal identification data, etc. This is sent to the FBI with the employee's fingerprints. If they show nothing in the FBI files that reflects on his loyalty, his agency is so notified, and that is the last of the matter unless information or a complaint about him is subsequently filed with the FBI. Sometimes these check-ups uncover fingerprints which were taken in a routine way in connection with previous jobs.

Similar questionnaires and sets of fingerprints covering applicants for jobs are sent to the FBI for checking by the Civil Service Commission. The Commission looks into the records of military and other departments, the local police, schools and colleges, and consults former employers and references given by the applicants. If allegations of disloyalty are developed, the case is then referred to the FBI by the Commission for a full field investigation.

Complaints and information filed with the FBI in the past have turned up at times positive proof of subversive connections without resulting in any action by the departments in which the subjects were working.

If any of these persons are still on the pay roll, the inquiry will be reopened in the loyalty check.

Take the case of Mr. C, the holder of an important government position who was recruited by the Communist party in December 1943. He was assigned a party membership card on January 2, 1944, and we had its number. The next month, our investigation showed, he was busy recruiting new members, and agents recognized him at various meetings during the year. Under questioning, he admitted Communist party membership, but only from February to July 1944. The claim of having quit the party was untrue; and we so reported to Mr. C's department. The department, nevertheless, decided there was no basis for further action against him.

Since 1945 the Communist party has operated on two levels. On the upper, or open, level are the admitted members of the party. The lower level, or underground, was devised to conceal members in key occupations—government, public utility, educational, and so on. The underground consists of a number of parallel groups whose size and membership are known only to a few top-ranking party members.

In the fall of 1946, members holding government jobs were ordered into the subcellar. Instructions were sent from party headquarters to dissolve all parallels comprising government workers. Cards were ordered destroyed and their issuance was discontinued. The group heads were told to function in an informal manner and to make only occasional contacts with party leaders in New York City and elsewhere.

These undercover Communists in government may see one another occasionally at a dinner or social gathering, or a pair may meet as if accidentally on the street and walk together for a couple of blocks, dropping in somewhere along the way for a cup of coffee or a drink. These maneuvers have all the trappings of a spy melodrama.

Many suspected persons resign under investigation without waiting for departmental trials. One government agency questioned the loyalty of an employee because in 1934 he had made pro-Russian statements. That is a good many years ago, and his later record might have cleared it up. The investigators got as far as verifying the fact that he had made such statements in 1934, when he resigned. There was nothing to do but close the case.

Often the source of allegations is vindictive. For example, charges were recently made that Mr. E, a skilled technician on a very confidential project, believed in the philosophy of national socialism, was sympathetic to Germany, and had argued that the history of the United States paralleled that of the Reich. He had been born in Yugoslavia and had been naturalized here. The source of the charges could not cite any overt act. A number of Americans who had known Mr. E ever since he came to the United States told our agents that he was loyal.

It developed that the informant was prejudiced against foreigners, and disliked Mr. E in particular. He had concluded that since Mr. E had criticized President Roosevelt and other government employees, he must be a Nazi.

Often the FBI cannot reveal the source of its information because that would cut off further valuable data about the same or other cases. Sometimes the informant, for his own reasons, asks that his name be kept out of it, and the FBI has to respect his confidence or the government would be deprived of his information. If he were called as a witness at a departmental trial, he would not be protected by a subpoena, as he would be in a court. When an informant's name cannot be used, the agent evaluates the reliability of the source.

So far as possible, oral information of a derogatory nature is reduced to writing and signed. If necessary, it can be passed on without a signature.

Although the FBI work is done with impartial thoroughness, it is most gratifying to me to be able to clear a person's name. The case of Mr. F, who holds an important job, is unique. He appealed for an FBI investigation because he thought the fact that he had a Communist brother would bring him under suspicion in the loyalty inquiry and embarrass his agency. The brother had put him through college, and Mr. F had paid the debt by setting his brother up in business. A complete investigation, going back to his college days, disclosed that Mr. F had a very creditable civilian and war record, and had often tried to change his brother's viewpoint. A report to the agency for which he worked fully established his loyalty.

The employee loyalty investigation is only one phase of the FBI's security operations. It also investigates espionage and sabotage, applications for Atomic Energy Commission jobs, and violations of the Atomic Energy Act. In all its security work it places great reliance on the cooperation of loyal Americans.

USE OF THE EVIDENCE [5]

The FBI is not a secret police organization in the European sense of the word. Mr. Hoover and his agents dig into situations upon order of the Attorney General, who reports to the President. Once they have gathered evidence, the use made of that evidence again depends upon decisions of the Attorney General or of the head of some other government agency that is affected. The decision can be to ignore the evidence or to use it as the basis

[5] From "Is FBI's Anti-Spy Evidence Wasted?" newsstory. *U.S. News & World Report.* 25:15-16. August 27, 1948. Reprinted by permission of *U.S. News & World Report,* an independent weekly magazine on national and international affairs published at Washington. Copyright 1948, United States News Publishing Corporation.

for prosecution or as reason to fire a government worker from his job. . . .

It is the FBI that supplies information to departments of government concerning employees supposed to be disloyal, or supposed to be members of subversive organizations. FBI reports, however, are not always acted upon. In some cases, persons named by FBI reports, or who are under investigation by FBI, have been given promotions or have been hired by other departments after information had been provided to departments hiring them. Two examples are provided to show what sometimes happens when FBI reports or investigations are ignored.

In a recent case, William Remington held three different jobs in the government where confidential information was available to him while he was under investigation by the FBI and the New York grand jury. . . .

In another case, the FBI was called upon to investigate charges against a government employee and submitted evidence that the man was a member of the Communist party.

The employing agency, however, conducted its own investigation and retained the man on the ground that he was a loyal and trusted employee. Later, the employee transferred to another agency. After working there a while, he resigned, with the announcement that he was taking a job as organizer for the Communist party. Subsequently, he was appointed to the party's National Committee, one of the top Communist jobs in this country. Under party rules, no Communist can serve on the Committee unless he has been a member in good standing for at least four years. There were some red faces after that incident.

The government's program of protecting itself from disloyal employees stems from an executive order issued by President Truman in March 1947. As long ago as May 1942, the then Attorney General Francis Biddle, held that the Communist party believes in and advocates overthrow by force and violence of the government of the United States. Mr. Truman held in his executive order that employment by the government of disloyal or subversive persons constituted a threat to democratic processes. As a result, loyalty tests now are made of all persons hired by the government.

The loyalty program, in actual practice, works out like this:

Applicants for jobs are investigated by the Civil Service Commission or some other designated department or agency. Much of this work is delegated to the FBI. The idea is to bar from employment any person who could be considered disloyal by reason of sabotage or espionage; treason or sedition; favoring revolution by force to overthrow the government; desire to serve a foreign government instead of the United States Government; or membership in, affiliation with or sympathetic association with any organization designated by the Attorney General as subversive, Fascist or Communist.

Those already employed also are subject to investigation. Heads of departments and agencies are held responsible for retaining only loyal employees. They may appoint loyalty boards to hear testimony and make recommendations. Workers under suspicion are entitled to hearings and written notice. Two appeals are open to them if the loyalty board recommends that they be fired. First appeal is to the head of the department or agency. A second appeal may be made to the Loyalty Review Board of the Civil Service Commission, which is the supreme court of the program.

Some disloyal employees have turned up as a result of the thousands of investigations conducted since the program was started more than a year ago. Latest official figures place at about 140 the total number of workers who have been fired or who have resigned after their loyalty had been questioned. Another 438 resigned while they were under investigation.

Congressional committees, inquiring into the progress of the program, are not satisfied that disloyal employees are being rooted out as fast as they should be. Their own investigations produced the spy stories that have been making headlines recently. From these investigations, the committees hope, there may emerge legislation tightening the espionage laws and making it easier to track down Communists. The investigations themselves, with their charges and denials, have pointed up the difficulty of determining who is loyal and who is not.

AEC INTERIM PROCEDURE [6]

Under the Atomic Energy Act, an FBI investigation and report to the Commission is required on the character, associations and loyalty of each employee of the Commission, and also on each employee of Commission contractors or licensees who is to have access to restricted data. The act thus requires that the investigation go beyond the question of loyalty, and include character and associations as well. The FBI reports on investigations are submitted to the Commission for the Commission's consideration in determining whether security clearance is to be granted.

The AEC stated that the present Interim Procedure is used in cases where a hearing has been determined to be appropriate because some information in the file has raised a question concerning the eligibility of the individual for security clearance. The Commission emphasized that the hearings are not considered to be in the nature of prosecutions, but are inquiries which will enable full development of relevant facts. The hearings thus play an important part in carrying out the security responsibilities of the Commission in a manner which will protect the atomic energy program and at the same time protect the individual concerned.

The basic points underlying the procedure may be summarized as follows:

1. The individual is notified at the outset of the reported information which has created a doubt as to his eligibility for security clearance. The statement furnished to the employee is prepared in as much detail as is possible, within security limitations, to enable the individual to present whatever facts he thinks may be relevant to amplify, explain, or correct the items reported.

2. The hearings are held before local boards of three members, designated, if the case arises in the field, by the appropriate Manager of Directed Operations, or, if the case arises in Washington, by the Assistant General Manager of the Commission. In the conduct of the hearing, the Board gives the individual

[6] From "AEC Interim Procedure for Local Security Boards," announcement made by the Atomic Energy Commission, May 20, 1948. *Bulletin of the Atomic Scientists.* 4:198. July 1948. Reprinted by permission.

an opportunity to present whatever information or witnesses he wishes, to examine witnesses, and to be represented by counsel. The Interim Procedure recognizes the fact that, because of the necessity of protecting confidential sources of information, it may not be possible for the employee to confront the persons who have reported information which may be derogatory to him. Within this limitation, the Commission is making every effort to have the information developed at the hearing as complete as is possible, and to give the employee fullest possible notice concerning any possibly derogatory information which may be contained in the file.

3. The local board makes a recommendation to the local manager, who, in turn, makes a recommendation to the General Manager of the Commission. If, after considering all of the factors, the local board is of the opinion that the granting of security clearance will not endanger the common defense and security of the United States, the board so recommends. In the event of an adverse recommendation, the employee is notified that he has a right to appeal to the Commission's Personnel Security Review Board, of which former Justice Owen J. Roberts is Chairman.

The entire proceedings at the hearing are taken down verbatim and transcribed into a written record, a copy of which is furnished to the employee.

The Commission said that the procedure is designated an Interim Procedure because it is intended to revise it in the light of practical experience in handling cases which are now pending before local boards. The Commission added that, in the interest of protecting the personal rights of employees involved in cases, it is the Commission's policy to refrain from any public comment upon individual cases.

SUCCESS OF AEC LOYALTY PROGRAM [7]

The Atomic Energy Commission makes the reassuring statement that the essential secret of the atomic bomb remains unviolated. . . .

[7] From "Great Precautions Taken to Guard Atomic Secrets," by Anthony Leviero, special correspondent for the *New York Times*. *New York Times*. 98:E5. September 26, 1948. Reprinted by permission.

Under the Commission regime, about fifteen of its employees have been summoned for hearings before personnel security boards. Most of these have not been completed, but such cases involve accusations concerning character and association with subversive groups or persons, and not with the theft of atomic secrets.

Security on the atomic project, as it is described by Commission spokesmen, is elaborated as thoroughly as it is possible to do so without frustrating either the employee or atomic development.

Apart from imposed safeguards, the atomic project is inherently strong because of its very complexity and newness. There is not merely an atomic secret. There are literally thousands of atomic secrets. The bomb itself is the greatest of all. Involved in its manufacture, however, are innumerable new formulas, processes and materials, many of which are important secrets in themselves.

It is the aim of the present security system to protect all of these many component secrets, which may be comprehended in the term "American know-how." For in the domain of science, there no longer is any secret about the basic theoretical science of atomic fission.

Under the principle of compartmentation, the worker is fenced in, physically and mentally. He operates in a strictly limited field.

Atomic scientists, accustomed to the untrammeled exchange of ideas in the pre-atomic age, complained bitterly of this compartmentation when they were freed of wartime restraints. They insisted that the extreme degree of separation within and between projects prevented an interchange of knowledge which might have hastened the production of the atomic bomb.

Whatever the merits of the controversy, compartmentation is a fundamental element of security and still prevails, but to a lesser extent than during the war, on the atomic project. The atomic worker is allowed to know only what he needs to in his particular operation.

Of necessity, higher officials possess the knowlege which bridges these compartments.

The personnel security system of the Commission is designed to detect the applicant with tainted character and loyalty and to bar him from its jobs. Every job applicant is investigated for the Commission by the Federal Bureau of Investigation.

The employees are rechecked periodically so that those who may have been corrupted after they came on the job can still be detected.

The investigating operation is colossal, for not only must the approximately 5,000 Commission employees be investigated, but also all of the 55,000 employees of private contractors of the Commission who handle restricted material.

Thus far the FBI has had to conduct 109,000 investigations for the commission, at a cost of about $100 each. Besides, the G-men have had to investigate all of the employees held over from the Manhattan Engineer District. . . .

A Commission spokesman estimated that it takes a total of about sixty days to complete the FBI investigation and the Commission's own screening of each employee.

Lieutenant General Leslie R. Groves, producer of the atomic bomb, recently said the Manhattan District hired more than 600,000 persons and that one could not expect every one of them to be perfect. The handful of persons arrested for violation of security and those named thus far by the Un-American Activities Committee as spy suspects were among that 600,000.

The evidence to date, however, is that even with some "unperfect" people, no critical secret has escaped, for the Commission states that no significant data pertaining to the bomb itself have leaked out or been violated. The few arrested have been former soldiers who merely kept photographs of restricted material as souvenirs.

LOYALTY VERSUS CIVIL RIGHTS

DISCUSSION

The federal loyalty program opened up a number of significant questions which had a definite bearing on the ultimate effectiveness of the program.

One of the first was the definition of loyalty itself. Under the President's Loyalty Order the basis of disloyalty was left pretty much to the enforcement officials, and could mean serious infringement of individual liberty.

Others revolved around the extra-legal concept of "guilt by association," the secret character of the charges, and the natural consequences of unjust accusations.

Much of the discussion has been favorable, constructive criticism, aimed in the direction of strengthening the loyalty program without invading the rights of the individual. The questions involve genuine problems of administration, although the fear of encroachment on civil rights is always present.

A PLEA FOR CAUTION [1]

There is still danger, however, in the thought which seems widespread that all the difficult problems presented by the loyalty cases can readily be solved by the provision for fair hearings before a loyalty board or a loyalty review board. Too little attention has been given to the question of how the requirements of the government for security and the requirements of the individuals concerned for fair play can in practice be reconciled. It is important to avoid confusing the two separate but related

[1] From "Loyalty Cases," a communication by Benjamin V. Cohen, formerly counselor of the Department of State, submitted to the *New York Herald Tribune* and the *Washington Post*, published by the *Washington Post*, December 18, 1947. Reprinted by permission.

problems which are involved in these loyalty cases. One is the problem of protecting the integrity of the government services where the security of the United States may be affected; the other is the determination of individual guilt or shortcoming.

Where the security of the United States is really concerned, any reasonable doubt ought to be resolved in a way that will protect the integrity of the government service. While it should not be possible to drive an official from public service simply by spreading rumors that he is a Communist or an associate of a Communist, there may be cases even where the responsible head of a department or the department's loyalty board is convinced of the trustworthiness of an individual and still the cloud of substantial suspicion that hovers about the individual makes it highly inexpedient to continue that individual in a strategic security position.

On the other hand, no individual should be stigmatized as disloyal or even as a poor security risk if there is any reasonable doubt as to his culpability. The branding of an individual as disloyal or a poor security risk may affect his life and livelihood no less seriously than his conviction for a serious crime.

A fair hearing in itself provides no easy way of reconciling the vital interests of the government and the vital interests of the individual. We must deliberately seek to develop procedure which will make it possible to protect the integrity of the service without stigmatizing individuals as disloyal or untrustworthy or even as being reasonably suspected of disloyalty or untrustworthiness.

The branding or punishment of individuals for disloyalty or breach of trust should be left for the court where the accused, in accordance with our common-law traditions, can be given the benefit of a jury trial and of every reasonable doubt.

Any individual in the government service who is satisfactorily performing his duties ought to have the right to resign without prejudice unless the evidence of disloyalty is such as to warrant prosecution by the Department of Justice. The duty of responsible administrative officials is to protect the intergrity of the government service, not to punish guilt or to proclaim suspicion.

If the responsible administrative head of a department or agency receives evidence of the disloyalty or untrustworthiness of an employee in a strategic position—that is, an employee who has power to make or influence decisions or has access to information which may affect the security of the United States—he should, of course, before taking final action, fully inform the employee of the charges against him and give him the opportunity to be heard with an appeal to a review board if the employee wishes it. But such proceedings, like grand jury proceedings, should be secret.

If the individual under suspicion is able to satisfy the administrative head that the charges against him are unfounded and that his continuance in the service would not be inimical to the best interests of the service, that should, of course, settle the matter. But if the individual under suspicion cannot meet this obviously onerous burden and the evidence against him is not such as to warrant prosecution by the Department of Justice, he should be given the right to resign without prejudice. If he does not do so, he should be transferred to a clearly non-strategic position or his employment should be terminated without prejudice.

Unless some such procedure is adopted, it will be difficult to protect adequately the security of the United States and at the same time protect adequately the traditional rights of the individual.

The government employees in strategic security positions may be fairly large in absolute numbers and they may range through segments of quite a number of departments and agencies, yet they are a relatively small part of the total government personnel. Individual investigation of the loyalty and trustworthiness of employees in strategic security positions is not only warranted, but is necessary. It is extremely difficult, however, to see the need for individual loyalty investigations of the myriads of other government employees who clearly do not fall within that category. . . .

We must see that those to whom matters vitally affecting the security of the United States are entrusted are unquestionably

loyal and trustworthy. But let us take care that in the name of
security we do not walk roughshod over the Bill of Rights and
exclude or drive from government those with inquiring, noncon-
forming minds.

THE NEED FOR ADDED SAFEGUARDS [2]

Investigation of "loyalty" did not begin with the executive
order issued by Harry Truman on March 21. As far as the
present generation of government employees is concerned, such
inquiries became systematic and widespread during the early
months of the Nazi-Soviet pact. They were carried on throughout
the war. In the war years the Civil Service Commission itself
investigated 395,000 employees. Of these 1,300 were removed
because there appeared "reasonable ground" for doubting their
loyalty. Approximately 700 of this group were in the Communist category. The FBI, Military and Naval intelligence, and
other groups staged similar inquiries. There were absurdities
committed, as anybody who inhabited wartime Washington
knows. Yet in perspective it may appear more significant that
we waged the most far-flung war in our history without even
faintly resembling a police state, that the sporadic "terror" was
usually more foolish than fierce, and that our liberties survived
the war without major scars.

All of which merely suggests that the fact of investigation
does not automatically breed a disastrous witch hunt, and that
a human equation—such as the presence of such conscientious
people as Arthur S. Flemming, Harry B. Mitchell, and Frances
Perkins as heads of the Civil Service Commission—can keep it
from going to excesses. But our wartime experience underlines
the nature of the risks involved and the character of the safeguards that must be invoked. From what we have learned it
now seems clear that the success or failure of the "loyalty" in-

[2] From "How to Rid the Government of Communists," by James A. Wechsler,
former staff member of *Nation* and *PM*, now in the Washington Bureau of the
New York Post. *Harper's Magazine*. 195:438-43. November 1947. Reprinted by
permission.

quiry will be determined by the resolution of these two unsettled questions:

1. Will accused employees receive protections that genuinely protect, inspiring the confidence of honest men rather than offering a field day for amateur and professional heresy hunters?

2. Will we evolve criteria of judgment that plainly differentiate nonconformists (on the left or right) from participants in underground conspiratorial movements run from a foreign capital or—as in the case of pro-Fascists—clearly identified with the now homeless Nazi international?

With respect to both questions the program enunciated by President Truman on March 21 was . . . unsatisfactory and inadequate. But the door is still wide open to elaboration and refinement of that order. A good many of the wiser officials in the capital have been sweating over these questions ever since the statement was promulgated. The important facts about contemporary Washington are that persons like Flemming, Mitchell, and Miss Perkins are deeply sensitive to the complexity of the issues and that the administration itself has shown little of the zeal for irresponsible persecution suggested by some of the more thunderous outcries on the left. Both Attorney General Clark and J. Edgar Hoover have manifested visible concern over liberal criticisms leveled against the terms of the program. While some conscientious detractors have hinted that this concern was "purely political," it is slightly gratuitous to complain when men in high office view liberal politics as sound politics.

As the loyalty machinery now operates more than a million federal employees will be subjected to at least routine review. (It is not true, as generally imagined, that all of them were investigated in wartime; tens of thousands went on the government pay roll in those hectic years without any scrutiny.) The FBI checks their names against its own records and all other current dossiers of subversion, including the notoriously unreliable files compiled by the peerless peep-hole artists of the House Un-American Activities Committee. If any "derogatory information" is revealed in any of these documents, the FBI conducts further inquiry, forwards a report—without recommendation—to the Civil Service Commission, which transmits the findings to the agency involved. If the administrator decides to act upon the data (and in the current political weather the pressure to do so will be strong) he must give the accused a summary of the charges, a chance to testify before counsel before a departmental review board, and an opportunity to seek personal review by the agency head. Then, finally, the case may be carried to a new, over-all Civil Service Commission review body which will presumably be composed of outstanding, disinterested citizens.

So far all this might be classified as progress; it formalizes heretofore shadowy rights of review and appeal and creates a supreme tribunal that is dependent on neither Congress nor government for favor. But the order also contains this crucial joker:

> The charges shall be stated as specifically and completely as, in the discretion of the employing department or agency, security considerations permit.

In effect this means that the FBI will retain its authority to decide how much of its case shall be disclosed. It means the victim may receive only the most fragmentary picture of the evidence on which he is being convicted and utterly no chance to confront the witnesses whose words may exile him from government.

The traditional defense for this course is that a security agency often cannot reveal the sources of its information—or even the full facts at its command—without permanently destroying the usefulness of its informers. Since stool pigeons are the key figures in most investigative cases, this explanation cannot glibly be thrown out of court.

But the exclusion of any man or women from government service is also serious business. Moreover, there are many cases in which informants are local janitors, women scorned, and village idiots who have no just claim to anonymity. Conceding that the problem isn't simple, the solution clearly rests in the hands of the proposed national review board and its regional counterparts.

This board must be empowered, in cases that it holds doubtful and inconclusive, to require the FBI to produce the full details of its findings and the witnesses from whom it was obtained. Admittedly this may make life tougher for the political G-men. But once again alternatives must be closely weighed.

The board's activities will also be gravely hampered if no records are kept of the lower-level hearings that precede final appeal. Each case will come up cold, with only the bare outline of general charge and categorical denial. All the previous appeals will be little more than waste motion.

Technically the decisions of the top board will be only "advisory." However, this is probably a verbal quibble, since few administrators will be likely to defy its conclusions, and most of them will welcome its existence as a powerful moral backstop for themselves.

Given these procedural weapons the review board can become a decisive restraint on reckless congressional clamor for a wholesale purge. It can help to take the issue of national security out of the dreary realm of partisan politics. It can give renewed courage to administrators who now defend the suspect at the risk of their own necks. And it can undermine the impression widely whispered in government circles that an argument with the FBI (or Congress) is a form of administrative suicide. For while the FBI reports are deadpan and no recommendation is set forth, their existence periodically "leaks" in wondrous ways. Congressmen can demand them and congressional "sources" are often remarkably outspoken.

Simultaneously the standards set forth in the order must be painstakingly clarified. Actually the Civil Service Commission made substantial progress in this direction during the war. Its progress may be nullified by some of the loose language in the loyalty order. Back in March 1942 President Roosevelt issued war service regulations which held that one of the grounds for disqualification for a federal employee was "the existence of a reasonable doubt of his loyalty to the government of the United States." But loyalty, as Professor Commager pointed out, has become a badly battered word. What we really mean is the existence of a competing allegiance so strong and clear that the person involved cannot be trusted inside a government office.

This problem is enormously complicated by emergence of the "fellow traveler" as a classic political phenomenon of our times. As the Canadian spy revelations showed, the fellow traveler may in some instances be just a well-intentioned fellow whose thoughts have been traveling along paths parallel to Communist lines; he may, however, be a clandestine party member who, for reasons of safety, is spared the formality of signing a party card.

Because the Communists, like the Nazis, have leaned so heavily on men who lead political lives, it is not enough to say that full proof of membership in the Communist party must be shown before any dismissal can occur. Under this criteria some of the most elusive and important Communist operatives might escape, while the clumsiest and least significant were apprehended.

In an effort to resolve this difficulty the loyalty order invoked the dangerous doctrine of guilt by association. The Department of Justice is now preparing a list of "proscribed" organizations held to be Communist and Fascist fronts. The Attorney General, in response to protests, has indicated that at least some of these organizations will be given a hearing before he hands down his ruling. But that doesn't settle everything. The crucial question is the significance that will be attached to membership in one of the organizations listed.

Mr. Clark might hold with some justification that the Southern Conference for Human Welfare has been utilized as a front for the Communists. Does that mean that Dr. Frank Graham, who has bitterly fought the Communists for control of the Conference but refused to abandon his membership in it, shall be barred from government employment? The question suggests the possible absurdity of the standard.

Mr. Flemming has indicated a far more plausible approach. "An employee will be dismissed only if evidence of membership in such an organization, *plus all the other evidence* in the case, leads to the conclusion that reasonable grounds exist for believing that he is disloyal to the government of the United States," he said recently. The order uses similar language, but it is later clouded by extensive reference to "association."

In effect Mr. Flemming is saying that the total pattern of behavior of the accused will be reviewed and a wide variety of human experience evaluated. Such subtleties are the qualities that distinguish reasonable inquiry from frenzied inquisition. Yet it should also be noted at this point that the Attorney General is given enormous "blacklist" authority, since membership in a front organization is the equivalent of at least one strike on the employee. Certainly the projected review board should have the right to make this final determination of "proscribed" groups, perhaps with the Attorney General occupying the role of prosecutor once he has reached his own decisions.

The recent dismissal of ten State Department employees— without hearings or even recitation of charges—forcibly dramatized the need for the safeguards outlined here. It also underlined what is not generally appreciated—that State, the military departments, and the Atomic Energy Commission run their own "purges" and more than 500,000 employees are thus not currently covered by even the limited protections of the President's executive order. State's arbitrary powers to fire (which the Department itself apparently reconsidered and modified in the case of the ten) derive from a congressional rider to its apropriation. The armed services invoke a wartime security statute. Atomic Energy similarly conducts its own security affairs by congressional sanction (or demand). There is little justification for this separation. The guarantees that preserve integrity and imagination in government are surely no less needed in the State Department than in agencies far removed from the diplomatic battlefield; and the same thing applies to the domain of the brass and braid.

There are some who contend that the whole loyalty program should be applied only to "sensitive" agencies, pointing out that the Labor Department or, let us say, the Fish and Wild Life Service would offer poor hunting ground for a foreign agent. Since military intelligence is primarily the art of correlating strangely diverse data, the argument is more entertaining than valid. Yet the review board might appropriately fix tighter standards for State, Atomic Energy, and the armed services than for clearly peripheral agencies. It could be plausibly argued that the "burden of proof" rests on the government in a non-security agency but that "reasonable doubt" would justify dismissal in the more strategic areas. It would also seem sensible to permit resignation without prejudice in any case short of an overt act.

In most of these matters the soundest course would be to let the review board draw these faint shadings rather than seek an advance blueprint.

The risks projected when police methods are applied to government will not be dissipated overnight even if the proposed review board consists of twenty of our wisest Solomons. Perhaps the most serious threat is the least tangible—the possibility that men in government will strive ostentatiously to conform, that the super-patrioteer will become a model public servant and the unorthodox mind will seek more congenial surroundings.

Dramatic and affirmative effort by the administration is plainly needed in view of the deepening demoralization in the government service. The caliber of the men appointed to the review board will decisively affect this atmosphere. They must command sufficient respect to withstand a change in national administration. They must dwarf the professional "know-nothings" in Congress. I know that such men are being earnestly sought. Their appointment must be accompanied by an emphatic clarification of the language used in the loyalty order, a swift assertion of the powers they will invoke, and a revised statement of the objectives of the inquiry.

With such moves the Washington air could be freshened. The petty bureaucrats who view the loyalty probe as a chance to plant knives in the back of competitors might be seriously discouraged; the citizen who wants to work for his government would no longer feel he was helpless prey for invisible informers. The "know-nothings" would promptly charge that the administration was "softening" again; the Communists would cry that these are empty bourgeois gestures. But the instinctive decency of American opinion would be crystallized. The same Gallup polls that show widespread support for exclusions of Communists from government also endorse full hearings for the accused.

The resilience of democratic society has repeatedly proved greater than the extreme right and extreme left have acknowledged. It faces a new test now. But on the basis of the evidence so far, the reports of democracy's death have once again been exaggerated. The loyalty program, despite a bad beginning, can still make sense.

LOYALTY TESTS AND GUILT BY ASSOCIATION [3]

Conflict in the policies of men and governments has become one of the authentic hallmarks of our time. It seems a commonplace to say that every day developments are occurring which, for generations to come, must inevitably affect the welfare of all mankind. Yet amid these grave mutations a few fundamental facts affecting the future of our nation stand out with clearness. One is that powerful and evil forces have been let loose against this nation and that the Soviet government, our recent ally whose friendship we sought, has chosen for the past two years to pursue an obstructive and unfriendly course. . . . Another fact that cannot be overlooked is that a warfare of ideas, accompanied by every deceitful device, is being waged against this country by propaganda and secret methods with which we are entirely unfamiliar, and with which, up to now, we have been unable to cope. Both of these developments present serious dangers for our country, not lightly to be dismissed . . . .

That our country has within its borders hostile agents cannot well be doubted. One of the most startling and, in a sense, appalling historical documents of our time is the Canadian White Book, relating the activities of Soviet agents in the Dominion of Canada and summarizing the evidence, including the confessions of participants. It is difficult to read that revelation without a sense of bewilderment at the unconscionable lack of ordinary standards of honesty and morality. Similarly, no one can read it without being convinced that there must have been,

    [3] From "Loyalty Tests and Guilt by Association," by John Lord O'Brian, lawyer, formerly general counsel for War Production Board. *Harvard Law Review.* 61:592-611. April 1948. Reprinted in *Bulletin of the Atomic Scientists.* 4:166-72. May 1948. Reprinted by permission.

and may still be, similar hostile activities being carried on in the United States. While it is to be regretted that the officials of our government having cognizance of these actions have not disclosed to us more of their nature, it seems nevertheless clear that the activities do, in fact, exist. The dangers from these activities are doubtless more serious and widespeard than they were in the years following the first World War. But from what is known of the established Communist techniques of deceit, we can scarcely hope to discover foreign agents or to detect their influence by means of wholesale inquisition of all persons in the federal service. . . .

One reason for the difficulties suggested is that they are implicit in the subject itself. All of us surely sympathize with the purpose of eliminating from public employment persons whose actions or advocacy constitute a real peril. We should not yield to emotion and too hastily condemn the loyalty order, and certainly we should give full support to the work of the Loyalty Board of Review, composed as it is of a group of unusually high minded and intelligent citizens. None of us want in positions of authority persons who are consciously advocating the overthrow of our institutions. On the other hand, if history in this field teaches anything, it is that any attempt to regulate or prescribe standards in the field of ideas should be taken with the utmost caution and only after profound study.

The question posed for present consideration is whether the measures which have been adopted, and others which are now being proposed, prescribing standards of loyalty, are either necessary or proper methods with which to carry on what must essentially be a battle of ideas. . . .

In determining the wisdom and effectiveness of the proposed measures, we should consider whether it is really necessary that secret investigations be made by government agents into the private lives of a million of our fellow citizens who happen to be in the public service. What is the ratio of the good results measured by the number of foreign sympathizers or truly disloyal persons thus discovered? . . . There are many who will support these new and proposed measures as desirable; but the price that we pay remains. No one familiar with the administration of a government department, however, can doubt that the mere existence of any law or order authorizing secret investigations will encourage suspicions, distrust, gossip, malevolent tale-bearing, character assassination and a general undermining of morale.

In considering the present agitation, one broad distinction should be recognized, based on the character of the dangers threatened. For example, searching examinations should obviously be made to determine not only the loyalty but the trustworthiness and even the emotional stability of that group of officials who, by reason of the strategic posts which they are to occupy, are in a position to betray secret information vital to the national security. The best example of this type is found in the personnel of the Atomic Energy Commission. The work of protecting secret information in an organization of that character presents problems separate and apart from the problem of detecting possible disloyalty in the vast number of run-of-the-mine employees and in those concerned with teaching. It is not intended to deal primarily with that problem at this time. Some of the conflicts evidenced in current discussions of what is broadly termed "disloyalty" arise from confusing this security problem with the problem of eliminating from the public service persons who hold treasonable views.

In most of the cases of alleged disloyalty or seditious conduct reported in the press, guilt or innocence has turned upon charges of association with other persons or with organizations tainted with suspicion. That is, these cases fall within the legal category of conspiracy. For this reason it is of first importance that in appraising methods dealing with disloyalty special attention should be given to the sinister developments which have been taking place in broadening the scope of our criminal conspiracy statutes and in the increasing acceptance of this doctrine of guilt imputed by association, so alien to our traditions. . . .

But this allusion to the broadening of the conspiracy statute is an allusion and nothing else. . . . Yet it may be largely responsible for our failure to take notice of the growing recognition in our law of the menacing doctrine of guilt by association, for

which traditionally we have had distrust amounting to abhor-
rence. There was no formal recognition of this doctrine in our
law prior to 1920. . . .

Congress for the past twenty-five years has been consistently
endeavoring to establish in our jurisprudence the doctrine of
guilt by imputation of belief, or "guilt by association." The
press reports of proceedings before certain of the congressional
committees during the last session of Congress corroborate this
assertion, and it may certainly be argued that the President's
loyalty order of March 21, 1947, gives it some support. Previously Congress had condemned "membership in" or "affiliation
with" a subversive group. The executive order considerably
expands this description. In prescribing standards its adds the
phrase "sympathetic association with." . . .

It may be left to others to discuss this order, including such
unprecedented features as the power conferred upon the Attorney General to designate *ex parte* organizations as subversive.
Only one broad aspect need be considered here—the administration of its provisions by secret investigations and secret reports. In fact, its enforcement makes necessary the use of these
devices of secrecy.

During the past quarter century Congress has seen fit to
authorize the establishment of investigating agencies of considerable size in various departments of the government. In particular it has steadily encouraged the expansion of the Federal
Bureau of Investigation as the chief over-all investigating agency
of the government. The questions here raised do not in any
way reflect or imply criticism of the integrity and conscientious
conduct of the chief of this agency or of any other investigating
agency. These comments are directed solely to the alleged necessity of maintaining these agencies on their present scale and with
their present characteristics.

Because the reports of these agencies are now to be the basis
for application of tests of loyalty or disloyalty by congressional
committees as well as by appointive or other administrative officers, their intrinsic character is a matter of first importance. The
public, generally speaking, has little or no knowledge of the way
in which information is gathered and the summary reports are

compiled. To understand the general character of these reports is all the more important because, as we have been repeatedly assured by the very efficient head of the Federal Bureau of Investigation, that agency simply reports the information without attempting to make or indicate any determination based upon the contents of the file. In other words, the Bureau reports what information it has obtained; it is then the function of the appointing officer to evaluate this information and form his own judgment as to the qualifications of the person investigated.

It is the function of every investigating agency to record all information, regardless of whether it is unreliable hearsay or authentic, which in any way may throw light upon the belief and personal character of the individual under investigation. This means that the typical file or dossier upon the individual investigated, in addition to the summary of the facts, usually contains other, miscellaneous information of varying degrees of importance. If conscientiously compiled it will contain not only information directly pertinent to the question of loyalty or disloyalty, but much incidental information as to private habits or lapses of moral conduct of the person investigated, as well as opinions of various anonymous persons on these subjects. In gathering information in such a great variety of fields, it is probable that much incidental information of fact and opinion is obtained and recorded regarding the lives of legislative, administrative and executive officials not directly under investigation. It seems reasonable to believe that the fact that assurances of secrecy are given to the persons questioned must sometimes lead to exaggeration. In many cases, also, agents in distant places seek answers to specific questions without knowing the purpose of the investigation, and there is consequent likelihood of irrelevant and misleading material being compiled therefrom. Because of the fact that ordinarily informants are not named, it is, to say the least, difficult for a reviewing officer to determine what weight should be attached to the statements made.

Because of the great variety of investigations in different fields, there exist today vast numbers of governmental secret dossiers filled with information as to the private lives and activities of public employees. In the course of its investigations into subversive and communistic elements, the House Committee on un-American Activities, according to public statements by its members, has listed in its files something between 600,000 and 1,000,000 persons and organizations. The Federal Bureau of Investigation must have hundreds of thousands of these individual files.

What must be the inevitable effect of this kind of institutional practice, with its secret investigations and vast numbers of secret dossiers, upon the freedom of the individual? Looking to the future, the Civil Service Commission estimates that the Executive Loyalty Order will necessitate clearing 1,466,000 cases through the FBI fingerprint and name files. The Commission has already flagged the names of 90,000 individuals after checking names of federal employees against FBI files which are supposed to contain some derogatory information. The Chief of the Bureau of Investigation estimates that the loyalty program will require investigation of charges of alleged disloyalty in 45,000 additional cases and also the check of the names and fingerprints in 2,181,108 cases. Thus, while the total number of files already in existence relating to private lives is unknown, it must, as above indicated, run into hundreds of thousands.[4]

To those citizens who maintain a lively and sensitive interest in protecting the civil rights of the individual, these astronomical figures, together with their implications, are, to say the least, disquieting.

Some may urge that a determination that the accused was in sympathetic association with a group designated by the Attorney General as subversive is not a finding of guilt against the accused, and that in any event no one has a vested right to public employment. But in practical effect the result of a finding of such asociation is analogous to that of a criminal conviction—loss of occupation, lasting disgrace to the individual, and a continued

[4] The FBI files are not the only ones to be examined. The loyalty order requires that: "An investigation shall be made of all applicants at all available pertinent sources of information." These sources are to include: FBI files, Civil Service Commission files, Military and Naval Intelligence files, the files of any other appropriate government investigative or intelligence agency, the files of the House Committee on un-American Activities, the local law enforcement files; also schools and colleges attended by applicant, former employers, references given by applicant and any other appropriate source. Exec. Order No. 9835, Part 1, Para 3, 12 Fed. Reg. 1935 (1947).

impairment of his ability to earn a livelihood. In fact, there is something peculiarly sinister and insidious in even a charge of disloyalty. Such a charge all too frequently places a stain upon the reputation of an individual which is indelible and lasting, regardless of his complete innocence later proved. Instances as far back as the first World War are easily recalled in which individuals loosely and falsely charged with disloyalty have never fully escaped from the effect of this attack upon their reputations.

Everyone who has had experience in the American public service knows that the overwhelming majority of employees in every branch of activity are self-respecting, loyal, patriotic and conscientious. What anxieties of mind, what prolonged periods of worry, what restraint upon their initiative will result from their knowledge that their private lives are being secretly investigated, no one can say. But neither can anyone assert that this shadow upon their activities, however intangible and subtle, will not act as a constraint upon their freedom and their sense of independence. Apparently we have departed a long way from the admonition to beware of treading too closely upon the borders of freedom of conscience.

There are political considerations also which must result from the enforcement of these federal and state loyalty programs. Their effect is not confined to those in the public service; they will inevitably affect persons outside the public service. Already, for example, alumni of some educational institutions are pressing for the expulsion from their faculties of professors and teachers solely because at one time or another they are alleged to have been members of one of the more innocent-seeming organizations recently proscribed by the Attorney General.

Much of the current discussion of these new conditions in the press and in legislative halls is concerned with the question of how an accused individual can adequately answer charges without knowing who expressed the opinions or gave the information on which a general charge against him has been based. Many of us hold the firm belief that the greatest safeguard in our law is the right of cross-examination. But it has long been the policy of the Federal Bureau of Investigation to refuse to identify its unnamed informants, and with admirable candor,

Mr. Seth Richardson, eminent lawyer and chairman of the Loyalty Board of Review, has stated: " . . . in the great majority of the cases, we apprehend that disclosure of evidential sources to the employee, and the resulting opportunity of cross-examination of such sources by him, will probably not be practicable." But problems like this, obviously of grave importance from a constitutional standpoint, do not go to the root of the matter. The plain fact is that if we are going to maintain a large-scale organization to gather information secretly and make reports of a secret character, we must pay the price for it. Are we prepared to do this? And is the result worth while? One of the inevitable results is that the accused will be denied some of those rights which we had supposed were guaranteed to him by the Constitution. In the past, secrecy in government has been generally regarded as inconsistent with the American polity. It is a commonplace of experience that secrecy in any aspect cannot promote confidence; it kills it. We have, at least up to these later days, agreed with Lord Acton that: "Everything secret degenerates, even the administration of justice; nothing is safe that does not show how it can bear discussion and publicity."

If this is true, and it is true, as to the operations of government, how much more important it is when the secrecy has a direct effect upon the reputation, the life, and the livelihood of the individual. How startling it is to realize that it will often, if not usually, be the secret undisclosed information which will determine the fate of the individual. What a shock would come to any lawyer if he were to witness a criminal trial and a conviction for crime based upon secret and undisclosed evidence. Yet, from a practical standpoint, is there any essential difference in terms either of the individual right or of the public interest between that situation and the result under the procedure on charges of disloyalty?

The practice of secret investigations is an aspect of government in which, up to now, no widespread interest has been aroused. How far, if at all, should we tolerate a policy of having our governmental officials build up, through secret investigations, these enormous numbers of secret dossiers dealing with the private lives of the people? For sound historical reasons the

founding fathers dreaded above everything else secret activities
in government operation. Must we take a different view? Is
this aberration from the principles guaranteeing the privacy of
the individual justified by any substantial proved facts? May
not all of this agitation turn out, as after the first World War,
to be an unreasonable and unworthy result of emotional in-
stability? . . .

Whatever may be thought of some of the considerations that
here have been emphasized, surely all may agree that determination of the fate of an individual upon secret evidence constitutes
a grave departure from our constitutional theory of the right
of the individual. Attempts to ameliorate the dangers of this
innovation by establishing appeals or other palliative procedural
measures will not eliminate this evil. Nor can they justify this
radical departure from historic policy.

THE PROBLEM OF LOYALTY [5]

It would be impossible to overemphasize the fact that because of the fundamental conflict between the basic tenets of
democracy and of communism concerning the nature of man, the
struggle of democracy against that ideology must take on something of the character of emergency measures in self-defense.
Democracies everywhere are faced with the question whether they
can remain true to themselves and allow free rein within their
borders to the adherents of an ideological system which negates
the basic democratic dogma, and which explicitly states that its
propagation shall and ultimately must be accomplished by force.

It has also been shown that the congressional investigative
committee, in particular the Committee on Un-American Activities, has been one of the main devices through which the government of the United States has attempted to uncover and to
deal with Communist propagandists in this country. The second
main device now in operation is the loyalty program which cen-
ters in the Loyalty Review Board set up on March 22, 1947.

[5] From "American Civil Rights in a Revolutionary Age. The Problem of
Loyalty," by Ellen D. Ellis, Professor Emeritus of Political Science, Mount
Holyoke College. Forum. 109:193-7. April 1948. Reprinted by permission.

The adoption of the present loyalty program does not represent the first attempt of the United States government to meet the problem of loyalty in a time of technical peace.

In order to understand the problem and the difficulties that attend it, some preliminary definition is necessary. What in effect is meant in this connection by loyalty? The term is obviously used here in its political connotation, i.e., as indicating, in dictionary phraseology, "fidelity to law or the lawful government or sovereign."

In the world of "sovereign states" of the past three hundred years, governments have had to depend upon this fidelity or loyalty for their defense against enemies external and internal. For the most part this dependence has been restricted to a state's own nationals, though under certain circumstances aliens have been drafted into military or other armed service. It is a commonplace that in the primary interest of self-defense a government must at all times be in a position to take action against those whose disloyalty goes so far as to lead them to use force against it—the government.

The most obvious form of disloyalty to government is known as treason. In English law, treason has included offenses not involving the direct use of force. The founders of the Constitution of the United States purposely framed a narrower definition whereby "treason against the United States . . . [should] consist only in levying war against them, in adhering to their enemies, giving them aid and comfort." Congressional legislation has closely followed the constitutional definition. For conviction for treason there must have been a specific overt act. The courts have held also that the mere use of force in resistance to the execution of the law, but with no public purpose in view, such, for example, as that of preventing the execution of an act of Congress, is not levying of war, and hence does not constitute treason, regardless of the degree of force employed.

Because of this restrictive definition of treason, both national and state governments have legislated in other terms concerning disloyalty, whether by word or deed, that falls short of the constitutional specifications of treason. . . .

During the past few years the problem of loyalty has assumed large proportions in the United States. Since 1939 the Congress has been giving especial attention to the matter of freeing the government service of "disloyal" persons. Conspicuous among its efforts in this direction was the inserting of a clause in an appropriation act in 1943 whereby R. M. Lovett, G. B. Watson, and W. E. Dodd, Jr., were ordered off the government pay roll for alleged subversive activities, on the recommendation of the Dies Committee. In March 1946, the Supreme Court invalidated this action as amounting to a Bill of Attainder and the three men were awarded the back pay due to them.

Congressional agitation culminated finally in the establishment by the Civil Service Commission of the Loyalty Review Board, and of agency and regional loyalty boards in November 1947. . . . The system as established provides for a checking against the records of the Federal Bureau of Investigation of the factual personal material required, together with his or her fingerprint, from every federal government employee or applicant for government employment; and for further investigation by the FBI of doubtful persons. Each employee "is required as a condition to employment to state under oath that he is not a member of an organization that advocates the overthrow of the government of the United States by force or violence." Information gathered will be sent to the appropriate government agency loyalty board and, if doubt persists, the employee or applicant will be faced with certain charges or questions. Hearings, which shall be private, will be granted if desired, with the assistance of attorney and witnesses. Further appeal of unfavorable decisions to the agency head and finally to the Loyalty Review Board is provided. Secrecy and privacy are to be maintained throughout.

The machinery thus set up has been the object of much criticism. It is claimed that the requirement to furnish the personal information requested is repugnant to the First Amendment to the Constitution. The fact that, while the report of the FBI is not binding on loyalty boards or agency heads, the employee or applicant will have no access to it or to its contents, and no opportunity to confront and cross examine witnesses has been pointed to as involving another violation of the Bill of Rights.

The answer of the government is, first, that here as elsewhere individual rights must be conditioned by preponderant public need—that the disclosing of the sources of pertinent information in the possession of the FBI might be prejudicial if not dangerous to the public good; and, secondly, that the loyalty hearings are not judicial trials and, therefore, not subject to the specific procedural guarantees of the Constitution. It is further maintained that the actual procedures to be followed allow to the employee every benefit of doubt possible under the circumstances, and that the only disability imposed under these proceedings is dismissal from office or failure to appoint, neither of which is comparable to punishment inflicted for crime. It is claimed that the government, like other employers is entitled to fix the qualifications of its employees, and that loyalty is the *sine qua non* for the holding of government office. Any mature judgment on the actual working out of these arrangements must await a longer period of trial.

The problem of loyalty is rendered especially difficult in the United States at present by the fact that this problem encompasses not only the question of the advocacy of force against the government of the United States. Because of the ideological implications of the present political situation, as well as of the nature of world Communist organization under the Communist party of the U.S.S.R., there is also involved the question of possible loyalty to another state. . . .

So long as the world is organized—or disorganized—on the basis of "independent sovereign" states, each of which must rely on itself alone for defense against enemies within and without, the question of loyalty within the borders of a given state, and especially of the loyalty of those within its governmental personnel, must remain a matter of prime importance. . . .

In closing, one may perhaps suggest that at this moment of history, under the impact of the dynamics of Russian communism and of Russian expansion, the application of the clear-and-present-danger doctrine would serve to render justifiable many of the activities of government which would otherwise appear repugnant to individual constitutional rights. To say this is not to deny that government must be constantly on the alert against abuses in this most difficult and delicate area. Nor is to say this to minimize the importance of eliminating misery and poverty which are among the most fertile breeding grounds for Communist ideology. At the present moment, however, efforts in this direction alone are not enough.

It is suggested also that while democracy must continually strive to give the maximum consideration possible under existing circumstances to preserving individual rights, there is a fundamental distinction to be drawn between temporary and emergency restrictions on the individual reluctantly imposed in order to defend against those who would destroy it, a democratic system dedicated to the development of the intellectual and moral capabilities of man, and restrictions which are, as under Russian communism, altogether in harmony with the concept of man inherent in the ideological system under which they are imposed.

WEAKNESSES OF THE LOYALTY PROGRAM [6]

Mr. A. is a government scientist. His work involves research and development in a field of national defense classified as secret. We may assume that he works in a laboratory where the government is developing an invention which will neutralize every atomic bomb within a 500-mile radius. This invention, we may imagine, is a radiation which can be rendered ineffective by counter-measures easy to develop and to apply, once the basic principle of the radiation is known. The United States has the neutralizer and the counter-measure, but wants to keep knowledge of both from potential enemies.

Mr. A. does not belong to the Communist party, nor is he a member of an affiliated organization. He is, however, sympathetic toward those ideals that the Communists insert in their propaganda as sucker-bait. Being one of those muddle-headed thinkers who conceive faith in Stalinist propaganda to be the mark of an intellectual, A. is antagonistic to all forms of military preparedness in the United States, though complacent toward

[6] From "What's Wrong with the Loyalty Program?" by a Federal Employee. *Plain Talk.* 2:1-5. September 1948. Reprinted by permission.

Russia's growing arms program. Moreover, he believes that exclusive possession by the United States of any militarily useful secret is a threat to world peace. He does not find it difficult to rationalize that the Soviet Union needs to know about new weapons in order to further its peaceful intentions.

Now A. is not quite muddled enough to extract secret papers from files and turn them over to a foreign agent, Hollywood style. He does not even disclose any information about the project. He does not need to. All he has to do is to drop a few hints at one of the Communist-inspired "get-togethers" he is so fond of attending. After he lets it be known, for example, that something of interest is going on in Section X of Division I in the Bureau, the plan to get information can be set in motion. A. can cooperate by pointing out that a position is open, and stating the qualifications—which are those of agent B. This cooperation may consist simply in recommending acceptance of an assistant who happens to be congenial and of the same mind as himself on things political.

Since throughout the government there is a continuing shortage of scientific and professional personnel as a result of the marginal parsimony practiced by Uncle Sam toward his employees, agent B. readily gets the job. Low salary is no deterrent to an earnest Communist whose prime motive is doing the party's work.

There are other ways in which A. can derange the program. He can deliberately stall and prolong its development by helping to create synthetic difficulties. He can clog the channels of essential contracts. Especially, he can exercise his authority in regard to whether or not certain matters should be classified as secret in the first place. A. does not need to be in a very high position in order to do this. If he is working on a project of importance to defense, he probably will be called in at times to pass judgment on whether or not suggestions and descriptions received in the government should be put in a secret category and the owners of the specifications notified to withhold the disclosures from publication. When, as is frequently the case, the suggestion or idea, or application for patent received from outside parallels the development that the government has classified as secret, obviously its publication will prove detrimental no matter what source discloses it. Disclosure of government information would involve A. in serious trouble. But simply by failing to take action to prevent disclosure by another person, he can accomplish the same disloyal end without violating any rule pertaining to his duties.

The case of A. is hypothetical, but by no means improbable. It shows why our loyalty investigations program is not getting results. The government could know, other employees could know, that scientist A.'s sympathies lay with communism, but they could not do one thing about it under the provisions of our present loyalty program.

Does A. advocate "force and violence to alter the constitutional form of government of the United States"? Not at all. A. advocates peace. He is, in fact, an avowed pacifist.

Is A. guilty of "unauthorized disclosure to any person, under circumstances that may indicate disloyalty, of documents or information of a confidential or nonpublic character"? He has not disclosed one iota of confidential information. True, he has seen classified information and information that should have been classified leaking out of the United States, and has done nothing to prevent it. But there is nothing in any official definition of loyalty that requires action on the part of an employee in such an event.

Is A. disloyal in the sense that he is a member of an association that advocates the overthrow of the government of the United States by force and violence? He is not. Therefore, though he may openly reveal his desire to see that government displaced by a dictatorship, he does not classify as disloyal, according to official definition.

Perhaps the government can get him on grounds that he has been acting in such a way as to serve the interests of another government in preference to that of the United States? After all, this definition of loyalty calls for action, and A. has done hardly anything that could be termed action. Can you hold an employee disloyal merely because he has not considered that a bit of information should be classified as secret? With the aid of legal counsel, it probably would be impossible to show that such non-classification could be construed as acting to serve, or being preferential to, a foreign government.

To suppose that the infinitesimal number of employees who have left the service as a result of loyalty investigations represents anything approaching the number of Communists and fellow travelers in the government is fantastic. The sights of the loyalty program have been so elevated that it shoots right over their heads.

According to the report of FBI Director J. Edgar Hoover on July 21, 1948, the FBI had "virtually completed" its obligations under the federal employees' loyalty program eleven months after the program had been undertaken. Mr. Hoover said that, of 2,020,975 federal employees checked under President Truman's loyalty program, 438 had resigned during investigations by bureau agents, and another 18 were found to be no longer on the government pay roll. Full field investigations were needed in only 5,510 of the cases processed, the report stated, and 2,632 of those were completed at the close of the fiscal year ended June 30, 1948.

Among the more than two million federal employees not given "full field invesitgations" by the FBI, how many were Soviet agents? There is no evidence that these employees have been investigated at all—unless requiring an employee to fill out a form, asking him whether he is a Communist, amounts to an investigation. True, federal employees have been fingerprinted, but this step is merely the beginning. It is doubtful whether detailed investigation would yield results. The FBI is limited by laws so heavily loaded with "overthrow of the government of the United States by force and violence" that action against the real enemy is hindered. Further, the removal of disloyal employees is rendered ineffective by laws that force procedural handicaps against those capable of moving against the offenders. J. Edgar Hoover reported to a congressional committee on March 26, 1947, "The FBI does not make recommendations. It merely reports facts and it is up to the interested government department to make a decision. Almost invariably, of course, subjects of investigations deny affiliation with subversive groups, often despite strong evidence to the contrary."

Among the requirements for "admission" to government service is an investigation for loyalty. Part I of Executive Order 9835 provides that such an investigation "normally will be conducted within 18 months after such persons enter on duty.' Then the door is securely locked against the marauder—after he has had 18 months to steal the horse. This, please note, is "normal." What went on during the abnormal times of the war, one can only guess. It would be nothing short of a miracle if Communists had failed to take advantage of this golden laxity to infiltrate the federal services. Normally, the "temporary" or "war service" employees who swarmed in during the emergency, not being under Civil Service, would have been released. But every pressure has been applied to retain them and to convert them into "permanent" employees with full Civil Service rights. All kinds of subterfuges are used for this purpose—for example, the giving of qualifying examinations years after the employee has entered upon his job, when he is able to pass as a result of his experience.

The Communist and fellow traveler have nothing good to say about the government of the United States and nothing unfavorable to say about the government of Russia. This attitude is typical of the conversation of a large number of federal employees. Of course, it *could* be just talk. But why, then, does it have timing and unison? Why is it concerted on certain themes? And why does it follow the party line so faithfully? Somebody who knows what he is doing has been flashing the signals. And somebody flashed the warning signal when the loyalty investigation program started. Such talk ceased abruptly. The boys are lying low until the heat is off.

I do not think for a moment that everyone who has been repeating such propaganda is a Communist. Some federal employees, though essentially loyal, permit themselves to be used as sounding-boards for the party line, merely because they are easy marks and too inert to realize the harm that these rumors do. That, of course, is one of the obscurities on which the propagandist relies—the fact that it is difficult to discriminate with certainty between the dupe and the Communist worker.

The present loyalty procedure is a welter of commissions, boards, recommendations, hearings, reviews, appeals, and all the paraphernalia of indetermination. It should be reduced to a small, simple organization vested with authority to decide, and with power to act.

The present program is slanted to protect the disloyal employee. It is he, backed by the party's lawyers, who will make the most of the "safeguards" that have been provided for his defense. The program should be designed, rather, to protect the loyal employee who has something to reveal about disloyal activities. I believe that if each government employee were called in for a confidential interview, some very interesting facts would be brought to light. The substance of these interviews, which might well be conducted by the FBI, should be held confidential, in order to protect the loyal employee from reprisals by pro-Communist supervisors.

The argument that most federal employees hold jobs under the policy-making level does not change the situation. Today government administration has reached new heights of complexity. It is impossible for the new head of a bureau or department, in the short time that he holds office, to inform himself fully as to all that goes on under his jurisdiction. So remote is the association of the working level with the supervisory and policy level that the "boss" is more dependent upon his employees than they are on him.

The gap betwen policy and performance recently was illustrated in the Voice of America case. Broadcasts were going out that sounded more like the Voice of Moscow. NBC, which hires the employee who was concocting the propaganda, apparently knew nothing about what he was doing. The State Department, which had let out the contract to NBC, knew nothing of what he was doing. And Congress was astonished and indignant when, at long last, they got wind of what was up. Meanwhile the harm had been done. The employee was a specialist—a scriptwriter who knew Spanish. Apparently that was all his superiors needed to know.

In legal fields—of which the government is full—specialization renders obscurity even more effective. Any little band of lawyers could keep the entire policy-making level of the government befuddled indefinitely. They could, if they were so minded, administer a law designed to aid business in such a way as to wreck business, without once committing any discernible act beyond the legitimate scope of debative opinion.

The government services are in urgent need of a real housecleaning. Our fine-spun legalistic definitions of loyalty ought to be abolished, and in their stead a standard of loyalty created that would insure the government against sabotage.

When investigation reveals evidence that raises a reasonable doubt as to an employee's loyalty to the United States, that employee should be promptly discharged. Reinstatement should follow only if the employee sustains the burden of proving that the charges are unfounded. Such procedure is not in accordance with the doctrine that holds no man guilty until he is so proved. But the issue at stake is not whether a defendant is guilty of a crime. It is whether the person is qualified to hold a government job. The procedure can and should be such as to cast no discredit on the person in the doubtful case.

To dispense with red tape and delay will result in some injustices. But, as between the interests of a few individuals and those of the people of the United States, there can be only one choice. To suppose that the enemy, sitting at government desks in Washington, can be routed by a program that holds the "right" to a job higher than the public safety, is a delusion. The normal privileges of the individual in a democracy have to be suspended at times in order that the system that protects those privileges may be preserved. Otherwise, we will fall subject to a system that will deprive all of us of our liberties.

LOYALTY CHECKS AND JUSTICE

DISCUSSION

While opinion generally tends to consider the loyalty program as a necessary evil during a troubled time in our history, the public has been exceedingly critical of the program in its practical application.

Numerous cases have been reported in the press where apparent injustice has characterized loyalty investigations. This has been particularly true in the scientific laboratories of the Atomic Energy Commission.

The most outstanding example of injustice was demonstrated in the Condon case. Although cleared by the federal loyalty program, Condon received the full effects of what has since been termed "Trial by headline." The House Un-American Activities Committee charged Condon with security violations, without allowing him opportunity for defense or public hearing. The result was sweeping and vigorous disapproval by the press and the scientific fraternity. While the case in fairness cannot be laid to the door of the federal loyalty program, it is an example of the extremes to which loyalty investigations can be carried.

The Condon case brought to a head the dissension which had been slowly developing throughout the nation, regarding federal information security measures. While the Atomic Energy Commission and the government attempted to provide additional safeguards to protect individuals under the program, the main problem of preventing possible injustices remained unsolved. Of particular significance was the question raised by the atomic scientists who asked in effect, "What right do you have to deprive men of a livelihood on the basis of slender evidence taken in secret without giving them the benefit of the constitutional right of trial by jury?"

THE CHARGES AGAINST CONDON [1]

Today I want to report to you about the continuing fight Congress is waging to force the executive department of your Federal Government, headed by the President, to fire Communists and fellow travelers from the government service. I want to report to you on a specific case—the case of Dr. Edward U. Condon, Director of the National Bureau of Standards. I want to tell you how Congress is having to pass legislation to force the President and Secretary of Commerce to turn over to it letters and information in the files of the FBI about Communists Congress seeks to expose on the government pay roll. I want to indicate to you how it is that Russia is possibly getting secrets on the atomic bomb with cooperation of our own governmental officials. It is a shocking story but one not uncommon in Washington. In the six years I have been in Congress there have been several hundred cases along the same line. . . .

First, who is Dr. Condon and why are we interested in him? Doctor Condon is Director of the Bureau of Standards. The Bureau is custodian of the nation's top scientific secrets. It is the nation's most important national defense research organization. It is engaged in projects at the present time concerning atomic energy, radar, proximity fuses, instrument landing systems, jet fuels and other vital and secret projects that affect the security of our nation. The Director of this agency has access to confidential records and information sought by virtually every foreign spy in the United States of America. . . . Let us look further into Condon's record. He has a most distinguished record as a top scientist. He was educated in this country and in Germany. He has held numerous government responsibilities prior to his appointment as Director of the Bureau of Standards. As far back as 1941 he was a member of the Roosevelt Committee on Uranium Research. The President also sent him to observe the effects of the atom bomb test made at Bikini Atoll, and similar jobs too numerous to mention.

[1] From a radio broadcast by Representative Marion T. Bennett of Missouri, reprinted in the *Congressional Record*. 94:A2558-9. April 22, 1948.

While a director of the Manhattan or atomic bomb project, Condon wrote a letter to his superior registering his impatience with the security regulations set up to protect the secret of atomic energy.

Dr. Condon is a member of the executive committee of the American-Soviet Science Society which is affiliated with the National Council of American-Soviet Friendship, Inc., an organization cited as subversive and as a Communist front by both the Attorney General and the House Committee on Un-American Activities. Condon has recruited ten other scientists in the Bureau of Standards to membership.

A member of Condon's immediate family is a member of an organization cited as a subversive Communist-front by the Attorney General.

Condon frequently associates with diplomatic representatives of the Russian, Polish, and Czechoslovakian governments. He has been entertained at their homes and has entertained them in his home, supplied to him by the United States Government.

He has associated with an individual who was dismissed from his job because of his Communist tendencies, and with others known to be Soviet spies and their friends.

It is conceivable that a person might associate with one or two individuals and have no knowledge of their Communist affiliations. However, when a person having access to vital information relating to atomic energy, associates with thirty or more individuals, whether directly or indirectly, who are engaging not only in the dissemination of communistic doctrine, but who are engaged in espionage activity, on behalf of the Soviet Russian Government, such association becomes a matter of national concern.

Condon recently wrote an article in the *Saturday Review of Literature,* in which he stated, "The restoration of freedom to science is one of the elements in the civilization we have been fighting for—freedom from secrecy and freedom from national barriers." No franker appeal has even been made for free exchange of scientific knowledge between nations, at a time when the atomic bomb is our greatest safeguard. Dr. Condon as head of the Bureau of Standards has permitted numerous Russian

Communist visitors to go through his Bureau, inspecting its secrets. On that point, the House Committee on Un-American Activities has the following to say in its official report:

Exchange of scientific material with the Soviet Union is a one-way street and our government is pursuing a dangerous and foolish policy of making scientific data available to the Soviet Union, since they will not permit us to inspect any of their bureaus, nor will they exchange any information with us. The Soviet Union, acting through its 'fronts,' has secured hundreds of thousands of patents from our Patent Office, and our present investigation along these lines reveals that even today they are continuing to order thousands of patents. We are convinced that what the Soviet Union is actually doing is setting up her own patent bureau by obtaining all of ours, at the rate of ten and twenty-five cents each. We should like to point out that the Russian Government has refused to give the United States a single patent since 1928.

The Patent Office is another bureau of the Department of Commerce, presided over by Secretary Harriman.

You will be interested, my friends, to know that Dr. Condon has been investigated by the FBI. On May 15, 1947, J. Edgar Hoover, Director of the FBI, sent a confidential letter about Condon to W. Averell Harriman, Secretary of Commerce. An investigator for the House Committee on Un-American Activities copied part of that letter but before he got through he was prevented from finishing his effort by orders of the department officials. He did record, as it is set forth in House Report 1753, that the FBI files show Condon has been in contact as late as 1947 with an individual alleged by a self-confessed Soviet espionage agent, to have engaged in espionage activities with the Russians in Washington, D.C., from 1941 to 1944. Names of others are given in the report. I cannot pronounce these Russian names so will not use them here.

When the House Committee on Un-American Activities asked the Secretary of Commerce, Mr. Harriman, to turn the FBI letter over to the Committee for examination, he refused on instructions of the President. When he was subpenaed by the Committee he still refused to bring it. The President issued a written order slapping censorship down on this letter and others of similar character which might show that Communists are working for the government. To say that this is astounding, is an understatement. Last week our committee on Interstate and Foreign Commerce, which has jurisdiction over legislation pertaining to the Department of Commerce and the Bureau of Standards which is in the Department, ordered hearings on a resolution to require the FBI letter to be turned over to Congress. The Secretary of Commerce refused to appear as a witness. This is the same Secretary of Commerce, Mr. Harriman, who was appointed this week by the President as our $25,000 per year roving ambassador, charged with the responsibility to see that the $17,000,000,000 European recovery money, provided by our taxpayers, is used in such a way as to stop communism abroad. A fitting reward for his failure and refusal to combat communism at home. How long will these fatal inconsistencies in foreign policy be permitted to continue? Not beyond January 1948, I trust.

The committee reported the resolution favorably, notwithstanding objections of Secretary Harriman. It will pass Congress but the President will probably kill it with a veto. This just goes to show the importance of having a President who will practice what he preaches when it comes to getting Reds out of the government of which he is head. It is futile to spend billions of dollars on atomic research and armaments if we are going to be betrayed by our own officials. The Congress and country would have never known of General Benny Meyers or Gerhart Eisler or Hanns Eisler, if Congress had not had access to the files of the executive branch of the government so that it could expose these rats in the public trough. Now the Congress has publicly charged that Dr. Condon, Director of the Bureau of Standards, is one of the weakest links in our atomic security. It is a grave charge. In justice to Condon, the administration and the Congress, all available evidence should be brought to bear on the subject. Why not? What has the administration to hide by refusing to let the FBI letter on Dr. Condon be made available in full to a proper committee of Congress?

Dr. Condon and other fellow travelers in science say Congress is retarding science by its attack on him. That is poppycock. Was J. Edgar Hoover retarding science when he wrote a three and a half page letter to the Secretary of Commerce, warning him about Condon's association and record? Was General Leslie Groves, director of the atomic bomb project, retarding science when he had Dr. Condon taken off a Soviet-bound plane in 1945, and refused to permit him to go to Russia as he desired, notwithstanding authorization of the trip by the State Department?

I grant that science may have been retarded by the arrest, conviction, and imprisonment for ten years of Alan Nunn May, professor of nuclear physics at Cambridge University, who was found guilty of the charge that he was a Soviet spy. His is not an isolated case. Other scientists are serving sentences in Canadian prisons for the same offense, friends of Condon's. Are we justified in having as a government employee, especially one charged with secrets of national defense, any who apparently see nothing wrong in associating with card-holding members of the Communist party and joining their associations? Is he not placing your welfare in jeopardy through such associations? Is not Congress entitled, in the public interest, to expose the fact and demand that the President quit protecting him and kick him out of office? Only the citizens of America, at the bar of public opinion can make effective and final answers to those questions. I have brought you the story. A story I could not, would not dare to tell over the radio, if I could not back every word of it with official government records and documents, yours for the asking by card or letter to your Congressman.

In considering the case of Dr. Condon, I wish to emphasize that what is involved is not a question of freedom of speech or research. The ruthless push of Stalin through Europe, in the opinion of Congress, necessitates a revision of the policy and thinking of this government and the people of the United States, regarding communism. We should bear in mind that the government is charged not only with the administration of public affairs, but it is also charged with the security of the people and the institutions of the United States. Whether we like it or not, we are engaged in a great epochal struggle; and not a struggle with guns, because the Communists don't fight that way, just yet.

They didn't take over Czechoslovakia with guns, they merely employed the strategy of getting a few men in the government, and then a few more and then they took over the entire government without firing a single shot or calling out a single regiment of soldiers.

They are conducting exactly the same kind of campaign in other countries, including our own. In this country they haven't gotten as far as they have in Czechoslovakia and a score of other nations now behind the iron curtain but they have got pretty far. They have duped a man who was Vice President of the United States and he is now their idol and favorite candidate for President. And he is the same man who recommended and appointed Dr. Condon as Director of the Bureau of Standards, which has atomic and other secrets of national defense.

SIGNIFICANCE OF THE CONDON ATTACK [2]

The attacks on Dr. Edward U. Condon during the last year serve the purpose, in my opinion, of aiding and abetting the efforts of some people to undermine the atomic energy legislation passed by the House and Senate some two years ago without a recorded vote of dissent. There are, obviously, other motives behind these attacks, but this is the basic and crucial one.

Let there be no mistake. These attacks on Dr. Condon seem to be a part of a general strategy to undermine the McMahon bill; and before we see the end of them, other eminent scientists, legislators, and citizens may be reviled, directly and indirectly. The objective seems glaringly apparent: By discrediting the scientists responsible for atomic energy and the legislators and citizens active in the establishment of the McMahon bill, and then by subsequent overt attacks on the Atomic Energy Commission, it is hoped that the McMahon bill will be revised or recanted and that a totally military bill will be substituted.

Now I do not believe that the National Defense Establishment—or its components, the Army, the Navy, the Air Forces— are behind this strategy. It is evident that the National Defense

[2] From remarks by Representative Helen Gahagan Douglas of California, before the House of Representatives. *Congressional Record.* 94:4572-7. April 14, 1948.

Establishment is cognizant of the worth of the present vast program for atomic energy, both with respect to its immediate military aspects and to future military developments based on further research, as well as with respect to the national value of the nonmilitary aspects of the work of the Commission. Rather, a very small minority of the Army . . . has consistently worked with a small but persistent and vociferous legislative minority in this direction. Now that the Atomic Energy Commission is about to come up for reappointment, we witness their opening guns in this attempt to undermine the McMahon bill and the present Commission. This is the basic significance of the attacks on Dr. Condon.

REPLY TO THE ATTACK ON CONDON [3]

For fifteen months we have witnessed an unparalleled publicity program by the House Committee on Un-American Activities in which the committee has attempted to smear the character and reputation of one of the nation's most distinguished scientists, Dr. E. U. Condon, Director of the National Bureau of Standards. In spite of a preliminary clearance, through an investigation requested by Dr. Condon himself on seeing certain attacks in the press in March of 1947 and conducted by Mr. W. Averell Harriman, then Secretary of Commerce and now Ambassador Extraordinary; in spite of clearance by the Loyalty Board, an investigation which he requested after the program was established; and now in spite of the clearance of the Atomic Energy Commission, after an exhaustive investigation the like of which has probably never occurred before—no doubt, a result of the atmosphere created by the House committee's publicity—in spite of all these investigations and clearances, backed by the FBI, we still see the committe continuing its oblique attacks by press releases.

What has this committee done in this case? . . .

First, March 1947: Two articles replete with vague innuendoes, appeared in the Washington *Times-Herald*, indicating that Dr. Condon would be investigated.

[3] From remarks by Representative Chet Holifield of California before the House of Representatives, *Congressional Record*. 94:9693-6. July 29, 1948.

Second, June 1947: Mr. Thomas, chairman of the House Committee on Un-American Activities, in a signed article in the popular magazine, *American*, attacked Dr. Condon and said that he would be subpenaed.

Third, June 21, 1947: Mr. Thomas again repeated the above attacks in *Liberty* magazine of this date.

Fourth, July 17, 1947: A headline press release was made by the committee which appeared in the Washington *Times-Herald* repeating past attacks. . . .

Fifth, March 1, 1948: A special subcommittee of the House Committee on Un-American Activities released a report in which it called Dr. Condon one of the weakest links in atomic energy, and pronounced judgment on him. This report was allegedly a report to the full committee, and yet at least one member of the full committee admitted that he was never given a copy; it was released to the press in a theatrical fashion at the hospital bedside of Chairman Thomas, shortly before the House was to consider the committee's appropriation. . . .

In between these major publicity campaigns, the committee continued to emit a steady stream of lighter missiles and these press releases repeat all the old innuendoes.

The reaction of the nation to the vicious report of March 1, 1948, should have settled this invidious publicity program of the committee, for the responsible press of the nation, from coast to coast, lashed out at the tactics and procedures of the committee. . . .

At the same time, eminent citizens and the distinguished professional societies and groups of the nation protested bitterly this unwarranted and vicious treatment of so distinguished a scientist and citizen as Dr. E. U. Condon, and those who knew and had worked with him made clear their views of his integrity. These, too, were summarized by the gentlewoman from California, the Honorable Helen Gahagan Douglas, on the floor of the House . . . [on] April 15, 1948.

Meanwhile the committee announced that it would devote its entire staff to secure evidence to substantiate its March 1, 1948, attack. Perhaps galvanized by the flood of reaction, it decided to hold a hearing. April 21, 1948, was set, only to be canceled and indefinitely postponed. Members of the committee subsequently assured Congress that hearings would be held prior to its adjournment, but adjournment time came and no hearings had been held.

Throughout this period Dr. Condon did his best to help the committee—without avail. On July 9, 1947, for example, Dr. Condon addressed the gentleman from New Jersey [Mr. Thomas] the following letter:

MY DEAR CONGRESSMAN: My attention has been called recently to your article in the *American Magazine* in which you say that I will be subpenaed to appear before your committee in connection with its desire to learn more about the American-Soviet Science Society. It will not be necessary to issue a subpena as I will be happy to supply the committee with all the information I have. When two of your staff assistants called on me last March, I showed them my complete file on this subject and would gladly do so again. Also I am assured that officers of the society, and the Rockefeller Foundation which is sponsoring the society, will be glad to furnish any information you desire on this subject.

I shall at all times be glad to cooperate with your committee in any way that I can help in its highly important work.

Sincerely yours,

E. U. CONDON, *Director*.

To this day he has never received even the courtesy of a reply. Shortly after this letter on July 17, 1947, Dr. Condon addressed each member of the committee as follows:

MY DEAR CONGRESSMAN: There have recently been newspaper and magazine articles in which it was stated that the House Committee on Un-American Activities intends to investigate me. I think it is important that you should have a copy (enclosed herewith) of the letter I wrote to the chairman of this committee soon after these things were called to my attention.

I shall be happy to cooperate with the committee in every way. Please allow me to suggest the desirability of proceeding without delay because of the grave importance of the issues raised.

Sincerely yours,

E. U. CONDON, *Director*.

From a few he received acknowledgments, but nothing happened. Then on March 5, 1948, after the sensational March 1 attack, Dr. Condon, this time in person, practically forced himself on several members of the committee in their chambers at the conclusion of a subcommittee session, renewing his standing offer to help, appear, cooperate, which he made eight months before. But, as before, nothing came of that either.

I will not go into the many times that Dr. Condon was cleared as a result of his association with many secret wartime projects, including clearance on the atomic bomb project, where he was under the supervision of Major General Leslie Groves. Then there was the initial investigation, requested by Dr. Condon because of the press attacks of March 1947. This was prior to the establishment of the Loyalty Board program, and Mr. W. Averell Harriman reported himself satisfied as to Dr. Condon's integrity. When the Loyalty Board was established, Dr. Condon, at his own request was again investigated and cleared with the concurrence of Mr. Harriman and the new Commerce Secretary, Mr. Sawyer. Finally, we have seen one of the most exhaustive and thorough investigations of all history undertaken by the Atomic Energy Commission: this investigation completely vindicates Dr. Condon of all the malicious smears, innuendoes, and gossip that has been peddled for these last fifteen months. That report bears repetition:

REPORT OF THE ATOMIC ENERGY COMMISSION AS
RELEASED ON JULY 15, 1948

The question before the Commission is the security clearance of Dr. Edward U. Condon, Director of the National Bureau of Standards. In view of Dr. Condon's past association with the atomic energy project, this question arises under the provisions of the Atomic Energy Act for reinvestigations of persons who were permitted access to restricted data by the Manhattan district. The question presented is whether Dr. Condon's clearance should be continued to permit him to have access to the restricted data pertinent to his duties as Director of the Bureau of Standards and related activities.

After examining the extensive files in this case, the Commission has no question whatever concerning Dr. Condon's loyalty to the United States. What we have for consideration, therefore, is whether the continued clearance of this distinguished American scientist, whose loyalty is unquestionable, would constitute a security hazard to the atomic energy program. Such a decision calls for a commonsense evaluation of the factors involved.

In considering the case, the Commission has taken note of the prior association of Dr. Condon with the atomic energy program, during which he was given access to information of a high degree of secrecy:

1. In 1940, Dr. Condon was appointed a member of the eight-man uranium subcommittee of the uranium section, National Defense Research Committee, which carried out the first over-all survey of problems related to developing nuclear energy from atomic fission for the defense program.

2. In 1941 and 1942, Dr. Condon served as associate director of research of the Westinghouse Corporation, during the period when Westinghouse took a prominent part in the production of the first substantial quantities of pure uranium metal.

3. Also in 1942, Dr. Condon was appointed a consultant to S-1 executive committee of the Office of Scientific Research and Development. This committee was charged with the responsibility for reviewing the basic program of the entire uranium project.

4. For a short period in 1943, Dr. Condon served as associate director of the Los Alamos Laboratory, at that time in the early stages of its organization as the unit of the Manhattan project which would finally turn out atomic bombs. While at Los Alamos he prepared a document known as the "Los Alamos Primer," which was used as an introduction to the subject of the explosive use of fissionable material, to introduce to scientific and technical personnel coming to the laboratory the fundamental ideas under investigation.

5. In 1944-45, Dr. Condon worked at the radiation laboratory of the University of California at Berkeley, which was under contract with the Manhattan district.

6. In November 1945, Dr. Condon, having been appointed by the President and confirmed by the Senate, took office in the position which he now occupies as Director of the National Bureau of Standards.

7. In December 1945, Dr. Condon was designated and thereafter served as scientific adviser to the Senate's Special Committee on Atomic Energy.

8. In 1946, Dr. Condon was named by the President as a member of the Evaluation Commission for Operations Crossroads, and in this capacity attended the Bikini tests.

During the war the Bureau of Standards conducted for the atomic energy program of the Manhattan district certain work of types which the Bureau was particularly suited to perform. The Bureau has continued to perform for the Atomic Energy Commission similar work which can be best carried out by the Bureau. Thus in his position as

Director of the Bureau of Standards, and in other related atomic energy activities in which he would participate, Dr. Condon has need for access to certain types of restricted data.

This meant that under the Atomic Energy Act Dr. Condon's security clearance required "reinvestigation"; that is, it was necessary for the FBI to investigate and report to the Commission on his character, associations, and loyalty, and for the Commission then to determine whether permitting him to have access to restricted data will endanger the common defense and security.

In defining the question before the Commission, it is recognized that, as is the case with thousands of other persons whose security clearances must be passed on by the Commission, Dr. Condon's clearance does not involve access to information on weapons or production or stock-pile data, for the reason that his duties do not require that such access be given.

The five members of the Atomic Energy Commission have personally examined with care the entire record. Although its Personnel Security Review Board expressed the opinion on June 7, 1948, that action by the Commission on the case might appropriately be deferred, pending reasonably prompt action by the House Committee on Un-American Activities with respect to that committee's own investigation and hearing as to Dr. Condon, the Commission considers that in view of its statutory obligations this is a case which the members of the Commission should themselves decide, and that it is our duty to proceed at this time to such a decision.

The record before the Commission includes reports compiled in two FBI investigations. In a most detailed and exhaustive manner, these present a very full picture of Dr. Condon's character, associations, and loyalty, since the FBI interviewed over three hundred persons to obtain information, and its investigations were conducted by a large number of agents on a countrywide basis.

In addition, the FBI supplied the Commission the pertinent information relating to Dr. Condon which it had obtained from the files of other government agencies. The thorough and painstaking investigations by the FBI, and other relevant information available to the Commission, provide the basis on which it is the Commission's responsibility to determine the question of Dr. Condon's security clearance.

In considering the record, the Commission has found that in the opinion of some persons, Dr. Condon's tact, judgment, and discretion appear to be subject to some degree of criticism. On the other hand, there are statements by persons who have been closely associated with Dr. Condon during his long work on classified information, which indicate proper care on his part in assuring that unauthorized persons should not obtain access to classified information.

The file contains unfavorable information of a relevant character concerning certain persons with whom Dr. Condon and Mrs. Condon have from time to time had contacts. The file also shows that Dr. Condon is a man of wide associations, and that his associates include many highly reputable members of the scientific community who have great confidence in him.

In deciding such matters, the Commission has a statutory responsibility to place in perspective the evidence both favorable and unfavorable, and to decide whether the common defense and security of the United States would be adversely affected if the individual concerned continued to have that access to restricted data which is required by the nature of his duties.

On the basis of the voluminous record before it, the members of the Commission are fully satisfied that, in the terms of the statute, Dr. Condon's continued clearance for the purposes stated above "will not adversely affect the common defense and security" of the United States. The Commission considers that his continued clearance is in the best interests of the atomic energy program.

DANGERS OF REPRESSION [4]

As charges of disloyalty are brought against such prominent Americans as the head of the Bureau of Standards, and as unnaturalized aliens accused of subversive Communist activities are seized for deportations, many thoughtful citizens wonder if the country is entering upon another Red scare. Their memories hark back to the days when a New York mob wrecked the office of the *Call* when veterans and "wobblies" clashed in the Northwest and when the "Buford" sailed for Russia with 240 radicals aboard.

We want no recurrence of such events. Yet as we look at the headlines, certain difficult questions are forced upon us. Just what is a dangerous Communist, and how can he be identified? How can precautionary measures be taken without imperiling liberals?

A salient difference between the anti-Red movement after World War I and that taking shape today needs to be pointed out. The principal root of all such movements is fear; fear

[4] From "What Is a Communist?" by Allan Nevins, Professor of American History, Columbia University; author. *New York Times Magazine.* p. 9+. May 2, 1948. Reprinted by permission.

usually mixed with prejudice, and heightened by hysteria. But the fear that had such baleful results in 1918-21 took a very different shape from whatever apprehensions are cropping out in this country today.

In the earlier period fear sprang chiefly from a sense of national disunity. Americans realized uneasily in 1918 that they had not yet created a closely welded nation. The war had revealed, indeed, a decided lack of homogeneity. The conflict had therefore been accompanied by a harsh intolerance of dissent. . . . Nobody worried about an external attack, but millions were apprehensive that the Reds (all bogies are given vague names) would foment class divisions so as to endanger orderly government and the economic structure.

Today few are troubled by ideas of domestic disruption. It is the external rather than internal peril that takes first place in men's apprehensions. National unity, as the second World War showed, has grown steadily in recent decades. . . . But, to our dismay and anguish, we are faced with an external threat. We are engaged in a cold war with Russia, we are pouring out billions to sustain Western Europe and China against her aggressors, and we are maintaining large armaments to meet possible attack. The threat may be exaggerated, but it exists.

The result is that we fear the Communist and Red, not as possible agents of an internal explosion, as in 1918-20, but rather as agents to aid a foreign attack. We fear the agitator much less and the accomplice much more. . . .

Unceasing vigilance is essential and in certain areas of government activity it is necessary to insist on a security check. We cannot let the armed services, our State Department personnel, or the agencies concerned with atomic energy, be invaded by men who may become secret agents of a foreign power. We have the example of Canada's spy ring to show what may be the penalties of laxity. But precautions regarding these limited sectors of national activity are not difficult to take; the records, associations, and expressed ideas of employees or prospective employees can readily be tested.

It is also true that certain precautions are necessary elsewhere. We have said that the general national unity in this year of 1948 stands at a high level. It must not be forgotten, however, that the Communist is not now greatly concerned with the general national unity of this country. He is seeking for the weak spots. He strives to enter the labor union, the discontented slum area, the groups of impressionable youth. Here he can be combated in two ways: by exposure of his aims and methods, and by the counter-encouragement of true liberalism. It is ironic nowadays to recall that in 1918-20 the groups most fiercely attacked were our Socialists. Today these Socialists, accepting the fundamental democratic premises, are among our stanchest opponents of communism. As we fight the Communist, we need to cherish the liberals of all schools and views.

In short, no real basis exists for such a "Red scare" as appeared just after the first World War; a scare which soon left our country heartily ashamed. Our worries about the internal situation then were greatly exaggerated; today such worries do not exist. The number of really dangerous Communists capable of betraying the United States to benefit the Soviet Union is small; their intelligence is open to question, for they certainly include a large proportion of mere crackpots; while their general influence is slight. Once certain areas of government are thoroughly protected, we may feel safe about the national situation in general. Such bodies as the Thomas Committee on Un-American Activities can be useful if they help guard these areas; they can be utterly pernicious if they follow the Mitchell Palmer Red-hunt tradition.

If we are to have a careful policing of governmental agencies —and it is certain that those offices and departments which deal with national security must be policed—we should at least have the work done with a careful regard to all parts of our Bill of Rights. It is the fundamental charge against the Thomas committee, not that it has acted clumsily, but that it has shown inadequate respect for the basic liberties written into our Constitution. Today even Great Britain, normally so slow to act in such matters, is purging her governmental services of Communists and their tools among the fellow travelers. But it is noteworthy that Britain has set up no body similar to our Committee on Un-American Activities.

If we grasp these facts, it is easier to approach the question. How can we deal with the dangerous Communists without hurting useful radicals and liberals? It is easier to answer because we can approach it without any sense of panic. One reason why our internal situation is so healthy is that radicals and liberals have been allowed free scope for expressing their opinions; another reason is that from 1929 onward many of their more valuable ideas were adopted and applied.

Repressive activities always defeat their own end. They arouse widespread antagonism, father the extremist doctrines at which they are aimed, and create martyrs and a martyrology—the most powerful agencies of propagandism known to history. We need not worry about the Utopian Communists; they can't but detest the Russian perversion of their ideals. We need not worry about liberals, who are the bulwark of our own system.

The more freedom of opinion and discussion we have, the better, for it will drive home to everyone some truths which still need enforcement. Fifteen years ago Harold J. Laski, declaring that capitalism and communism were running a race for the allegiance of the masses, stated that each had certain tests to meet. Capitalism had to remove the fear of insecurity which haunted the worker's life. It had to abolish competing imperialisms. Above all, it had to cut away the jungle growth of vested interests which impaired its efficiency and its social equity. As for communism, wrote Laski, it had to put an end to the perpetual postponement of consumption for the sake of a future which never arrived. It had to terminate the dominating grip of one party and its small cabal of leaders, introduce truly representative institutions, and permit political freedom.

While Mr. Laski thought that communism had the better prospects, we can now see that in this competitive rivalry the capitalist states have made by far the better showing. In one Western democracy after another, and particularly in Britain and the United States, effective measures have been taken to remove the fear of insecurity. The power of the vested interests has been healthfully diminished. Imperialism has been almost completely abolished, and where it exists it has taken on a greatly improved character. Meanwhile, in Russia, the era of consumptional plenty still recedes, while the tyrannical grip of a small oligarchy of rulers has been tightened, not relaxed. In nearly every respect in which it is possible to compare the recent development of capitalistic democracy with that of Russian communism, the advantage lies manifestly with the former. These are facts which free discussion, and only free discussion, can bring forth.

Repression is an indispensable part of the Soviet regime; it is not needed in the United States, and is hostile to every American tradition. Precautions against treason we may well take, and we can always punish individual violations of our statutes; but beyond that no arm of the government can afford to go. We may well recall the words of Charles E. Hughes at a time when a sweeping attempt to deny radicals their rights simply because they were radical had carried away the New York Assembly:

> I count it a most serious mistake to proceed not against individuals charged with violation of the law, but against masses of our citizens combined for political action, by denying them the only resource of peaceful government; that is, action by the ballot box and through duly elected representatives in legislative bodies.

If we restrict the security check to its proper and very narrow areas, and elsewhere guarantee free opinion, free speech, and a free vote, we are safe.

EXAMPLES OF CLEARANCE PROCEDURES [5]

This Committee mailed, in November 1947, a general request to members of the Federation of American Scientists to inform us of any cases known to them of allegedly unfair clearance procedures. In this manner we learned of seventy-six cases, of which fifty-six involve scientists.

In general, it is difficult to obtain such information. If an individual is denied clearance, he hesitates to inform even his friends because of the implied reflection on his character, however unwarranted the clearance denial may be. Therefore, the

[5] From: "Some Individual Cases of Clearance Procedures," by the Committee on Secrecy and Clearance, Federation of American Scientists. *Bulletin of the Atomic Scientists.* 4:281-5. September 1948. Reprinted by permission.

response to our request probably represents a small fraction of the total number of cases.

In view of the widespread interest in clearance problems, this Committee has felt it desirable to make public a selected number of these individual cases in detail. We have, of course, no way of checking the veracity of each letter sent to us. We can state only that, in each case described below, the facts are taken directly from a letter in our files. . . .

The Case of Dr. A: Dr. A. was offered a post as Physiologist P-6 in an Army laboratory. He was informed that he had been cleared by Military Intelligence. Turning down other offers, he moved to the East coast from California, where he had been living for twenty years, to assume his duties. Prior to this, he had had fifteen years of research experience at universities. . . .

Two months after I arrived here I was abruptly informed that the clearance I had received was only an interim one and that I was not cleared. I was offered the alternative of resigning "without prejudice" or of being suspended. I was curtly informed an appeal would be fruitless and if suspended I would be ultimately dismissed "with cause" and it would be so entered into my record. . . . I was told that there were no charges against me but that Military Intelligence considered me a potential "risk" for the following reasons:

1. The birthplace of my parents
2. I was a member of the Federation of Atomic Scientists
3. I was a member of the Independent Citizens Committee of the Arts, Sciences and Professions
4. I knew too many left wing people . . .

On the basis of the above, I was considered to be either a Communist or a "fellow traveler." . . . I am not now, nor ever have been a Communist or "fellow traveler." . . . In addition to a good academic research reputation I have a 4½-year record of accomplishment as Responsible Investigator for OSRD-cmc and BuMed and Surgery Projects. These were carried on during the war . . . and were highly classified.

Dr. A. . . . was suspended "in the interests of national security" without a hearing. Five months later, the Secretary of the Army ordered his reinstatement and stated that the "action taken was unjustified." He received his back pay and an apology. He then resigned to accept a better position. . . .

The Case of Dr. C: Dr. C. is a biologist of nineteen years experience who has published more than sixty papers. In 1946, he was made chief of a section at a U.S. Army research laboratory. This position terminated without notice or explanation after he had been there for several months. . . .

Colonel X, the director of the Y laboratory . . . told me he had received an order from the Commanding General of Y to terminate my services, because I could not be cleared for access to classified documents. I explained that I had already been cleared during the war, had read numerous secret documents in the course of my work, and was myself an author of a number of classified publications, and the holder of patents pending with the Army and Navy, likewise classified. . . .

Dr. C. then spent several weeks trying vainly . . . to ascertain the charges against him. . . .

I might state here that I have never been a member of the Communist party, and know practically nothing of their activities. . . . Both my parents were born in Kovno, Lithuania (formerly Kovno, Russia). I subscribe to *PM, In Fact,* the *New Republic, Consumers' Union,* and receive about a dozen scientific publications. After the war I received a letter of commendation from the group leader and a certificate of effective service from the OSRD.

After five months of unemployment, Dr. C. secured another position doing unclassified work. . . . He was not able to learn the charges against him, much less contest them. . . .

After having been at the Z laboratory about six months, I was informed only recently that the Army's Central Intelligence Bureau, unsolicited, sent representatives to the Assistant Director of Z, and to the chief of the laboratory I have been working in, to make representations concerning me. It appears that the Army proposes to "hound" me out of any position I may succeed in obtaining. There is no question that the Y dismissal has made it difficult for me to obtain another job as my subsequent attempts demonstrated. . . . It may be appropriate to point out . . . that these . . . are as yet unclassified projects." . . .

The Case of Mr. E: The author of the following letter was refused clearance and dismissed from the research laboratory of a prominent electrical manufacturing company. . . .

A year ago I . . . was abruptly told to submit my resignation because I had not been cleared by the Army. . . . This came as a complete shock as I had been employed by the Laboratory for seven and a half years, including the war years when I had been covered by Security Clearance. . . . No appeal was possible. I was subsequently informed that the one month period initially given me "to get out" was modified to cover such time, up to several months, as was necessary for me to find employment elsewhere. . . In no manner, to repeat, was I given either the opportunity to appeal my case or to learn any more definitely the reasons for my failure to receive clearance.

To make matters worse, the V Co. was able to use me on non-secret work at their J Laboratory, for I was asked to make a visit there for an interview. This interview, however, was canceled by the J people after "checking with the Research Lab in ――――." Similarly while I was visiting [a separate industrial firm] where clearance was no issue, my interview was abruptly terminated—they informed me they had "checked with the V Research Laboratory."

The Case of Mr. G: Mr. G. is a chemist who has traversed a complex path of clearances and denial of clearance for a period of two years. For four years previous to the events described below, he had worked on various classified projects including three years during the war with the Manhattan District. During this time his clearance status was not questioned. Early in 1946 he was asked to join a group urgently need at Los Alamos to work on the Bikini atomic bomb tests. . . . The day before his planned departure, a telephone message was received stating that he had not been cleared. . . .

This came as a shock to my wife and me. . . . I knew of absolutely no reason why I should not be cleared. I have never belonged to any subversive organizations nor taken part in any subversive activities, nor has my wife. . . . Accordingly, on February 21, I sent a telegram to General Leslie R. Groves asking either that I be cleared or be told the reason why clearance was refused. . . . On February 26, I received a reply . . . "Apparently there has been some misunderstanding concerning your clearance status PD I have checked into this matter and find that you have been cleared for employment at Los Alamos PD End Maj. Gen. L. R. Groves Manhattan Dist. Washington, D.C.

When Mr. G. returned from Los Alamos he inquired about the possibility of becoming a consultant-without-pay to the AEC laboratory at which he had been employed during the war. . . . Mr. G. waited for three months and was then told he could not be cleared. In February 1947 he wrote a long letter appealing his case directly to the Atomic Energy Commission. Twelve months later he was granted partial clearance for "access to files" to complete his thesis. He has not yet been told whether he can be employed again at an AEC laboratory. . . .

The personal results of [my] security difficulties have been many: [I] have suffered financial loss, personal discomfort, and great personal embarrassment. . . . The implications, moreover, are far reaching in their effect and can quite conceivably prejudice one's status for many years. . . . Since first being employed by the Manhattan District, I have planned to make this field my life work and to go back to work in one of the National Laboratories concerned with atomic energy when I have obtained my Ph.D. degree. Now, unless a change in decision is made, this is no longer possible. . . .

However, the broader implications of the denial of clearance are, of course, the more important, far reaching ones. The fact that a man can be judged without knowing what is held against him and without having a chance to clarify his position is intolerable. A security system based upon such false premises seems entirely incompatible with a democracy. It is only reasonable and just that one should know the facts in his own case and have an opportunity to speak in his own behalf. I should welcome an opportunity to do so.

THE OAK RIDGE HEARINGS [6]

Two scientists at the atomic laboratories here have been suspended pending determination of their loyalty, three others have been called up before a loyalty board and it is expected that as many as thirty more cases may be heard in the immediate future.

The charges upon which these men are being heard are not sworn, but consist of anonymous accusations of Communist leanings. In most cases the accusation is admitted to be thin even by the men who are hearing the cases. One charge, for example, read: "A former landlord of yours has reported that in 1943, after you moved from the premises in which you had been residing, certain magazines and pamphlets which may have been left on the premises by you may have included a copy of the magazine *New Masses*." Another charge reads: "A neighbor has

[6] From "Report on Oak Ridge Hearings," by Stephen White, staff reporter, *New York Herald Tribune*. (Condensed version of the reports which appeared May 18, 19, and 29 in the *New York Herald Tribune*) *Bulletin of the Atomic Scientists*. 4:194-6. July 1948. Reprinted by permission.

stated that she believes a close relative by marriage is a Communist." The man against whom these charges were made is one of the two who has been suspended.

It is the nature of the charges rather than the fact that hearings are being held that has created a state of acute apprehension here that is shared by the scientists, the administration and the examining board alike. There are many here, not normally pessimistic, who fear that the outcome is likely to be the annihilation of Oak Ridge as a major contributor to atomic energy research.

The disorganization of morale at the laboratory became acute in January after the commission made sizable alterations in the research program that had been set up. Soon afterward, the suspension of two scientists, the announcement of hearings for three more and the threat that thirty others would be called hastened the exodus from the Tennessee research center, one of the most important under commission rule.

Although the figures show that one third of the sixty senior physicists and chemists have been lost by resignation, the situation is actually worse than that. Many of those who have made no final decision to depart are seeking other work in industry or education, and it is not unlikely that the numbers will grow in the next few weeks.

Of thirty senior physicists, ten have departed since the beginning of the year. Of thirty chemists, three have departed and eight others have committed themselves as going in the next few months.

Hearings are held before a board which includes one member of the AEC administration here, one member of the technical staff and one Knoxville lawyer. The accused are permitted to have counsel and to present witnesses; they are given transcripts of the record and are permitted all latitude in conducting their defense. They are not allowed to know the names of the people who have submitted accusations against them, however, and may not confront their accusers. They are not given access to the Federal Bureau of Investigation dossiers upon which the charges are based, but in the letters calling them for hearing some of these charges are itemized.

All those who have appeared agree that the hearings are eminently fair, and that there is no attempt being made to "get" anybody. The local board, however, does not have the final disposition of these cases. Both the AEC in Washington and its own loyalty board, headed by former Associate Justice Owen Roberts, of the Supreme Court, supplement the local board, and perhaps the joint congressional committee as well.

The men who have been examined are between the ages of twenty-two and thirty-eight, and the positions they hold vary in importance. In more than one case the person's background is associated so closely with work on atomic energy that discharge from Oak Ridge would be equivalent to loss of the ability to earn a livelihood.

The hearings have been going on for more than a month, while the Association of Oak Ridge Scientists and Engineers debated the advisability of making the situation public. Once the decision was made, the association went all out. This reporter has spoken to the men who have undergone hearings, and has read transcripts. At the request of the men involved, names are omitted from this account.

At best, it is freely granted by John C. Franklin, area director for the AEC, that the charges brought do not appear to carry much conviction. To this reporter the persons against whom the charges were brought point out that they also abound in errors of fact or acute misconceptions, all of which are subject to simple check.

Thus, the camp referred to in [one case] is run by a cooperative organization headed by Jerry Voorhis, former Democratic Congressman from California, and bars Communists as officers. The "member of several subversive organizations" in [another case] was editor, until he died, of two technical journals, and almost every research scientist in that field corresponded with him of necessity. The newspaper referred to in [the same case] is violently anti-Communist. Similar errors occur in almost all cases.

The young scientist [in still another case] whose transcript was turned over to this reporter, figuratively threw up his hands at the hearings. The charge, he told the board, could only stem from pure malice. "I have to admit," said S. Frank Fowler, Knoxville attorney who was one member of the board, "that I squirmed a little listening to him try to defend himself against a charge of that sort. He said, 'Who is this man that says I am a Communist? He has no name, no face, no social security number.' I must say," Mr. Fowler remarked ruefully, "that I sympathize with him."

The most immediate impression of the loyalty investigations is that no one finds them anything but distasteful.

Not unnaturally, the scientists who have been called up, and those who fear they may be next to undergo the procedure, find it entirely hateful. John C. Franklin, director of Oak Ridge for the Atomic Energy Commission, winces visibly when the subject is broached, for he knows that it may mean the end of his great research institute. The board that hears the cases is composed of men who are sunk in gloom at the task they must perform; the best they can say is that the law directs that the job must be done, and therefore they must go ahead and do it.

The worst of it seems to be that no person at Oak Ridge came to this reporter's attention who thought that any of the men are "loyalty risks" under any reasonable test that could be devised. The men who actually hear the cases, of course, could not with any propriety make such statements, but even their remarks indicated that they have not been impressed by the dossiers upon which they must base their search.

It is clear that in an organization as tightly integrated as Oak Ridge, where almost all the technical people live and work in close association, a man whose loyalty was suspect would soon be known to his fellows. The men and women here insist that no such person exists in Oak Ridge, or, if one should have stolen in, his mask is so supremely excellent that he will escape the coarse-grained net that the AEC is casting.

The scientists already called—two physicists, two chemists and a mathematician who asked that their names be withheld—do not complain about the manner in which the hearings are carried out. Without exception, they expressed confidence in the three men who have heard their cases: Charles Vanden

Bulck, administrative assistant to the director; John Swartout, a member of the technical staff; and S. Frank Fowler, Knoxville attorney.

At the hearings the suspected worker is furnished a list of charges against him, he may present witnesses and retain counsel, at his own expense, and he is given a transcript of the hearing. In the transcripts furnished this reporter it was clear that the person heard had an entirely reasonable and sympathetic audience, which tried at least as hard to find out favorable evidence as unfavorable.

The atmosphere was best expressed by Mr. Fowler himself. "We do not consider ourselves prosecutors," he said. "We are not trying to convict anybody. We are trying to judge these men by their words and their bearing. It's really a job for a psychoanalyst, not a lawyer."

But the men who have been heard are incensed, not at the hearing procedures but at the fact that what they consider the flimsy and trifling evidence that has been brought against them should be given any attention at all. Basically, they feel that the AEC is letting them down. The dossiers, they say, should have been read and discarded if the worst that they provided were the charges that have been brought. "Any self-respecting radical," one of them said, "would be ashamed of charges like those."

They believe that most of the charges could have been checked without any trouble before the hearing procedure was invoked. One of the two who have been suspended was able to controvert with unmistakable evidence the charges brought against him. It is expected he will soon be reinstated. "Why didn't the Federal Bureau of Investigation do that before they submitted them?" he said. "Just one phone call would have assured them that my sister was not a member of the Joint Anti-Fascist Refugees Committee, or that the camp my wife belongs to has no connection with communism or leftism."

"Sure, they'll clear us all," another said. "What does that prove? They'll probably fire the hearing board and appoint a new one. If they are willing to try us at all, under these charges, it can only mean that they will keep on trying us until a certain number of us have been fired."

It is this type of fear that is leading to a full-scale exodus from Oak Ridge, since there are a limited number of scientists today, most of whom are entirely employable in private industry, and the competition for their services is high.

B. W. Menke, director of the area's security division, explained that up to now the dossiers have been read and charges prepared in Washington, and instructions sent to Oak Ridge that certain men be heard. A new procedure, only now coming into effect, will supplant this with a system where his office checks the dossiers and brings charges. In any case, after recommendations by the board and the director, cases go back to Washington for final disposition.

"The law says we have to do this," he said. "We are responsible for seeing that no potentially disloyal people work on restricted data. How would you have us go about it?"

But one of the men took a slightly different view. "They are throwing the baby out with the bath," he said.

THE PRICE OF INJUSTICE [7]

In March 1948, shortly following the publication of charges of disloyalty against Dr. Edward U. Condon, the Atomic Scientists of Chicago surveyed its membership with respect to their reactions to security clearance procedures applied to scientists working on classified research projects. Replies were received from 72 per cent of the organization's 144 members. Of those replying, 45 per cent were currently employed on government-sponsored classified projects; 11 per cent on government-sponsored unclassified projects; 48 per cent in non-government-sponsored scientific work; 9 per cent were not currently employed in scientific work. However, all but 2 per cent had, at one time or another, been employed on classified projects.

[7] From "Loyalty Investigations—A Poll of Atomic Scientists," by Shirley A. Star, study director of the National Opinion Research Center, Denver, Colorado. *Bulletin of the Atomic Scientists.* 4:218. August 1948. Reprinted by permission.

The overwhelming majority of these scientists—85 per cent—thought that some kind of security clearance procedure was necessary at the present time; only 4 per cent said they were unnecessary; while 11 per cent were undecided. Those who regarded clearance procedures as necessary almost invariably explained their position in terms of safeguarding national security in the light of the present international situation. Typical of this attitude is the following: "In these days of international unrest, it would be folly not to employ some type of security clearance on work which affects the national security."

The few who regarded security clearances as unnecessary did so from a belief in the necessity of free communication to scientific progress. Those who were undecided most frequently said they saw the conflict between the principle of scientific freedom and the needs of national security. As one said: "I am not certain that the cost to the country in delayed work, inefficient operation and reduced total effort isn't too high to pay for a transitory security."

While most of these scientists accepted the necessity of security clearance procedures of some sort, they did not, for the most part, approve of the methods now being used. They were asked: "On the whole, do you approve or disapprove of the methods now being employed in making security clearances of scientists employed on classified projects?"

Eleven per cent approved, 54 per cent disapproved and 34 per cent were undecided (1 per cent failed to answer the question). The few who approved said that the present system usually worked fairly or that they could not think of any better system. The rather large proportion who did not express a definite opinion usually explained that they did not have reliable information about the procedures being used. The disapproving majority offered as their major objections:

1. The lack of legal procedures. They felt that scientists refused clearance were not permitted to defend themselves, to know the nature and source of the charges against them, or to offer anything in rebuttal. There was some feeling that this amounted to considering a man guilty merely because an accusation had been made.

2. The kind of evidence employed. Many scientists felt that too much weight was being given to hearsay in making queries of scientists' acquaintances. In addition, they thought that mere association with suspect persons or organizations was being taken as proof of disloyalty.

3. The definition of disloyalty. Some scientists felt that all political liberalism was being identified as disloyalty.

The majority of these scientists felt that a scientist who has been refused clearance before employment should be permitted (1) to know the charges against him, (2) to cross-examine the sources used against him, and (3) to make some kind of appeal from the decision against him. There was less agreement among these scientists as to whether a scientist who has not been cleared should have ultimate recourse to the federal courts, but this right was more often favored than opposed. In the case of a scientist whose clearance has been withdrawn after employment, there was even more emphatic agreement that he should be permitted these four rights.

In view of this endorsement of a procedure which permits the scientist refused clearance to know the charges against him, to cross-examine the sources used against him, and to appeal the decision in some way, it is all the more striking that most of these scientists do not believe that these rights are granted by current procedures. There is also a good deal of uncertainty and confusion about current procedures, as evidenced by the proportions saying they just don't know whether current procedures permit these rights or not.

About three fourths of these scientists regarded the existing personnel clearance procedures as a disadvantage of working on classified projects as compared with unclassified projects: 43 per cent said it was "a great disadvantage," and 34 per cent thought it was "somewhat of a disadvantage." Only the publication policy of classified projects was more often given as a disadvantage of working on them. They recognized, of course, that there were as well certain advantages to working on classified projects, especially in the size of research budgets and in access to special materials and instruments.

The charges made against Dr. Edward U. Condon, in particular, had the effect of making many of these scientists reluctant to accept government employment. Ninety-nine per cent of them had been following the news about Dr. Condon, and 75 per cent had either decided to decline government offers or were more reluctant to accept them in the light of his treatment. The scientists were asked: "How did the manner in which the charges were made against Condon affect your willingness to accept responsible government positions?"

Made me decided to decline any such offer.... 12%

Made me reluctant to accept................. 63

Had no important effect.................... 23

Made me more willing to consider such an offer. —

No answer............................... 2

_____

100%

Interestingly enough, scientists currently employed on government-sponsored projects were just as likely to feel reluctant about accepting government employment as a result of the Condon case as were those not employed by the government.

The question just presented indicates only one aspect of these scientists' reactions to the charges made against Dr. Condon. In order to tap a wider range of attitudes, the survey concluded by asking the scientists to reply in their own words to the question: "As a scientist, what is your own reaction to the Condon affair?"

Their answers fell into three main groups:

1. Thirty-nine per cent made comments critical of the House Committee on Un-American Activities. Some typical expressions: "The activities of Un-American Committee are, to put it mildly, *un-American*; their actions violate civil rights." "I am outraged about the methods employed, in particular, about the freedom of the Committee on Un-American activities and its employees to make public accusation without the substantiation of such charges being required. The committee members and employees should be subject to the libel laws."

2. Thirty three per cent were critical of the attack on Condon, without specific references to the House Committee. Some comments illustrative of this group are: "The charges should never have been made unless substantiated with infallible evidence." "Whether the charges are valid or not, this is not the way to proceed in such a matter."

3. Eighteen per cent commented that the effect of such incidents was or would be to lose the best scientific talent from government projects. Seven per cent made miscellaneous comments. Three per cent did not answer the question.

(The total adds to more than 100 per cent because some of the scientists were engaged in more than one type of work.)

BIBLIOGRAPHY

An asterisk (*) preceding a reference indicates that the article or a part of it has been reprinted in this book.

BOOKS, PAMPHLETS, AND DOCUMENTS

Bernays, Edward L. Safeguarding civil liberties today. 158p. Cornell University Press. Ithaca, N.Y. '45.

Casey, Ralph D.; Smith, Bruce Lannes; Lasswell, Harold D. Propaganda, communication and public opinion. 445p. Princeton University Press. Princeton, N.J. '46.

Commission on Freedom of the Press. Free and responsible press; a general report on mass communication. 138p. University of Chicago Press. Chicago. '47.

*Commission on Freedom of the Press. Government and mass communication; a report by Zechariah Chafee, Jr. 2v. 829p. University of Chicago Press. Chicago. '47.

Cushman, Robert E. Safeguarding our civil liberties. Public Affairs Pamphlet No. 43. 31p. Public Affairs Committee. New York. '40.

*Cushman, Robert E. New threats to American freedom. Public Affairs Pamphlet No. 143. 43p. Public Affairs Committee. New York. S. '48.

Gordon, Matthew. News is a weapon. 268p. Knopf. New York. '42.

*Hildebrand, Joel H. How not to control atomic energy. American Library Association. 10p. Chicago. S. 1, '47.
Same. American Library Association Bulletin. 41:273-81. S. 1, '47.

Hocking, William Ernest. Freedom of the press. 239p. University of Chicago Press. Chicago. '47.

Kinsley, Philip H. Liberty and the press. 99p. The Chicago Tribune. Chicago. '44.

Matthews, Blayney F. The specter of sabotage. 255p. Lyman House. Los Angeles. '41.

Riegel, O. W. Mobilizing for chaos. 231p. Yale University Press. New Haven, Conn. '35.

*United States. Congress. Act for the development and control of atomic energy. (S. 1717) (Public law 585, 79th Congress) 22p. [Approved August 1, 1948] Supt. of Docs. Washington, D.C. '46.

United States. Department of State. Pub. 2498. A report on the international control of atomic energy. 61p. Supt. of Docs. Washington, D.C. '46

*United States. Department of State. Pub. 2520. Atomic energy: agreed
    declaration by the President of the United States of America and
    Prime Minister of the United Kingdom, and the Prime Minister of
    Canada, signed at Washington, November 15, 1945. 5p. Supt. of
    Docs. Washington, D.C. '46.
*United States. Department of State. Pub. 2702. International control
    of atomic energy: growth of a policy. 282p. Supt. of Docs. Wash-
    ington, D.C. '46.
United States. Department of State. Pub. 3024. Report by the President
    to the Congress (second annual report on the UN). 359p. Supt.
    of Docs. Washington, D.C. '48.
United States. Department of State. Pub. 3161. International control
    of atomic energy: policy at the crossroads. 252p. Supt. of Docs.
    Washington, D.C. Je. '48.
*United States. Department of the Army. Memorandum No. 360-25-1.
    Release of military information. Washington, D.C. Ja. 7, '48.
*United States. Senate. Document No. 96. Letter from the chairman and
    members of the United States Atomic Energy Commission trans-
    mitting the second semiannual report of the United States Atomic
    Energy Commission, July 22, 1947. 80th Congress, 1st Session.
    27p. Supt. of Docs. Washington, D.C. '48.
*United States. Senate. Document No. 118. Letter from the chairman
    and members of the United States Atomic Energy Commission trans-
    mitting the third semiannual report of the United States Atomic
    Energy Commission, February 2, 1948. 80th Congress, 2d Session.
    49p. Supt. of Docs. Washington, D.C. '48.
*United States. Senate. Special Committee on Atomic Energy. Atomic
    energy: hearings, November 27, 1945-February 15, 1946, pursuant to
    S. Res. 179. 79th Congress, 2d Session. 5 pts. 573p. Supt. of Docs.
    Washington, D.C. '45, '46.
*United States. War Department. Army Regulations No. 380-5, Sec-
    tion V. Washington, D.C. Ag. 15, '46.
    Memorandum No. 380-5-1. Military information; restrictions on publication
of operating or financial statements by companies engaged in war production. Ag. 7,
'46; Memorandum No. 380-5-2. Military information. S. 10, '46.

PERIODICALS

*American Bar Association Journal. 34:645-8+. Ag. '48. Communism
    vs. the Constitution: the power to protect our free institutions.
    Frank B. Ober.
*American Political Science Review. 42:486-99. Je. '48. The federal
    loyalty program: background and problems. Roger S. Abbott.
Annals of the American Academy of Political and Social Science. 185:
    182-9. My. '36. The freedom of the press. Chester H. Rowell.
Annals of the American Academy of Political and Social Science. 250:
    26-31. Mr. '47. Government control of sources of information.
    K. E. Mundt.

Annals of the American Academy of Political and Social Science. 254: 137-9. N. '47. Freedom of press, radio, and screen. Byron Price.

Atlantic. 180:115-16. Jl. '47. Press and its critics. L. M. Lyons.

Atlantic. 180:3-7. S. '47. The Atlantic report on the world today— Moscow.

Atlantic. 180:27-32. S. '47. Freedom of science in America. James R. Newman and Byron S. Miller.

Atlantic. 180:12. N. '47. Atlantic report; what is disloyalty?

Atlantic. 180:15+. N. '47. Atlantic report; atomic energy.

Atlantic. 180:29-32. N. '47. Atomic war or peace. Albert Einstein (as told to Raymond Swing).

Atlantic. 180:93-4. N. '47. Witch-hunting then and now. Sumner T. Pike.

Atlantic. 182:19-23. Ag. '48. Subversive of what. Julian P. Boyd.

Atlantic. 182:36-41. Ag. '48. I'd do it again. Edward Kennedy.

*Bulletin of the Atomic Scientists. 3:233-4. S. '47. Two years after Hiroshima.

*Bulletin of the Atomic Scientists. 3:321-4+. N. '47. Security regulations in the field of nuclear research. Bart J. Bok, Francis Friedman, and Victor Weisskopf.

Bulletin of the Atomic Scientists. 3:335-8. N. '47. Atomic energy is your business. David E. Lilienthal.

Bulletin of the Atomic Scientists. 4:45-8. F. '48. Loyalty procedures of the A. E. C.—a report and recommendation. Byron S. Miller and Harrison S. Brown.

*Bulletin of the Atomic Scientists. 4:163-5. Je. '48. How far should military censorship extend? report by the Committee on Secrecy and Clearance, Federation of American Scientists.

Bulltin of the Atomic Scientists. 4:173. Je. '48. Freedom of thought and the future of America. Robert M. Hutchins.

Bulletin of the Atomic Scientists. 4:174+. Je. '48. A state governed by fear ceases to be civilized. Edward U. Condon.

Bulletin of the Atomic Scientists. 4:175. Je. '48. We must protect the last increment of ability. Harold C. Urey.

Bulletin of the Atomic Scientists. 4:193-4. Jl. '48. 'Security risk' cases —a vexed question. T. H. Davies.

*Bulletin of the Atomic Scientists. 4:194-6. Jl. '48. Report on Oak Ridge hearings. Stephen White.

Bulletin of the Atomic Scientists. 4:197+. Jl. '48. AEC loyalty procedures and civil rights. M. Gerson and M. L. Lesser.

*Bulletin of the Atomic Scientists. 4:198. Jl. '48. AEC interim procedure for local security boards, announcement by AEC, May 20, 1948.

*Bulletin of the Atomic Scientists. 4:211-12+. Jl. '48. American Society of Newspaper Editors reports on atomic information problems, report by Gideon Seymour.

*Bulletin of the Atomic Scientists. 4:218. Ag. '48. Loyalty investigations—a poll of atomic scientists. Shirley A. Star.

Bulletin of the Atomic Scientists. 4:277-9. S. '48. New legislation to replace the McMahon Act. Walter DeCew.

*Bulletin of the Atomic Scientists. 4:281-5. S. '48. Some individual cases of clearance procedures. Committee on Secrecy and Clearance, Federation of American Scientists.

Christian Century. 64:611. My. 14, '47. Find peril to freedom in loyalty tests.

Christian Century. 65:76-8. Ja. 21, '48. Spy scares. F. J. McConnell.

Christian Science Monitor. 40:5. Jl. 22, '48. UN concerned by link with subversives.

Christian Science Monitor. 40:1. Ag. 5, '48. Spy suspect kept U.S. job despite navy ouster effort.

*Christian Science Monitor. 40:1. Ag. 5, '48. Kremlin talks: Top secret.

Christian Science Monitor. 40:10. Ag. 5, '48. Complete airings slated in loyalty charge quiz. Mary Hornaday.

Christian Science Monitor. 40:14. Ag. 5, '48. The aim vs. the method.

Christian Science Monitor. 40:1. Ag. 6, '48. Reason for keeping alleged Communists on U.S. job aired. Mary Hornaday.

Christian Science Monitor. 40:6. Ag. 6, '48. Alger Hiss denies Communist party tie. Mary Hornaday.

Christian Science Monitor. 40:16. Ag. 6, '48. Politics and education. Mary Hornaday.

Christian Science Monitor. 40:1. Ag. 7, '48. Public hearings halted in Senate loyalty probe. Mary Hornaday.

Christian Science Monitor. 40:3. Ag. 7, '48. McDowell reasserts Soviets received uranium shipments.

*Christian Science Monitor. 40:10. Ag. 7, '48. Loyalty checks enhance stature at spy trials.

Christian Science Monitor. 40:9. Ag. 18, '48. Spy hearings stir quiz on loyalty laws needed. Mary Hornaday.

Christian Science Monitor. 40:1. Ag. 25, '48. State of the nation. Where did Moscow get uranium 235? Roscoe Drummond.

Christian Science Monitor. 40:1. Ag. 26, '48. Hiss vs. Chambers tilt deepens spy mystery. Mary Hornaday.

Christian Science Monitor. 40:5. Ag. 26, '48. Hiss demands verdicts based on facts.

*Christian Science Monitor. 40:9. Ag. 26, '48. Censorship censured: news blackouts cast shadow on west. William H. Stringer.

Christian Science Monitor. 40:14. Ag. 27, '48. To keep it in the course.

*Christian Science Monitor. 40:1. Ag. 28, '48. Congress probes tighten tests for employee loyalty. Mary Hornaday.

Christian Science Monitor. 40:3. S. 2, '48. Evidence of "spies" seen nil in UN agents admitted to U.S.

*Christian Science Monitor. 40:5. S. 2, '48. Berle links Hiss to pro-Soviets.

Christian Science Monitor. 40:14. S. 2, '48. What hysteria can do.

*Christian Science Monitor. 40:14. S. 3, '48. "Secret" vs "open" diplomacy.

Christian Science Monitor. 40:2. S. 4, '48. Teacher's dismissal affirmed as negative.

Christian Science Monitor. 40:14. S. 7, '48. Perspective.

Christian Science Monitor. 40:3. S. 8, '48. Director of A-bomb project to disclose story of spies.

Christian Science Monitor. 40:5. S. 8, '48. Spy hearings backed and censured. Mary Hornaday.

Christian Science Monitor. 40:6. S. 8, '48. Britain suspends atomic researcher.

Christian Science Monitor. 40:14. S. 9, '48. How it should be done.

*Christian Science Monitor. 40:1. S. 11, '48. Atom secrets tie anti-trust case in knot. Roscoe Fleming.

Commonweal. 45:604. Ap. 4, '47. Communist man-hunt.

*Congressional Record. 94:4572-7. Ap. 14, '48. Remarks before the House of Representatives by Helen Gahagan Douglas.

Congressional Record. 94:A2241. Ap. 19, '48. Address by Senator Eugene D. Millikin.

Congressional Record. 94:4894-902. Ap. 22, '48. The Condon case, remarks on the floor of the House.

Congressional Record. 94:4912-13. Ap. 22, '48. Why were the Condon hearings postponed?

*Congressional Record. 94:A2558-9. Ap. 22, '48. Radio address by Marion T. Bennett.

Congressional Record. 94:A2574-8. Ap. 22, '48. Edward U. Condon.

Congressional Record. 94:A2608-9. Ap. 26, '48. Memorandum by the Department of the Army, Public Information Division, Press section, in reply to an open letter by Drew Pearson.

Congressional Record. 94:A2615. Ap. 26, '48. Atom scientists hit un-American activities group.

Congressional Record. 94:A2622-3. Ap. 27, '48. On sticking to the facts in the Condon matter. C. P. Ives.

*Congressional Record. 94:5339-41. My. 3, '48. Remarks before the House of Representatives by John W. Byrnes.

Congressional Record. 94:5386-8. My. 4, '48. Remarks before the House of Representatives by F. Edward Hebert.

*Congressional Record. 94:5849-50. My. 12, '48. Remarks before the House of Representatives by Clare E. Hoffman.

*Congressional Record. 94:5963. My. 13, '48. Remarks before the House of Representatives by J. Percy Priest.

Congressional Record. 94:A3091-136. My. 13, '48. Report on the Communist party of the U.S. as an advocate of overthrow of government by force and violence, issued by the House Committee on Un-American Activities.

Congressional Record. 94:A3213. My. 14, '48. Remarks by Richard B. Vail before the House of Representatives.

*Congressional Record. 94:6045-6. My. 17, '48. Report of the Joint Committee on Atomic Energy presented to the U.S. Senate. Bourke B. Hickenlooper.

Congressional Record. 94:A3205. My. 17, '48. Subversive activities control bill, 1948.

*Congressional Record. 94:6169-70. My. 18, '48. Remarks before the House of Representatives by George A. Dondero.

Congressional Record. 94:A3210. My. 18, '48. The truth about the Mundt-Nixon bill.

Congressional Record. 94:A3319. My. 20, '48. Mundt-Nixon bill.

Congressional Record. 94:A3333. My. 20, '48. Danger to freedom.

Congressional Record. 94:A3656-7. Je. 2, '48. Memorial day address. Joseph W. Martin, Jr.

Congressional Record. 94:A3709. Je. 4, '48. The Mundt-Nixon bill.

Congressional Record. 94:A3847. Je. 9, '48. Control of subversive influences.

Congressional Record. 94:A3940. Je. 11, '48. The Mundt-Nixon bill.

Congressional Record. 94:9126-7. Je. 18, '48. It's no time for secrecy. Hanson W. Baldwin.

*Congressional Record. 94:9693-6. Jl. 29, '48. Remarks before the House of Representatives by Chet Holifield.

Congressional Record. 94:9793-4. Ag. 2, '48. Remarks by Bartel J. Jonkman.

*Congressional Record. 94:9935-9. Ag. 4, '48. Remarks before the House of Representatives by Edward H. Rees.

Congressional Record. 94:10059-60. Ag. 5, '48. Remarks by George A. Dondero.

Congressional Record. 94:A5160-2. Ag. 5, '48. Executive papers—the President and the Congress, address by Peter Campbell Brown.

Congressional Record. 94:10185. Ag. 6, '48. Uranium material furnished to Russia. John McDowell.

Congressional Record. 94:A5217-20. Ag. 6, '48. Testimony before House Committee on Un-American Activities, Ag. 5, '48, by Fred E. Busbey.

*Congressional Record. 94:10272-7. Ag. 7, '48. The Iron curtain at home. Homer Ferguson.

*Congressional Record. 94:5502-3. Ag. 17, '48. Remarks before the House of Representatives by Edward H. Rees.

Dallas Morning News. 63, sec. II:3. Je. 24, '48. FBI always tries to get basic facts of any case. J. Edgar Hoover.

Dallas Morning News. 63, sec. II:7. Ag. 29, '48. Old friend's advice changes Clark's mind on 'spy' cases. Robert S. Allen.

Dallas Morning News. 63, sec. II:3. Ag. 31, '48. Hiss-Chambers issue causes row in Thomas committee. Robert S. Allen.

Editor & Publisher. 80:5. N. 1, '47. Secrecy rules softened in response to protests. James J. Butler.

Editor & Publisher. 80:7. N. 22, '47. Security board retreats to modified 'gag' stand. James J. Butler.

Editor & Publisher. 80:8. D. 6, '47. Open hearings demanded in Texas.

*Editor & Publisher. 80:10. D. 6, '47. ASNE, atomic board join in security study. James J. Butler.

Editor & Publisher. 80:34. D. 20, '47. Back to secrecy.

*Editor & Publisher. 81:8. Ja. 10, '48. Justice Department studies 'break' on speed plane.

*Editor & Publisher. 81:34. Ja. 24, '48. Self-censorship.

Editor & Publisher. 81:5-6. Ja. 31, '48. How Soviet press is run: directives come under seal. By a former Soviet journalist.

Editor & Publisher. 81:36. F. 7, '48. U.S., UN find agreement on accreditation.

Editor & Publisher. 81:42. F. 7, '48. UN and free press.

Editor & Publisher. 81:12. F. 14, '48. Not a word—lock you up! Barked at Soviet editors. By a former Soviet journalist.

Editor & Publisher. 81:56. F. 28, '48. Girl army aid admits "leak" on Foust story.

Editor & Publisher. 81:9+. Mr. 6, '48. Seek plan to guard security information.

Editor & Publisher. 81:32. Mr. 6, '48. Covenant protects fundamental rights. Zechariah Chafee, Jr.

Editor & Publisher. 81:36. Mr. 20, '48. Straw man.

Editor & Publisher. 81:12+. Ap. 3, '48. Media security advisors suggested to Forrestal.

Editor & Publisher. 81:15. Ap. 3, '48. Army rules press correspondents may criticize.

*Editor & Publisher. 81:36. Ap. 3, '48. Security problem.

Editor & Publisher. 81:80. Ap. 10, '48. Shop talk at thirty. Robert W. Brown.

Editor & Publisher. 81:50+. Ag. 21, '48. Much data available on atomic projects. Charles W. White.

*Editor & Publisher. 81:30. Ag. 28, '48. Atomic news.

*Fortune. 32:170-1+. N. '45. Military security and the atomic bomb. Louis N. Ridenour.

Forum. 109:106-11. F. '48. Loyalty board. S. W. Richardson.

*Forum. 109:193-7. Ap. '48. American civil rights in a revolutionary age: the problem of loyalty. Ellen D. Ellis.

Harper's Magazine. 195:193-9. S. '47. Who is loyal to America? Henry Steele Commager.

*Harper's Magazine. 195:438-43. N. '47. How To rid the government of Communists. James A. Wechsler.

*Harvard Law Review. 61:592. Spring, '48. Loyalty tests and guilt by association. John Lord O'Brian.
    Same. Bulletin of the Atomic Scientists. 4:166-72. My. '48.

Journalism Quarterly. 23:5-10+. Mr. '46. New world journalism demands background and responsibility. Martin Eban.

Journalism Quarterly. 24:315-22. D. '47. Atomic energy and the press: two years after Hiroshima. Neal O. Hines.

Ladies' Home Journal. 65:11-2+. S. '48. Climate of a free press. Dorothy Thompson.

*Liberty. 25:14+. Mr. '48. How the FBI finds disloyal government workers. J. Edgar Hoover (as told to Stacy V. Jones).

Liberty. 25:14-5. My. '48. Reds in the Panama Canal Zone. J. Parnell Thomas (as told to Stacy V. Jones).

Life. 21:84-5+. Jl. 29, '46. U. S. Communist party. Arthur M. Schlesinger, Jr.

Nation. 162:536-8. My. 4, '46. Canadian spy case. B. K. Sandwell.

Nation. 167:251-2. S. 4, '48. The case of Alger Hiss. Thomas Sancton.

Nation's Schools. 40:17-18. N. '47. What is loyalty? A. B. Moehlman.

New Republic. 119:11. Ag. 9, '48. Witch-hunt in the northwest.

New Republic. 119:6-7+. Ag. 16, '48. Trial by Congress. Michael Straight.

*New York Times. 97:E4. N. 16, '47. 'Secrets' arouse foes of censorship. Hanson W. Baldwin.

*New York Times. 98:3. Ag. 29, '48. Summary of report on spy inquiry.

New York Times. 98:20. S. 7, '48. Eight scientists assail Thomas committee.

*New York Times. 98:E5. S. 26, '48. Great precautions taken to guard atomic secrets. Anthony Leviero.

New York Times Magazine. p. 7+. N. 2, '47. What is loyalty? a difficult question. Arthur M. Schlesinger, Jr.

*New York Times Magazine. p. 9+. My. 2, '48. What is a Communist? Allan Nevins.

New York Times Magazine. p. 7+. Ag. 22, '48. Should we outlaw the Communist party? Henry Steele Commager.

Newsweek. 30:15. Nov. 24, '47. Red inquiry.

Newsweek. 30:24-25. D. 8, '47. Hollywood super-purge.

Newsweek. 30:23. D. 15, '47. Blacklist.

Newsweek. 30:43. D. 15, '47. Reports on British state of confusion.

Newsweek. 30:51+. D. 15, '47. Atomic age: year six.

Newsweek. 30:23. D. 22, '47. Campus cause célèbre.

Newsweek. 30:31. D. 29, '47. Japan: confidentially, some confidential shades of FEC-230.

Newsweek. 31:54. Ja. 5, '48. U. S. vs. UN.

Newsweek. 31:21-2. Ja. 12, '48. The atom strike danger.

Newsweek. 31:48. F. 2, '48. Atomic look-ahead.

Newsweek. 31:50+. F. 9, '48. MacArthur and the press.

Newsweek. 31:21+. Mr. 1, '48. The right to investigate.

Newsweek. 31:48. Mr. 1, '48. Press vs. MacArthur.

Newsweek. 31:54. Mr. 8, '48. Red faced.

Newsweek. 31:54. Mr. 8, '48. Secret sources.

Newsweek. 31:25+. Mr. 15, '48. The Condon case.

Newsweek. 31:36. Ap. 5, '48. Purge with care.

Newsweek. 31:31+. Ap. 19, '48. Hobble for reds.

Newsweek. 31:67. My. 17, '48. Hoffman's sleeper.

Newsweek. 31:24. My. 31, '48. Rider dodgers.

*Newsweek. 31:16. Je. 21, '48. Exports to Russia.

Newsweek. 31:27. Je. 21, '48. Much faster than sound.

Newsweek. 32:20-1. Jl. 19, '48. Assaying the Reds.

*Newsweek. 32:20-3+. Ag. 2, '48. The case of Mary and the spy ring shrinks to the case against the Reds.

*Newsweek. 32:20-1. Ag. 23, '48. Truth, half-truth, untruth.

*Newsweek. 32:24. O. 4, '48. Spy probe: the finger points.

Nieman Reports. 2:3-4. Ap. '48. The MacArthur censorship. Robert P. Martin.

Nineteenth Century. 140:302-13. D. '46. Royal commission. F. A. Voigt.

Plain Talk. 1:27-39. O. '46. The State Department espionage case. Emmanuel S. Larsen.

Plain Talk. 2:1-6. My. '48. They knife General Clay. Blair Taylor.
    Also reprinted in Congressional Record. 94:A2894-5. My. 5, '48.

Plain Talk. 2:32-3. My. '48. So runs the world—the case of Dr. Condon. Isaac Don Levine.

*Plain Talk. 2:1-5. S. '48. What's wrong with the loyalty program? A federal employee.

Public Opinion Quarterly. 9:140. Summer '48. Maintaining a healthy public opinion. Byron Price.

Publisher's Auxiliary. 82:1. ·N. 15, '47. President hits ASNE protest of censorship.

Queen's Quarterly. 53, no. 3:369-78. [Ag.] '46. Report of the Royal commission on espionage. Wilfrid Eggleston.

*St. Paul Pioneer Press & Dispatch. Ap. 18-25, '48. Communist links with the State Department, series of eight articles. Gustaf A. Nordin.
    Reprinted in Congressional Record. 94:A2554; A2572; A2628; A2666; A2689; A2705; A2753-4; A2822-3. Ap. 21-My. 3, '48.

Saturday Evening Post. 219:18-19+. Ja. 25; 24+. F. 1, '47. How the Russians spied on their allies. S. M. Shalett.

Saturday Evening Post. 221:92. Ja. 3, '48. Aid with a sneer will win us no friends.

Saturday Evening Post. 221:132. F. 21, '48. Even a "cold" war must have peace terms.

Saturday Evening Post. 221:15-16. Je. 19, '48. The atom general answers his critics. Leslie R. Groves.

Saturday Evening Post. 221:144. Je. 19, '48. Can we protect freedom without losing it?

Scholastic. 50:15. Ap. 14, '47. Testing loyalty.

Scholastic. 51:11-12. O. 13, '47. Checking up on loyalty.

School & Society. 64:27-8. Jl. 13, '46. Wanted: a new pledge of allegiance. Gilbert Byron.

School & Society. 66:145-50. Ag. 30, '47. All God's chillun got wings. W. H. Cowley.

Science Digest. 19:27-30. Je. '46. Five steps that make a spy. S. J. O. Alsop and Thomas Braden.

Science Teacher. 14:166-7+. D. '47. Scientists want freedom. Joseph Singerman.

Survey Graphic. 36:283-7+. My. '47. President's loyalty purge; with highlights of executive order no. 9835. R. E. Cushman.

Time. 50:70-3. Ag. 25, '47. Dangerous knowledge.

Time. 51:40. Mr. 29, '48. Transfer.

Time. 51:60. My. 3, '48. How to lose scientists.

Time. 52:42-3. Je. 28, '48. Stand up and be counted out.

Time. 52:52. Jl. 26, '48. The new freedom.

Time. 52:14-16. Ag. 9, '48. The network.

Today's World. 2:4. Ja. '48. Dismissals from War Department on account of disloyal connections.

Today's World. 2:22-3. Ja. '48. Subversive list called farcical.

*United States News & World Report. 25:15-16. Ag. 27, '48. Is FBI's anti-spy evidence wasted?

United States News & World Report. 25:11-13. S. 24, '48. U. S. tactics in the "cold war": gains that outweigh losses.

*University of Chicago Law Review. 15:799-821. Summer '48. A law is passed—the atomic energy act of 1946. Byron S. Miller.

*University of Chicago Law Review. 15:839-54. Summer '48. The atomic energy act: public administration without public debate. Herbert S. Marks.

Vital Speeches of the Day. 14:702-4. S. 1, '48. U. S. information program. G. V. Allen.

*Yale Law Journal. 56:769-802. My. '47. Control of information relating to atomic energy. James R. Newman.

Speech and Debating

Anthology of Public Speeches. Mabel
Platz, comp. 895p. 1940. $3.75.
Selections from speeches repre-
senting all cultures from Pericles
and Cicero to Chiang Kai-shek and
Neville Chamberlain.

**Competitive Debate: Rules and Strat-
egy.** By G. M. Musgrave. 128p.
1945. $1.25.

**Extempore Speaking: A Handbook for
the Student, the Coach, and the
Judge.** D. L. Holley. 115p. 1947.
$1.50.

**High School Forensics: An Integrated
Program.** By A. E. Melzer. 153p.
1940. 90c.

**Oral Interpretation of Literature in
American Colleges and Universities.**
By M. M. Robb. 242p. 1941. $2.75.

Representative American Speeches. By
A. C. Baird, comp. Published annually in The Reference Shelf.
Eight volumes now available. Prices
vary.
Each volume contains representative speeches by eminent men and
women on public occasions during
the year. Each speech is prefaced
by a short sketch of the speaker and
the occasion.

**Selected Readings in Rhetoric and
Public Speaking.** By Lester Thons-
sen, comp. 324p. 1942. $3.